An Interpretative History of
ALASKAN STATEHOOD
★

An Interpretative History of
ALASKAN STATEHOOD

★

By CLAUS-M. NASKE

Published by ALASKA NORTHWEST PUBLISHING COMPANY
Box 4-EEE, Anchorage, Alaska 99509
1973

Copyright © 1973, ALASKA NORTHWEST PUBLISHING COMPANY
Box 4-EEE, Anchorage, Alaska 99509

All rights reserved. No part of this book may be reproduced or transmitted in any form or by any means, electronic or mechanical, including photocopying, recording or by any information storage and retrieval system, without written permission of Alaska Northwest Publishing Company.

Printed in U.S.A.

Library of Congress Number: 72-92091
International Standard Book Number: 0-88240-014-2 (Paperbound)
International Standard Book Number: 0-88240-017-7 (Hardbound)

DEDICATION
To my parents,
Alfred and Kathe Naske of Goslar, West Germany.
They kept the faith.

PREFACE

Three events in twentieth-century Alaskan history are surely destined to stand out among all others. The Second World War revolutionized the territory, the struggle for statehood completed Alaska's process of modernization, and the discovery of oil on the North Slope gives promise of large revenues. Alaska's modest population together with a large income will make it possible for the state, if it so desires, to pioneer in building a unique model community with the comforts and conveniences of twentieth-century life in proximity to and in harmony with the natural environment.

Ernest Gruening published his *The Battle for Alaska Statehood* in 1967. Since it was based primarily upon the recollections of one of the participants, a re-examination of the movement based on a variety of sources seems in order. That, at least, is the excuse for the present study. The main sources utilized included the files of the Department of the Interior, Office of Territories, and the papers accompanying Senate and House bills in the National Archives. Personal interviews with a number of the participants in the Statehood crusade provided valuable insights. The Records of the Office of the Governor of Alaska, 1884-1958, Federal Records Center, Seattle, furnished much material, as did the Anthony J. Dimond and E. L. Bartlett Papers and the James Wickersham Diary in the University of Alaska Archives, College. Congressional hearings on statehood also were important sources.

I want to thank the librarians of the various depositories who always extended unfailing help. I am particularly grateful to Professor David H. Stratton of Washington State University, mentor and friend, for helping to shape many of my ideas and for his untiring editorial efforts. I would also like to thank my wife, Dinah, who has given me help, encouragement, understanding and support over many years.

ABSTRACT

In an age when oil is of great national and international importance, the recent discovery of "black gold" on Alaska's North Slope has brought prominence to the forty-ninth State. But for most of its history since 1867, Alaska was regarded as remote, noncontiguous, and of little importance by a nation preoccupied with more immediate concerns. The Klondike gold rush of the late 1890's attracted only temporary attention to Alaska, although it resulted in the development of a significant colonial economy based on natural resource extraction. These absentee business interests soon dominated Alaska politics.

Although demands for self-government began early, Alaska did not become an incorporated Territory until 1912, an act which predestined it for eventual admission to the Union. The first statehood attempts, beginning in 1915, failed because of the Territory's small population and geographic remoteness, the apathy of Alaskans and of Congress, and the opposition of the special interests. But historical precedent and the course of events were running in Alaska's favor.

When the Japanese occupied Kiska and Attu during the Second World War, the United States government and the American public suddenly realized Alaska's strategic importance. Vast military expenditures transformed America's northern Achilles heel into a bastion of defense. An influx of wartime immigrants drastically changed the population, and spawned a vigorous statehood movement. Led by Delegate to Congress Edward L. Bartlett and Governor Ernest Gruening, it soon developed into a crusade. At first this movement was narrowly based, involving the Territory's more established residents. In 1953, when lengthy congressional hearings were held in Alaska, the statehood campaign entered its "populist" phase, as thousands of hitherto uninvolved citizens joined in the struggle.

The Truman administration backed the admission of both Alaska and Hawaii, but the Eisenhower administration only advocated the admission of Republican-leaning Hawaii. From 1916 to 1958, statehood opponents employed the same general arguments. Alaska was noncontiguous, its population too small, and its economy lacking in the development necessary for the financial support of statehood. Its admission would result in disproportionate congressional representation, especially in the Senate. Also, Alaskans were too liberal politically. As a result, the conservative Republican-Southern Democratic coalition, seeing the tradition of the filibuster and cloture threatened and fearing the racial consequences, blocked Alaska statehood. In Alaska, the main opposition came from the special interests, particularly the canned salmon industry, and some old-time residents. Statehood advocates argued that admission was a moral and historical right derived from the Territory's incorporated status.

In 1955-56, with statehood bogged down in Congress, Alaskans took it upon themselves to hold a constitutional convention, adopt a "Tennessee Plan" of admission, and, in effect, invite themselves into the Union. A determined campaign, waged by Alaskans and their powerful friends in Congress and elsewhere, brought statehood in 1958. The factors accounting for success included the idealism generated by the Second World War, the defense necessities of the Cold War, the social and economic revolution which was transforming America, and the leadership of Alaskan statehood advocates.

TABLE OF CONTENTS

PREFACE	vii
ABSTRACT	ix
Chapter	**Page**
I. INTRODUCTION	1
II. LITTLE GOVERNMENT FOR THE FEW	13
III. WICKERSHAM AND THE SECOND ORGANIC ACT	23
IV. THE FIRST STATEHOOD CAMPAIGN	35
V. THE FEDERAL ROLE IN ALASKA	47
VI. BARTLETT AND GRUENING: CRUSADERS FOR STATEHOOD	67
VII. CONTROLLING THE SPECIAL INTERESTS	85
VIII. THE FIGHT FOR STATEHOOD BECOMES NATIONAL	95
IX. ALASKANS DEMAND "STATEHOOD NOW"	111
X. THE CONSTITUTIONAL CONVENTION	131
XI. STATEHOOD ACHIEVED	151
BIBLIOGRAPHY	175
INDEX	187

TABLE

1. Votes in Southeastern Alaska in the 1946 Statehood Referendum ... 73

CHAPTER I

INTRODUCTION

After negotiating for three weeks, Secretary of State William H. Seward and Baron Edouard Stoeckl, the Russian Minister to the United States, met at Seward's home in Washington, and during a long night of phrasing and rephrasing the wording, they finally completed the Treaty of Cession of Russian America. Early in the morning of March 30, 1867, the two weary men signed the document.[1] Even before the money for Alaska was paid to Russia, the Territory was officially taken over by the United States. President Andrew Johnson appointed General Lovell H. Rousseau of Kentucky to act as commissioner for the United States government in the ceremonies, with General Jefferson C. Davis to command a military force of about 500 men, stationed at five posts, to maintain peace and order.[2] In a speech at Sitka on August 12, 1868, Secretary Seward dedicated Alaska to future statehood, when he stated, "Nor do I doubt that the political society to be constituted here, first as a Territory, and ultimately as a state or many States, will prove a worthy constituency of the Republic."[3]

President Johnson, when notifying Congress of the transfer which took place at Sitka on October 18, 1867, commented on the indefinite status of Alaska: "Possession having been formally delivered to our commissioner, the territory remains for the present in care of a military force, awaiting such civil organization as shall be directed by Congress."[4] Congress did not respond to President Johnson's veiled suggestion that some sort of civil government should be established in the new acquisition. Instead, the Fortieth Congress (1867-1869) merely passed an act which made Alaska a customs district of the United States. Violators were to be prosecuted in the United States district courts of Washington, Oregon, or California. Whatever semblance of civil government existed was exercised without any definite legal authority by the commanding general of the troops stationed at Sitka. And, in 1877, the troops were withdrawn from Alaska to help put down the Nez Perce Indian uprising in the Pacific Northwest.[5]

Control of the Territory was then officially handed over to the Treasury Department which already was struggling to enforce the customs, commercial, and navigation laws, and to prevent smuggling and the use or importation of liquor and firearms. For the next two years there was no real federal authority at all in Alaska, except what the customs collector at Sitka could conjure out of thin air. In the summer of 1878, the citizens of Sitka, fearing a native uprising, petitioned for help from the British who responded by sending the warship *Osprey* under the command of Captain H. Holmes A'Court for their protection. Shortly thereafter the American sloop of war *Jamestown* under Commander Lester Anthony Beardslee arrived.

Commander Beardslee had been instructed by Secretary of the Navy R. W. Thompson to restore "harmonious relations" between settler and native, and in the absence of civil government and law, to use his "own discretion in all emergencies that might arise."[6] Much to the discomfiture of Commander Beardslee, his arrival inaugurated a five-year period during which the Navy exercised the role of the sole effective government for Alaska. This role was not terminated until 1884, when the passage of the First Organic Act made Alaska a "civil and judicial district" with a governor, district judge, clerk of court, marshal, four deputy marshals, and four commissioners, who had the functions of justices of the peace. The general laws of the state of Oregon then in force were declared to be the law of the district of Alaska, in so far as they might be applicable and not in conflict with the provisions of the act or with the laws of the United States.[7] One historian has declared, "As finally passed, S. 153 was evolved from a composite of honest intentions, ignorance, stupidity, indifference, and quasi-expediency."[8] In short, the First Organic Act provided for a total of thirteen officials who would be responsible for some 586,000 square miles and a population of 32,000 souls, of whom 430 were white.

The settlers who came to Sitka with the Army in 1867, and those who subsequently made the long journey to Alaska, came largely from the other Territories and from the States. Most of them had some knowledge of how frontiers in the United States had developed, and they believed that, in the normal course of events, after a suitable period of territorial government, Alaska would join the Union as a State. Alaska, however, did not follow the usual Territory-to State pattern. It was not until 1884 that, as previously mentioned, the First

Included was a system of taxation, the first levied in the district. License fees for some forty occupations were imposed. These varied from $250 per year for banks to $500 for breweries. Mercantile establishments paid on a sliding scale, with a $500 per year fee for those who did a $100,000 business. The sale of liquor was legalized, but a tax was imposed on the dealer. Railroads were taxed $100 for each mile of their operation and salmon canneries were taxed at four cents per case. The funds derived from these taxes and license fees were to pay for the government of Alaska, and the surplus was to go into the United States Treasury.[17] This system of taxation, with only minor modifications, persisted for over fifty years.

A great many Alaska bills were introduced in the Fifty-sixth Congress (1899-1901), including measures pertaining to native welfare, reindeer, education, the fisheries, the judiciary, and a recurrent request for an Alaskan delegate to Congress. In 1900 Congress passed a civil code and a code of civil procedure. With this last piece of legislation, Congress began to deal directly with the problem of providing a general governmental system for Alaska. The district of Alaska was divided into three parts, and courts were established at Sitka, Nome, and Eagle City on the Yukon, with authority to convene elsewhere when necessary.[18] Within the framework of the Organic Act of 1884, which had established Alaska as a civil and judicial district of the United States, the 1900 act provided for the presidential selection of three district judges. It also made possible the incorporation of municipalities for the first time. Communities with 300 or more permanent inhabitants were allowed to organize local governments. The first step was a petition to the United States district court, which had to approve the proposal. At a subsequent local election, the new local governmental scheme was to be approved or disapproved by the inhabitants. In 1904, amending and codifying legislation was passed, and this, together with the act of 1900, was the beginning of statutory local self-government in Alaska.[19] The Klondike gold rush had brought about some legislation for Alaska. But most important, Alaska had secured official recognition as a pressing problem.

Bills to provide Alaska with a delegate to Congress, as mentioned, had repeatedly been introduced in Congress. In the Fifty-fifth (1897-99), Fifty-sixth (1899-1901), and Fifty-seventh (1901-03) Congresses, delegate bills made some progress, but not enough for enactment. Not until the Fifty-ninth Congress, in 1906, did both houses of Congress take favorable action. The bill provided for the election of a delegate for the short term, that is, the rest of the Fifty-ninth Congress, and for the subsequent election of one for the full session of the Sixtieth Congress (1907-1909).[20] The territorial delegate acted as a nonvoting member of the House of Representatives. He received the same salary and allowances as his colleagues; he served on committees, spoke on the floor, and introduced bills. Since the Federal Government and its various departments and bureaus played such an important social and economic role in the life of all Alaskans, this representation was extremely important in deciding Alaska's future.

It was not until 1912 that Congress passed the Second Organic Act, which gave an elected legislature to Alaska. Technically, this body was a creature of the Federal Government, and its work was subject to the veto of a federally appointed governor and to approval (or disapproval) by Congress. The act prescribed the structure of the territorial legislature, the nature of its membership, the method of electing members, and its general internal organization and procedures. Additionally, specific limitations were placed on its authority.[21] Broad responsibility was given to the appointed governor. As a result, territorial legislators, who usually distrusted the Alaskan chief executive, spent much of their time and energy in thwarting this control. They created various boards and elective positions, which eventually resulted in a patchwork of duplication and overlapping of responsibility, making territorial government cumbersome and unwieldy.

Viewing the Alaskan government some three decades after its creation, the National Resources Planning Board concluded in 1941:

> In many respects Alaska is a Federal province: The Governor is a Federal appointee, the law-enforcement and judicial system is administered by the United States Department of Justice, part of the local taxes are imposed by Act of Congress and collected by Federal officers, the fisheries and wildlife are under the jurisdiction of Federal and quasi-Federal agencies, about 98% of the land is in Federal ownership, the national defense program now changing the economic life of the Territory in a radical way is entirely in Federal control. This picture is remarkably different from the simple pattern of Federal activities that prevailed during territorial days in the States.

On the other hand, the Territory of Alaska is in many respects treated as a state and is expected to assume responsibilities similar to those carried by the states. It is, for example, expected to maintain its own system of elementary, secondary, and higher education . . .; to maintain a system of social security which will comply with standards laid down for states; to maintain certain technical services in aid of mining and agriculture.[22]

The whole structure of territorial government could have been made more responsive to the popular will had Congress seen fit to make the position of governor elective and to enlarge the powers of the legislature. This would have necessitated an amendment of the Second Organic Act. Proposals for such amendments were introduced time and again by Alaska delegates to Congress but evoked no response in Washington. Delegate E. L. "Bob" Bartlett, who served in the nation's capital from 1945 to 1958, expressed his frustration on this point when he declared in 1947:

. . . we have lived under a very limited form of territorial government for 35 years. Delegate James Wickersham . . . tried to get reforms for the [sic] organic bill. He failed. Anthony J. Dimond failed and I have failed and I have reached the point where I am convinced that it would be just as simple to get a statehood bill through Congress as to get through a new organic act.[23]

But despite all its apparent defects, the Organic Act of 1912 ended Alaska's mysterious legal and constitutional status. It specifically stated, "The Constitution . . . shall have the same force and effect within the Territory of Alaska as elsewhere in the United States." As early as 1868, Alaska had been referred to as both the "District of Alaska" and the "Territory of Alaska." These two terms also were used interchangeably in subsequent debates and committee reports, and the First Organic Act of 1884 added to the confusion by making Alaska "a civil and judicial district."[24] The distinction between a Territory and a district was a crucial one, because the former was thought capable of exercising at least a limited measure of home rule through a locally elected legislature, while the latter was considered to be incapable of exercising self-government.[25]

It was the Northwest Ordinance of 1787 which had established the philosophical and structural framework for the American territorial system. The outstanding characteristic of this scheme was its transitional and progressive character looking toward ultimate statehood.26 Under the provisions of the ordinance the United States had grown from the original thirteen States to forty-eight States, when the last two contiguous Territories, New Mexico and Arizona, were admitted to statehood in 1912. The legal and historical precedents of admitting Territories, therefore, had deep roots in American history.

Complications had arisen, however, when the United States acquired the Hawaiian Islands and other noncontiguous lands as a result of the Spanish-American War of 1898. Alaska, although acquired by purchase in 1867, was noncontiguous, remote, and contained an Indian, Eskimo, and Aleut population of modest size. It was grouped with the new lands. The question soon came up whether or not these new acquisitions, populated largely by alien people, were eligible for eventual statehood. The Supreme Court attempted to give an answer in a number of decisions, known as the "Insular Cases," which distinguished between two types of Territories, "incorporated" and "unincorporated."27 In one of these cases, *Downes v. Bidwell*, the Court dealt with the question of whether or not the constitutional requirement that duties, imports, and excises should be uniform "throughout the United States" applied to Puerto Rico. Specifically, would it invalidate a provision in that island's Organic Act establishing a schedule of custom duties on its merchandise entering the continental United States? The Court decided that Puerto Rico was not a part of the United States for the purposes of this constitutional provision because it had not been incorporated into the United States. Secretary of War Elihu Root reportedly said of this rather nebulous distinction established by the Court, ". . . as near as I can make out the constitution follows the flag—but doesn't quite catch up with it."28

Historically, statehood was tied to the territorial classification, and, after the Insular Cases, specifically to the incorporated status. On a number of occasions the Court recognized Alaska's incorporated status,29 and also decided that once an area had been incorporated it could not revert again to an unincorporated status. Furthermore, once Congress had incorporated a Territory, it subjected itself to certain limitations to legislate for that region, although these restrictions did not apply when it exercised authority to make laws for an unincorporated area. Most importantly, the act of incorporation was consistently looked upon as a commitment on the part of Congress ultimately to admit the incorporated Territory as a State.[30]

Because of such strong historical and judicial precedents, Alaska's eventual admission to statehood was as certain as anything can be in the American political system. But the admission process had often been influenced by political considerations. An example is the case of Nevada. During the Civil War the Republican hierarchy in the Senate had elevated that Territory to statehood to give Abraham Lincoln more electoral votes in 1864 and to help ratify the Thirteenth Amendment, although Nevada had a population of only 20,000.[31]

When Delegate James Wickersham introduced Alaska's first statehood bill in 1916, the Territory had a citizenry of roughly 58,000. At this point the population had not been sufficiently "politicized," and the first statehood movement died due to apathy. When Warren G. Harding visited the Territory in 1923, the first President to do so, it gave only a momentary boost to the Alaska statehood movement. The Second World War, however, revolutionized Alaska. Billions of dollars in defense monies flowed into the Territory. The dramatic impact of this influx was reflected in Alaska's population growth. Of a total of about 75,000 inhabitants in 1940, approximately 1,000 were members of the military forces. By 1943, the number of people in Alaska had risen to 233,000, of whom some 152,000 were members of the military. Although the total number of inhabitants declined to approximately 99,000 in 1946, the Cold War years and the associated increase in military expenditures again raised Alaska's population to approximately 138,000 in 1950.[32]

The influx of this new population and money during World War II and the Cold War transformed the Territory socially and economically. Together with these momentous changes, a new and vigorous movement to gain statehood arose in the mid-1940's. This modern statehood movement consisted of two phases. The first lasted from 1943 to 1953. It was propelled by Alaska's governor, the delegate to Congress, and a cross-section of the Territory's established business and professional men and women. It had a fairly narrow base. A referendum on statehood was held in 1946. Alaskans, by a margin of three to two, expressed their desire for statehood. In 1949, the territorial legislature responded by creating an official Alaska Statehood Committee. Several congressional hearings were held in which most of the testimony was favorable to statehood. By 1950, the year an Alaska statehood bill for the first time passed in either house of Congress, the opposition to statehood had crystallized. It was led by the Alaska Canned Salmon Industry, Inc., a trade organization, and included a number of Alaska's newspapers. In Congress, the main support came from representatives and senators of western public land States, while the opposition was centered mainly in the South.

The second or "populist" phase of the statehood movement began late in 1953 and lasted until 1958. It involved thousands of ordinary Alaskans not connected with any official group or agency. It culminated in a constitutional convention in 1955-56 and the adoption of a constitution in the spring of 1956 by a substantial majority of Alaska's voters.

Throughout the two phases, national as well as local support for Alaska statehood grew. A combination of these pressures resulted in the passage of an Alaska statehood act in 1958 by both houses of Congress.

FOOTNOTES FOR CHAPTER I

1. United States Army, Alaska, *The Army's Role in the Building of Alaska* (Headquarters, United States Army, Alaska: Public Information Officer, Pamphlet 360-5, April, 1969), p.1. See also Frank A. Golder, "The Purchase of Alaska," *The American Historical Review*, XXV (April, 1920), 411-25; Victor J. Farrar, "The Background of the Purchase of Alaska," *Washington Historical Quarterly*, XIII (April, 1922), 92-104; R. H. Luthin, "The Sale of Alaska," *Slavonic Review*, XVI (July, 1937), 168-82; Thomas A. Bailey, "Why the United States Purchased Alaska," *Pacific Historical Review*, III (March, 1934), 39-49.

2. Stuart Ramsay Tompkins, *Alaska, Promyshlennik and Sourdough* (Norman: University of Oklahoma Press, 1945), p. 191.

3. *Speech of William H. Seward at Sitka, August 12, 1868* (Washington: Philip and Solomons, 1869), p. 16.

4. James D. Richardson, ed., *A Compilation of the Messages and Papers of the Presidents* (New York: Bureau of National Literature, 1912), V, 3778.

5. Mel Crain, "When the Navy Ruled Alaska," *United States Naval Institute Proceedings*, LXXXI (February, 1955), 199, states that United States troops were withdrawn as an economy measure by president Rutherford B. Hayes in 1877. Jeannette Paddock Nichols, in *Alaska: A History of Its Administrations, Exploitation, and Industrial Development During the First Half Century Under the Rule of the United States* (Cleveland: The Arthur H. Clark Company, 1924), p. 59, states that the troops were withdrawn because they were needed to quell the Nez Perce Indian uprising in the Pacific Northwest. Ernest Gruening, in *The State of Alaska* (2nd ed.; New York: Random House, 1968), p. 36, echoes Mrs. Nichols.

6. Crain, "When the Navy Ruled Alaska," p. 198.
7. Gruening, *The State of Alaska*, pp. 33-52.
8. Nichols, *Alaska*, p. 72.
9. Earl S. Pomeroy, *The Territories and the United States 1861-1890: Studies in Colonial Administration* (Philadelphia: University of Pennsylvania Press, 1947), p. 2.
10. Jack E. Eblen, *The First and Second United States Empires: Governors and Territorial Government, 1784-1912* (Pittsburgh: University of Pittsburgh Press, 1968), p. 151; *Ibid.*, p. 8.
11. Richard E. Welch, Jr., "American Public Opinion and the Purchase of Russian America," in *Alaska and its History*, ed. Morgan B. Sherwood (Seattle and London: University of Washington Press, 1967), pp. 274-88.
12. "Speech of Hon. Charles Sumner, of Massachusetts, on the Cession of Russian America to the United States," in U.S., Congress, House, House Executive Document No. 177, 40 Cong., 2 Sess. (Washington: Government Printing Office, 1868), p. 188. For an excellent description of early Alaska, see William H. Dall, *Alaska and its Resources* (Cambridge: University Press, John Wilson and Sons, 1870).
13. Quoted in Welch, "American Public Opinion and the Purchase of Russian America," pp. 276-77.
14. George W. Rogers and Richard A. Cooley, *Alaska's Population and Economy*, vol. I, *Analysis* (College, Alaska: Institute of Business, Economic and Government Research, 1963), pp. 16-19.
15. Richardson, *Compilation of Messages and Papers of the Presidents*, VIII, 6269; *Ibid.*, IX, 6400; *Ibid.*, IX, 6401.
16. Gruening, *The State of Alaska*. p. 105.
17. *Ibid.*, pp. 107-13.
18. Nichols, *Alaska*, pp. 180-83.
19. Thomas A. Morehouse and Victor Fischer, *The State and the Local Governmental System* (College, Alaska: Institute of Social, Economic, and Government Research, March, 1970), p. III-8.
20. Gruening, *The State of Alaska*, pp. 138-39.
21. U.S. *Stats. at Large* 512 (1912).
22. National Resources Planning Board, "Postwar Economic Development of Alaska," in *Regional Development Plan—Report for 1942* (Washington: Government Printing Office, December, 1941), pp. 21-22.
23. U.S., Congress, House, *Alaska*, Hearings before the Subcommittee on Territorial and Insular Possessions of the Committee on Public Lands, Committee Hearing No. 31, 80 Cong., 1 Sess. (Washington: Government Printing Office, 1947), pp. 366-67.
24. 37 U.S. *Stats. at Large* 512 (1912); 15 U.S. *Stats. at Large* 240 (1868); 23 U.S. *Stats. at Large* 24 (1884).
25. Max Farrand, "Territory and District," *The American Historical Review*, V (July, 1900), 676-81.
26. For an elaboration of this view, see Eblen, *The First and Second United States Empires*, pp. 201-36; Pomeroy, *The Territories and the United States*, pp. 1-5.
27. *De Lima v. Bidwell*, 182 U.S. (1901); *Downes v. Bidwell*, 182 U.S. 244 (1901).
28. Robert H. Wiebe, *The Search for Order 1877-1920* (New York: Hill and Wang, 1967), p. 228.
29. See *Rasmussen v. United States*, 197 U.S. 516 (1905); *Nagle v. United States*, 191 Fed. 141 (1911); *United States v. Farwell*, 76 F. Supp. 35 (1948).
30. See *Balzac v. People of Porto Rico*, 258 U.S. 298 (1922); *McAllister v. United States*, 141 U.S. 174, 188 (1891); *O'Donoghue v. United States*, 289 U.S. 516, 537 (1933). George Washington

Spicer described and analyzed some thirty-five key court cases in *The Constitutional Status and Government of Alaska* (Baltimore: The Johns Hopkins University Press, 1927). Alaska statehood proponents in the mid-1940's borrowed heavily from Spicer in their efforts to establish a judicial framework for their cause.

31. Ray Allen Billington, *Westward Expansion: A History of the American Frontier* (3rd ed.; New York: The Macmillan Company, 1967), p. 627.

32. George W. Rogers, *The Future of Alaska: Economic Consequences of Statehood* (Baltimore: The Johns Hopkins Press, 1962), p. 95.

CHAPTER II

LITTLE GOVERNMENT FOR THE FEW

In the eighteenth century, the European exploration of the North Pacific Coast opened up an entire new frontier to the Russian and British fur traders and trappers. This northern region offered an abundance of pelts to meet the growing world demand. With the extension of the trade into Alaska, the basis for an enduring colonial economy was created, an economy which was characterized by destructive exploitation of the fur bearing animals as well as numerous other natural resources.[1]

In the 1740's, the Russians began to harvest the fur seals and sea otters together with a variety of land animals bearing valuable pelts. Men from other nations later joined this quest. By the end of the nineteenth century, the sea otters had been virtually destroyed. By the first decade of the twentieth century, the Pribilof fur seal herd, which had numbered in the millions, had declined to no more than 100,000 animals. The unbridled killing of the Pribilof seals had ceased by 1911 as the result of an international treaty which outlawed pelagic sealing, and, in addition, the United States government took over from private concessionaires the utilization and management of this seal herd. Whaling was big business from 1849, when the first whalers passed through the Bering Strait, until the 1880's, when, due to the growing scarcity of these huge mammals and the substitution of petroleum products for whale oil, the industry began to decline.

Although the fur trade dwindled after the United States acquisition of Alaska in 1867, salmon fishing, which had merely provided for local needs under the Russians, expanded into a thriving business. The first American saltery was set up in 1868, and the first cannery began operation at Klawock on Prince of Wales Island in 1878. By 1898, there were fifty-nine canneries in Alaska. Prospectors created another component of Alaska's colonial economy. Some men searched for minerals, principally gold, in Southeastern Alaska as early as the 1860's. Actually it all may be said to have started in 1848 when gold was discovered in California. Soon restless miners spread out from there and began to search for the precious metal elsewhere, in Nevada and Colorado, Washington and Idaho, among other places, and northward into British Columbia as well. In 1857 prospectors found gold at the juncture of the Fraser and Thompson Rivers in British Columbia. Miners followed the Fraser River toward its headwaters and discovered gold deposits in the Cariboo district in 1860 and the Cassiar district in the early 1870's. From the Cassiar district miners filtered into southeastern Alaska via the Stikine River route and added to the prospecting population in the region. Gold was discovered in the Sitka area in the early 1870's and in 1880 Joseph Juneau and Richard T. Harris made a big strike at the present site of Juneau. Late in the same year the two men entered a townsite claim which they named Harrisburgh.

While hard rock mining grew slowly in southeastern Alaska, a few prospectors found their way into the Yukon Valley in the early 1870's by way of Hudson's Bay Company route from the Mackenzie River. A little later, miners penetrated the Yukon Valley over the coastal mountains by ascending the Chilkoot Pass and reaching the upper part of the Yukon River. The discovery of placer gold in the Yukon Valley led to the establishment of a number of small mining settlements along that river and its tributaries.

Although the economic development at this time was modest, it resulted in a substantial influx of white fortune seekers. The first official census in 1880 reported 33,426 inhabitants, of whom all but 430 were aboriginal Alaskans. The next census, in 1890, showed an increase of 3,868 whites and a decline among the Eskimos, Indians, and Aleuts of 7,642, due to the usual traumatic collision between Caucasian and Native cultures.[2]

By 1884 Congress had passed Alaska's first Organic Act, sponsored principally by Indiana's Senator Benjamin Harrison. This framework of government was so patently inadequate that it caused Alaskans to agitate for a territorial form of government and encouraged them to create their own institutions.[3] As Professor Ted C. Hinckley has observed, Alaska was "no different from other Western territories" in that it was "granted a great deal of administrative freedom" from the very beginning.[4] As in so many other regions of the frontier West, Alaskan miners' meetings and law—the so-called miner's code—helped fill the local governmental void. By the authority of this code the miners not only made their own regulations for their claims, but they also enacted rules and regulations which concerned community affairs. Alfred H. Brooks, at one time head of the United States Geological Survey in Alaska, has stated, somewhat romantically:

> ... there developed democracies of the purest type, resembling in a manner the government in some of the cantons of Switzerland and the earliest colonial settlements of New England. The miners met and by majority vote enacted a mining civil and criminal code. If any member of the community believed that a wrong had been done him, he called a miner's [sic] meeting and the case was settled by majority vote. Similar action was taken in criminal cases. As imprisonment was impractical, there were only three punishments: hanging, banishment, and fines. In the code established at Circle City in 1893, murder was punished by hanging, assault and stealing by banishment, and minor infractions by fines.[5]

The miner's code thus helped to fill the local government needs which existed. In the larger settlements, local law enforcement officers, rudimentary court systems, and elected mayors, councils, and other officials began to appear in time.[6]

Meanwhile, the governor, whose office had been established by the First Organic Act of 1884, was marooned in Sitka, Alaska's capital city located on an island in the Alexander Archipelago. Legally, the chief executive was obligated to perform a long list of duties for which he was endowed with an impressive amount of authority. But as one of the governors ruefully remarked, "... authority to require performance of duty, in the absence of any power to compel it, amounts to nothing...."[7] Since the governor had limited means of transportation, he usually was out of touch with most of Alaska. Although still a problem today, the physical and geographical features of Alaska presented almost insuperable barriers to the early pioneers. Southeastern Alaska, where the majority of the white population lived and worked in the 1880's, had ready access to the "outside" (as anything south of Alaska is still referred to in old-fashioned Alaskan idiom) by water transportation. On the other hand, the Gulf coastal area, or the "Westward," and the land mass north of the Alaska Range, or the "Interior" or "Northward," were practically inaccessible and isolated.

Bearing in mind his isolated situation, the governor's annual reports to the President are studies in Alaskan politics and territorial administration. If read critically, they give a good insight into many aspects of the history of Alaska. These reports also served to keep territorial affairs before the executive branch of the Federal Government. Alaska's frontier politicians, Professor Hinckley comments,

> "confronted more ponderous problems than those found in many territories. They frequently became very peevish and censorious because of what they felt was glaring inconsideration from Washington, D.C. Damning congressional apathy was a venerable Western habit."[8]

Alaskan governors were especially critical of the Organic Act of 1884. Alfred P. Swineford, the Territory's second chief executive, perhaps was typical. In every one of his annual reports he complained about the shortcomings of the Organic Act and expressed doubt that it could be

> construed into anything more in harmony with the fundamental principles of free representative government than could one which explicitly declares a qualified executive absolutism. That act, following, as it appears, the always exceptional treatment of Alaska, presents an anomaly of law, by expressly excluding all legislative or representative power from the people.[9]

What Alaska lacked was people, the foundation of any booming frontier. From the lack of population, as Professor Hinckley has written, "everything else suffered. And because it was basically a problem that could not be remedied by Alaskans, they blamed their government... [for all their ills]."[10]

Governor Swineford considered a delegate to Congress a necessity and a right which had been extended to every Territory except Alaska. He dismissed as inconsequential the argument that Alaska's population was too sparse to entitle it to a delegate. Where the question of right was concerned, he asserted, numbers had no significance.[11] Without a legislature and a delegate to Congress, Governor Swineford stated, Alaska could not develop its wealth and potential. In this last regard he struck a theme which was to be repeated throughout the years, and which finally found a focus in the statehood movement in the 1950's. Economist George W. Rogers has remarked that Alaskans, like other colonial peoples, conceived of economic development as essentially political in nature. Thus the modern statehood proponents asserted that without two senators and one representative in Congress, the Territory would be unable to realize its economic potential. Lack of progress, this same group maintained, was due to the absentee salmon canning, gold mining, and

Seattle shipping interests.[12] While there is no doubt that absentee economic interests played a significant role in Alaska, as they do in any colonial economy, they also served as a symbol of the Territory's ills and helped to rally citizens to the statehood cause.

When Congress did not remedy any of the deficiencies of the Organic Act which Governor Swineford had criticized so vehemently and so long, he concluded in utter frustration that "the civil government of Alaska is little, if any, better than a burlesque both in form and substance."[13] Swineford's successors echoed and amplified his dissatisfactions, and the politically articulate public in southeastern Alaska also criticized the shortcomings of the district's governmental structure. As a matter of fact, political consciousness in southeastern Alaska became evident soon after the passage of the Organic Act of 1884, and "from this time onward" there was a "desire for home rule, marked by fairly definite stages."[14] These stages took the form of political conventions which met in Harrisburg in 1881 and in Juneau in 1890. In each instance a delegate was elected and dispatched to Washington to plead for, among other things, representation in Congress. Both times the memorials fell on deaf ears.[15]

After these unsuccessful ventures, concerned Democrats and Republicans of southeastern Alaska decided to work through the regular party machinery. Alaskan Democrats already had received recognition by their national party when two of their delegates had been seated at the Democratic National Convention in 1888. Four years later, both territorial Democrats and Republicans attempted to seat their representatives at their respective national conclaves. The Democrats again placed their two men. The Republicans for the first time were granted two delegates. Both territorial organizations were also granted a national committeeman.[16] Partly as a result of these political activities by Alaskans, occasional measures for a delegate had been considered in Congress. One such bill even received a favorable committee report in 1896 but died in the House of Representatives.[17]

In that same year, however, there occurred an event in Canada which profoundly influenced Alaska's political history. In August of 1896, news of a gold strike came from an obscure creek on the upper Yukon River. George Washington Carmack, his Indian wife, and his two brothers-in-law, Skookum Jim and Tagish Charlie, had found gold on Rabbit Creek, later renamed Bonanza Creek. This stream flowed into the Klondike River, a tributary of the mighty Yukon. News of the strike spread rapidly, and, before that fall ended, most of the ground around the creeks that emptied into the Klondike and Indian Rivers was staked out. At the junction of the Klondike and Yukon Rivers a tent camp on a marshy riverbank developed into the frontier city of Dawson.[18]

The rush to the gold fields of the Klondike was on, and since the two major routes led across Alaskan soil, the Territory was brought to the attention of millions of Americans. Reported widely in newspaper columns, in scores of magazine articles, and ultimately in "not fewer than three hundred bound volumes of personal experiences as well as fuller compendia"[19] the Klondike gold rush publicized the northland as nothing before had done.

It has been estimated that between 200,000 and 300,000 people started for the Klondike and that approximately 50,000 actually reached the interior of the Yukon Territory and Alaska. Thousands of "stampeders," who were disappointed with the New Eldorado, spread down the Yukon River and up its tributaries into Alaska panning for gold. Just as the Klondike excitement was abating, gold was discovered on the Seward Peninsula near Cape Nome, and the whole story of the Klondike was repeated, and in some respects magnified, because access to the new find was much easier. In 1896, the Seward Peninsula, which forms the nearest approach to Asia in Alaska, was populated by a few hundred Eskimos and a handful of whites. Ten years later it had a permanent population of roughly 4,000 and the summer inhabitants numbered 10,000. In 1902, a gold strike in the Tanana Valley in the interior of Alaska gave birth to the city of Fairbanks. During all this excitement, a great deal of gold was taken from these areas. Between 1896 and 1906, the Klondike produced $118,725,000 worth of the yellow metal, and the Seward Peninsula, between 1898 and 1906, shipped out $37,247,000 in gold.[20]

In 1897, Governor John G. Brady described the effects of the gold rush on Alaska by stating that thousands of fortune seekers had started to the Klondike at once, thousands were waiting for more news from the gold fields, and in addition

> Shipload after shipload of goldseekers and their freight has *[sic]* been rushed to the extreme limit of salt-water navigation, and there they have been literally dumped upon the beach, some

7. *Report of the Governor of Alaska for the Fiscal Year 1888* (Washington: Government Printing Office, 1889), p. 46. Hereafter cited as *Annual Report of the Governor of Alaska* with appropriate year in parenthesis.

8. Hinckley, "Reflections and Refractions: Alaska and Gilded Age America," p. 101.

9. *Annual Report of the Governor of Alaska* (1885), p. 15.

10. Hinckley, "Reflections and Refractions: Alaska and Gilded Age America," p. 101.

11. *Annual Report of the Governor of Alaska* (1885), p. 17.

12. Rogers, *The Future of Alaska*, p. 170.

13. *Annual Report of the Governor of Alaska* (1888), p. 45.

14. Nichols, *Alaska*, pp. 121-24, 125.

15. *Ibid.*, pp. 66-68, 127-29.

16. *Ibid.*, pp. 125,134.

17. *Cong. Record*, 54 Cong., 1 Sess., p. 4675 (May 1, 1896).

18. Gruening, *The State of Alaska*, p. 103. By far the best book on the gold rush is Pierre Berton, *The Klondike Fever: The Life and Death of the Last Great Gold Rush* (New York: Alfred A. Knopf, 1958).

19. Gruening, *The State of Alaska*, p. 104.

20. Clark, *History of Alaska*, pp. 98-115.

21. *Annual Report of the Governor of Alaska* (1897), p. 32.

22. *Ibid.*, p. 37.

23. *Ibid.* (1898), p. 47.

24. *Ibid.* (1899), p. 49.

25. David S. Jordan, "Colonial Lessons of Alaska," *Atlantic Monthly*, November, 1898, pp. 582, 591.

26. Nichols, *Alaska*, pp. 145-46.

27. U.S., Congress, Senate, Committee on Territories, *Conditions in Alaska*, 58 Cong., 2 Sess., S. Rept. 282 to accompany S. Res. 16 (Washington: Government Printing Office, 1904), p. 32.

28. Nichols, *Alaska*, p. 246.

29. U.S. *Stats. at Large* 169 (1906).

30. Gruening, *The State of Alaska*, p. 139. The view that a delegate to Congress was a legal, historical, and moral right is elaborated upon in Everett S. Brown, *The Territorial Delegate of Congress and Other Essays* (Ann Arbor, Michigan: The George Wahr Publishing Co., 1950), pp. 3-38.

CHAPTER III

WICKERSHAM AND THE SECOND ORGANIC ACT

Much of Alaska's history has been a conflict between the nonresident special interests, principally the mining, shipping, and salmon canning industries, and the aspirations of Alaskans for a greater measure of self-government. From 1884 until 1912, these interests worked in Washington to obtain special privileges from an unconcerned Congress, and successfully thwarted territorial desires for home rule. After 1912 and the appearance of a territorial legislature, the special interests also exerted their influence and authority in Alaska. Territorial residents were not totally helpless in counteracting these pressures. This was especially true after the passage of the 1906 delegate act, when James Wickersham, Alaska's third delegate to Congress and the Territory's most dominant political figure for the first three decades of the twentieth century, built a highly successful political career primarily on a platform of fighting the "Alaska Syndicate."[1] Wickersham was greatly aided in his battle against the lobby by the conservation issue, highlighted by the famous Ballinger-Pinchot controversy in 1909-10, which drew the nation's attention to its northern Territory.

Four years before the Ballinger-Pinchot affair rocked the administration of President William H. Taft, territorial Democrats and Republicans had held conventions to select their first candidates for the new position of delegate. Despite vigorous campaigns, the major party candidates were defeated by the "Independent" nominees of the Seward Peninsula and Tanana region miners. In accordance with the 1906 act, Frank Waskey, a prosperous, young miner was elected to serve for the rest of the current congressional session, while Thomas Cale, a middle-aged, popular but financially unsuccessful pioneer, was victorious for the first full term to start in 1907. The Waskey-Cale platform had included a demand for a territorial form of government. The Democrats had also supported full territorial government, while the Republicans had proclaimed their faith in the general principle of self-government but did not think the Territory was quite ready for it.[2] Governor Wilford B. Hoggatt, who had not backed the delegate bill and who also was against a change in the governmental structure, stated nevertheless: "... it is to be hoped that Alaska will be benefited by a ... representative of its people and that the hopes of those who have been asking for representation in Congress for many years may be fully realized."[3]

Shortly before Congress convened late in 1906, President Theodore Roosevelt asked Waskey and the Governor to submit to him statements outlining Alaska's political needs. Delegate Waskey wrote to the President that what the Territory most urgently needed was special mining legislation, but that the most important matter politically was territorial government. "We are all Americans," Waskey stated, "and as such believe in the inalienable rights and privileges of self-government." Governor Hoggatt disagreed with Waskey and remarked that the conservative businessmen of the Territory were almost unanimously opposed to territorial government. He pointed out Alaska's tremendous size, small population, widely scattered settlements, and the instability of the placer mining camps. Most importantly, the cost of such a government would have to be borne by the permanent residents of Alaska. Hoggatt felt that much of the agitation for territorial government came from the "saloon element" in Alaska which wanted to decrease the high license fees then imposed upon that business. In addition, the Governor stated, some of the demand for self-government had been generated by demagogic statements which claimed that Alaskans were deprived of some of the essential rights of American citizenship.[4] Hoggatt's views made him unpopular with many of the Territory's citizens and also had an effect in making home rule a prominent issue in Alaska.[5] The hostility between the Governor and the Delegate continued during the term of Waskey's successor, Thomas Cale, which began in March, 1907.

Cale had hardly taken office before speculation arose as to who would replace him, and it soon became apparent that James Wickersham was the favorite. He had come to Alaska in 1900 as a district judge commissioned by President William McKinley. Wickersham first took up his duties in Eagle on the Yukon River, then moved to Nome in 1901, to Valdez in 1902, and to Fairbanks in 1903. He served in that city[6] until he handed in his resignation in 1907, but agreed to stay on until a new judge had been appointed, although no later than March, 1908. In his capacity as judge, he had become widely known in the northern part of Alaska, and many respected him for his efficient handling of the court's business.

The Judge had at first taken a dim view of the movement for territorial government when he had written to Governor Hoggatt early in 1907:

> I regret very much that Waskey and Cale have started off on the mistaken idea of putting territorial government ahead of all other things for Alaska. It certainly is a great mistake and one which will cost the territory dear. You are right in opposing it and you ought not to hesitate. The population is too sparse and the taxable wealth is too small to sustain local self-government. The population is unsettled, and probably out of the six thousand or eight thousand men in this mining camp not a hundred of them will admit that they intend to remain in the territory the rest of their lives; nor would one-tenth of them remain if the placer mines were worked out as they are in Dawson and will be here inside of a few years. It is my judgment that a large majority of the people of this district are opposed to local self-government, although there is no difficulty in scaring up resolutions in Fourth of July language in favor of it. You should pay no attention to such resolutions except to try to explain to congress and the president that they come from a small number of people with nothing else to do and are simply goodnaturedly mistaken about what to do.[7]

Hoggatt made this letter public at a congressional hearing in 1908 which was considering two territorial government bills, both introduced by Delegate Cale and one of which had been drafted by Wickersham.

By then, however, the Judge had given his support to a limited form of territorial government only. As a man who was heavily involved in the mining business of the Tanana Valley, he apparently shared the fears of the canning and mining interests that a full territorial form of government would induce legislators to tax capriciously and spend public funds unwisely. The territorial government bill Wickersham had drafted reflected some of these fears. The measure provided for an appointed upper house and property holding as a qualification for office in the lower house. Wickersham was acutely embarassed by the letter because he had since changed his position. He also had political ambitions in 1908, and recognized that home rule was a powerful emotional symbol. As a pragmatist, he did not intend to jeopardize his political future by adhering to an unpopular position. In addition, both the territorial Republican and Democratic parties endorsed the theory of home rule.[8]

At the territorial convention in 1908, the Regular Republicans nominated "Seattle John" Corson, and the Democrats, John Ronan. J. P. Clum ran independently in the hope of securing support from the interior; Joseph Chilberg was chosen by the northern miners and ran on a pro-labor platform; and Cale was nominated by the Independent Republicans.[9] Wickersham, who had believed that Cale would not run again and wanted to utilize Cale's organization for his own campaign, entered the race for delegate on June 23, 1908.[10] Telegrams announcing his candidacy were sent to various newspapers in Alaska. Shortly thereafter, since Cale had not withdrawn from the race, Wickersham gave up his candidacy. "With both local newspapers against me," he wrote ruefully in his diary, "no money—and no organization—with my friends at Skagway, Valdez [sic] and Nome for Cale it is a mistake to continue longer in the scramble...." And again, on July 7, Wickersham reflected, "I am sorry that I made such a damned weak display of myself—I went up a little ways in a little baloon [sic] & forgot to take the parachute along." When Cale withdrew from the race in July, however, the irrepressible Judge announced that "at the persistent request of many friends throughout the territory I am a candidate for delegate to Congress."[11]

At that point the Alaska Syndicate became involved in the campaign. The Syndicate was a combination of the J. P. Morgan and Guggenheim fortunes. In Alaska the principal mining venture of this organization was the Kennecott-Bonanza copper mine. In order to tap this deposit it began construction of the Copper River and Northwestern Railroad, ruthlessly suppressing competition wherever possible. In addition, the "Guggies" carried on constant warfare against other railroad companies struggling to survive.[12] Since the Syndicate apparently had inexhaustible capital and reportedly controlled steamship transportation and a major part of the salmon canning industry, many Alaskans feared that the wealthy combine would shortly dominate Alaska's politics. It was also common knowledge in the Territory that the Syndicate lobby in Washington had successfully postponed the delegate bill and opposed any further extension of home rule.[13] A representaive of the Morgan–Guggenheim interests, David H. Jarvis, strongly advised candidate Wickersham against running for Congress. The Judge's anti-

Guggenheim sentiments were well-known and the lobby did not want to see such a foe in a potentially influential office.

Wickersham construed the Syndicate advice as a challenge and a threat. He immediately revised an address to the people on his candidacy and included a strong plank against Guggenheim domination in mining and transportation matters in Alaska.[14] Then and there the Judge recognized the political potential of the nonresident control of Alaskan affairs by the lobby. He ran on an anti-Syndicate platform; in short, one which was generally designed to appeal to many Alaskans. In addition, Wickersham advocated the same form of limited local self-government as recommended by President Roosevelt, and expressed the hope that this government would be as simple and inexpensive as possible and that the elective territorial legislature would be endowed with carefully restricted powers.[15]

In the ensuing campaign, the control of territorial affairs by the Syndicate and the outspoken personality of the Judge were the main issues. Wickersham won the election. His Republican opponent, "Seattle John" Corson, was defeated because of his Guggenheim backing. John Ronan, the Democratic candidate, ran a poor third because the voters identified him as anti-labor.[16] Wickersham's victory, one eminent Alaskan politician and historian has remarked, put "a lusty and resourceful battler" into the position of delegate to Congress "who was able to make the most of the turbulent political situation that was developing."[17]

In November, 1908, Delegate-elect Wickersham further explained his stand on an elective Alaskan legislature in a telegram which he sent to President Roosevelt. He asked the President to include in his annual message a recommendation that Congress give the Territory a bicameral legislature with carefully limited powers. Specifically, these limitations would include a prohibition against territorial or municipal bonded indebtedness, no county form of government, a fixed limit on the legislature's powers of taxation, and whatever other restrictions might be necessary to give Alaska sufficient, yet simple self-government.[18]

No action was taken under the Roosevelt administration. Delegate Wickersham met the new President, William H. Taft, for the first time in Washington in April, 1909. The Delegate used the occasion to urge the Chief Executive to support a territorial government for Alaska.

The President remained unconvinced on the ground that Alaska's population was too sparse and transitory. Instead, Taft favored giving Alaska a commission form of government. Wickersham disagreed wholeheartedly with the President's plan and resolved to fight it.[19] On June 9, 1909, he therefore introduced a bill to establish a legislative assembly in Alaska. He mailed numerous copies to the territory in order to get the reactions of Alaskans to his home rule measure.[20]

In September, 1909, the President came to Seattle to attend the Alaska-Yukon-Pacific Exposition and to deliver an address. The inspiration for this fair had initially come from a group of Alaskan gold rush pioneers who wanted to establish an Alaska exhibit in Seattle to advertise the Territory. The idea grew and eventually resulted in the exposition which was to advertise Seattle's pivotal position in relation to the Pacific Rim countries.[21] Upon his arrival in Seattle, President Taft was greeted by a telegram from Alaska which had been signed by sixteen of the Territory's nineteen newspapers, seven mayors, and two chambers of commerce. The telegram asked the President to support territorial government.[22] Alaskans at the exposition were greatly disappointed when the President recommended a commission form of government instead of the hoped for home rule.

The reaction in the Territory to Taft's proposal was bitter. An editorial in the *Fairbanks Times* stated that the President even intended to legislate the office of delegate out of existence by relegating it to a mere advisory position. It was obvious, the newspaper observed, that President Taft's Philippine experience, in which he administered a commission form of government, had been with people who were not born to self-government. "Withhold self-government from a Malay, and he will not know the difference. Deprive an Anglo-Saxon of the same thing, and he feels enslaved." Wickersham remarked that Taft was surprised at the Alaskan reaction. If the President anticipated trouble from the Territory over his proposal, the Delegate concluded, it was likely to occur, for "I intend to make some myself."[23] If anything, the President's plan for a commission form of government had a unifying effect in Alaska where many changed from mere interest in a local legislature to active advocacy. This became evident when Wickersham asked his constituents to strengthen his position in Washington by holding mass meetings on October 18, 1909, the anniversary of Alaska Cession Day, and by passing resolutions in favor of home rule. Many citizens in the Territory complied with his request, and the Delegate returned to Washington fortified with these favorable expressions.[24]

Washington in early 1910 was turbulent. The famous Ballinger-Pinchot controversy had erupted and put Alaska in the national spotlight. This conservation issue centered on thirty-three coal land claims in Alaska and culminated in a joint congressional investigation.[25] Even though the committee, voting along party lines, absolved Secretary of the Interior Richard A. Ballinger of wrongdoing, public sentiment sided with Gifford Pinchot, the Chief Forester in the Department of Agriculture.

The trouble with the coal land claims reached back to 1906 when President Roosevelt, on the advice of Pinchot, had withdrawn all coal lands in Alaska from entry. Before this executive order became effective, Clarence Cunningham and a group of associates had filed claims in the Bering River area of Alaska. Ballinger, then Commissioner of the General Land Office, had to judge the legality of the claims in the light of the executive order. The investigation by his agent, Louis Glavis, seemed to show that the Cunningham group intended to turn their claims over to the Guggenheims in violation of the law. Ballinger validated the claims, but Secretary of the Interior, James R. Garfield, overturned his decision. Ballinger left the Land Office in 1908 and returned to Seattle while Glavis pursued the matter of the Cunningham claims. As an attorney in Seattle, Ballinger represented the Cunningham group in Washington. When Ballinger became Secretary of the Interior, he removed Glavis from the investigation on a pretense, whereupon the latter complained to Pinchot. The Chief Forester disliked Ballinger and believed Glavis' account. He arranged a meeting between President Taft and Glavis. The Chief Executive examined the evidence, upheld his Secretary of the Interior, and fired Glavis. Pinchot felt that the decision had been unfair, and provided information to the press, and finally brought the matter to a head in Congress. Taft dismissed Pinchot, and Ballinger resigned in 1911. The Cunningham claims were eventually denied.[26]

The controversy helped bring about the election of a Democratic House in 1910 and a rift between Roosevelt and Taft. According to Wickersham, the affair destroyed the friendship between Theodore Roosevelt and President Taft; split the Republican party into two great factions; defeated President Taft for re-election in 1912; elected Woodrow Wilson President of the United States; and changed the course of history of our country.[27]

In this charged atmosphere, Senator Albert J. Beveridge of Indiana, chairman of the Senate Committee on Territories, and Representative E. L. Hamilton of Michigan, Chairman of the House Committee on Territories, introduced complementary proposals for a commission form of government without consulting Wickersham. In 1910, hearings on these two bills were held. It soon became evident that there was strong opposition to the President's plan. After some political maneuvering the administration abandoned its proposal. The defeat of these measures was in no small part due to Wickersham's skillful use of the conservation issue to obtain support for Alaskan home rule. The Delegate pointed out that the resources of Alaska should be used for the benefit of the entire country. Yet, so far, the Territory had been exploited by a few large, absentee-controlled corporations, such as the monopolies which harvested the fur seals and salmon and mined the copper deposits. Home rule, Wickersham asserted, would allow proper utilization of the Territory's wealth.[28]

During the conservation controversy, and as a result of it, home rule for Alaska gained measurably. In 1911, there were manifestations of support from the legislatures of Washington and Oregon and commercial associations of those states. The senators and representatives from these areas were instructed to vote for Alaska home rule. Democratic presidential aspirants, such as Woodrow Wilson, Oscar Underwood, and William J. Bryan, were pledged to support the home rule plank of their party. In this favorable atmosphere, hearings on Wickersham's home rule bill began in the spring of 1911 before the House Committee on Territories under its new chairman, Henry D. Flood of Virginia. By late summer of 1911, the passage of the Wickersham measure seemed reasonably assured.[29]

Some Alaskan papers, such as the *Alaska Daily Times* of Fairbanks, were unhappy with the limitations of the Delegate's measure. Several newspapers in the Territory, the editor stated, "do not enthuse over the bill to establish a debating society in the territory of Alaska, but that does not justify anybody in asserting that they are hostile to home rule."[30] In the face of such remarks, Wickersham wrote in his diary: "[Such editorials]... show how fully the Guggenheim publicity bureau under Gov. W. E. Clark, Governor of the *District* of Alaska, is at work to kill my elective legislative bill...."[31]

In a special message to Congress on February 2, 1912, President Taft dealt extensively with Alaska. He urged Congress to enact legislation which would help the Territory develop its resources.[32] On April 24, 1912, the House unanimously passed Wickersham's elective legislative assembly bill. "It was a glorious Victory!" a jubilant Wickersham exulted in his diary. On July 24, 1912, the Senate passed the Delegate's measure in essentially the same form in which its author had drafted it. At that time Wickersham wrote this candid assessment in his diary: "I have won this victory by a single handed fight against all odds—simply by standing at my station and never ceasing the effort." On August 24, 1912, the President signed the Wickersham measure into law. As the author of the Organic Act of 1912, who had also piloted the measure through Congress, the Delegate seemed to be content with the provisions of the act. He confided to his diary that the Senate and House conference "agreed to all those things in dispute which I wanted in our Home Rule Bill!"[33]

The Organic Act of 1912 gave Alaska a senate of eight members and a house of sixteen to be chosen equally from the four judicial divisions. Since both senators and representatives represented the same constituency, there had been no real reason why Alaska could not have been granted a unicameral legislature, except for the tradition which divided American legislative bodies into two. The 1912 act directed that the existing executive and judicial structures provided by the First Organic Act of 1884 (as amended in 1900 and thereafter) were not changed by the territorial legislature. Both of these branches were to remain appointive by and responsible to the President. The legislature also was prohibited from passing any laws which would deprive the judges and officers of the district court of Alaska of any authority, jurisdiction, or function exercised by similar judges or officers of district courts of the United States. The legislature was further forbidden to deal with the laws relating to the game, fish, and fur resources. The Federal Government retained jurisdiction and management of these very important resources. And there were numerous other restrictions on the powers of the legislature which would cause Alaskans to make tireless efforts to amend and change the Second Organic Act.[34]

FOOTNOTES FOR CHAPTER III

1. The role of the special interests is extensively described in Gruening, *The State of Alaska*, and Nichols, *Alaska*.
2. Nichols, *Alaska*, pp. 274-76.
3. *Annual Report of the Governor of Alaska* (1906), p. 6.
4. U.S., Congress, Senate, *Needs of Alaska in Matters of Legislation and Government*, S. Doc. No. 14, 59 Cong., 2 Sess. (Washington: Government Printing Office, 1906), pp. 4,2.
5. Nichols, *Alaska*, p. 280.
6. U.S. Congress, House, *Biographical Directory of the American Congress, 1774-1961*, H. Doc. 442, 85 Cong., 2 Sess. (Washington: Government Printing Office, 1961), p. 1811. This source states that Wickersham resigned to run for delegate to Congress from Alaska. Wickersham, in his diary, says that he resigned from the bench because he "was a poor man and just then had a reasonable and proper opportunity to re-enter the law practice with a fair prospect of accumulating a stake before opportunity failed or old age overtook...[me]." In addition, the Senate had never confirmed him and he had served under repeated recess appointments by President Roosevelt. The Judge did not think that those Senators who had always opposed him would relent now. At that time he had also had a falling out with Alaskan Governor Wilford B. Hoggatt over a court case involving the career of a young lawyer in which he had rendered a decision contrary to the Governor's views. The latter thereupon refused to give proper support to the court and Judge Wickersham. On top of it all, his wife Debbie had been in ill health for a number of years and he felt that he had been unable to give her needed personal attention. See James Wickersham Diary, September 9, 1907, Microfilm, University of Alaska Archives, College, Alaska; hereafter cited as Wickersham Diary.
7. *Alaska Record* (Juneau), May 27, 1908, quoted in Nichols, *Alaska*, fn. 575, pp. 302-03.
8. Nichols, *Alaska*, pp. 301-04.
9. *Ibid.*, pp. 300, 295, 303, 312-14.
10. Wickersham Diary, June 23, 1908. Wickersham's progress from retired judge to active politician is chronicled in the following excerpts from his diary:
"...the end of my political career was reached without a pang of regret—with real genuine feeling of relief—I can now begin to organize my home—library—and my own private fortune." (September 8, 1907)
"McGinn [a Fairbanks Republican leader] came to see me again and insisted that I ought to run for Delegate to Congress but can't make up my mind to do so." (February 20, 1908)
"McGinn came today—told him that I would not be a candidate for Delegate to Congress—nor to the National Convention—that I am out of political life and intend to remain out." (March 2, 1908)
"I BECAME A CANDIDATE!!" (June 23, 1908)
11. *Ibid.*, July 1, 1908; July 6, 1908; July 7, 1908; July 14, 1908.
12. James Penick, Jr., *Progressive Politics and Conservation: The Ballinger-Pinchot Affair* (Chicago and London: The University of Chicago Press, 1968), pp. 82-83.
13. Nichols, *Alaska*, pp. 306-09. For the story of the Guggenheims, see Harvey O'Connor, *The Guggenheims: the Making of an American Dynasty* (New York: Covici Friede, 1937).
14. Wickersham Diary, July 17, 1908.
15. "James Wickersham Address to the Voters of Alaska," unidentified clipping in Wickersham Diary, July 17, 1908.
16. Nichols, *Alaska*, p. 316.

17. Gruening, *The State of Alaska*, p. 143.
18. Wickersham Diary, November 17, 1908.
19. *Ibid.*, April 1909; May 31, 1909; June 5, 1909.
20. *Ibid.*, June 7, 1909.
21. George A. Frykman, "The Alaska-Yukon-Pacific Expositions, 1909," *Pacific Northwest Quarterly*, LIII (July, 1962), 89-99.
22. Nichols, *Alaska*, p. 329.
23. Editorial, *Fairbanks Times*, October 3, 1909, clipping in Wickersham Diary, October 3, 1909. For a favorable comment on Taft's commission plan, see Brownell Atherton, "Wanted: A Government for Alaska," *Outlook*, February 26, 1910, pp. 431-40. For the opposite view by "An Alaskan," see "President Taft Does Not Favor Home Rule," *Alaska-Yukon Magazine*, August 1909, pp. 470-71.
24. Wickersham Diary, October 13, October 18, 1909.
25. See U.S., Congress, Senate, *Investigation of the Department of the Interior and of the Bureau of Forestry*, S. Doc. 719 pursuant to H.J. Res. 103, 61 Cong., 3 Sess. (Washington: Government Printing Office, 1910). A modern account of the controversy between Ballinger and Pinchot is rendered in Penick, *Progressive Politics and Conservation*. For Clarence Cunningham's views on the whole matter, see Cunningham to Martin Harrais, United States Commissioner, September 16, 1935, Harrais Papers, University of Alaska Archives, College, Alaska. For Alaskan views on the Ballinger-Pinchot controversy and the conservation issue, see "Conservation Gone Crazy," *Alaska-Yukon Magazine*, February, 1910, pp. 171-73; "Conservation That Locks Up," *Ibid.*, April, 1910, pp. 290-93; and the entire issue of *Ibid.*, May 1910. For a protest against the exploitation of Alaska, see Casey Moran, "A Land to Loot," *Collier's*, August 6, 1910, pp. 19-24.
26. Penick, *Progressive Politics and Conservation*, pp. 77-142.
27. James Wickersham, July 21, 1923, Juneau, Alaska, in Introduction, Nichols, *Alaska*, p. 17.
28. *Ibid.*, pp. 349-58.
29. *Ibid.*, pp. 325-84.
30. Editorial, *Alaska Daily Times* (Fairbanks), September, 1911, clipping in Wickersham Diary, September, 1911.
31. *Ibid.*, September, 1911. The Delegate not only had trouble with some newspapers over his home rule bill, but also with some irate citizens. After a debate with a local politician in Fairbanks, Wickersham wrote in his diary: "I intend to try to convince the people that my legislative bill is good and sufficient...."*Ibid.*, October 27, 1911. Another article in the *Alaska Daily Times* (Fairbanks), October 29, 1911, attacked the Delegate and his bill bitterly. Clipping in *Ibid.*, October 29, 1911.
32. Gruening, *The State of Alaska*, p. 150.
33. Wickersham Diary, April 24, 1912; July 24, 1912; August 17, 1912.
34. 37 U.S. *Stats. at Large*, 512 (1912).

CHAPTER IV

THE FIRST STATEHOOD CAMPAIGN

Many Alaskans were not enthusiastic about Wickersham's home rule measure, and the Delegate knew it. Addressing a joint session of the first Alaska legislature in 1913, Wickersham emphasized the positive aspects of the Second Organic Act. He told the lawmakers that they could deal effectively with a wide variety of matters, including such diverse and important fields as health, vital statistics, education, and welfare. If the legislature acted in all of these areas, the Delegate predicted, it would have a busy and fruitful sixty days ahead of it.[1]

By 1916, Wickersham had developed second thoughts about the efficacy of the Organic Act. He blamed the fishing and mining interests, those "invisible forces which organized the opposition to a more perfect government for the people of Alaska under both administrations," for having stymied efforts to amend the act. These "powerful interests," he believed, "desire to seize, own, and exploit the great undeveloped resources of Alaska, free from governmental control." He had hoped that the Wilson administration would remedy the defects of the Organic Act. Instead, opposition to a full territorial form of government now came from the President and his administration. At the time of its passage Wickersham had expressed entire satisfaction with the Organic Act of 1912. But now, recalling the origins of the measure, he complained:

> The big interests engaged in exploiting Alaska finally contented themselves with procuring the insertion of amendments in the bill [the Organic Act] limiting the power of the Alaska legislature over the fisheries, schools, roads, and other important matters of the local concern which had always theretofore been controlled by a Territorial legislature.[2]

Wickersham thought that organic acts for territories always had been, always were, and always would be deficient. Since a plank in the Alaska Democratic platform of 1912 referred to territorial government as but "a temporary makeshift and a preparatory step to complete statehood," the Delegate advised Alaskans that the governmental powers they sought could be obtained "through Statehood more certainly than in any other way."3

That Wickersham had already given some thought to statehood was evidenced by an article he had written for *Collier's* in 1910, under the suggestive title "The Forty-Ninth Star." Alaska was destined to become a State, he argued, pointing out that the Supreme Court had declared that "under the treaty with Russia ceding Alaska and the subsequent legislation of Congress, Alaska has been incorporated into the United States and the Constitution is applicable to that Territory." Accordingly, Alaska was no different from all the other territories which had become States, and therefore had "the constitutional right to Statehood." The Delegate failed to mention that Alaska's noncontiguous status might be an obstacle. In his article, Wickersham did state his intention to introduce a statehood bill for Alaska late in 1910, but for some reason he failed to do so.4

In the meantime, advocates of greater home rule in Alaska sought a number of rather modest objectives. They desired a territorial court system, expansion of the powers of the legislature, and Alaskan control over its natural resources. In order to achieve these goals, the second Alaska legislature, meeting in Juneau in the spring of 1915, petitioned Congress to amend the Organic Act of 1912 to give the people of the Territory "the power to enact laws as fully as the people of the territories of New Mexico, Arizona, Nevada, Montana and Oklahoma and many other territories of the United States have enjoyed." Another memorial from the same session of the legislature requested Congress to remove the restrictions of the Organic Act and to grant Alaska full control and regulation of her fisheries.5

Also in 1915, territorial Senator O. P. Hubbard introduced a senate concurrent resolution which asked Congress for statehood for Alaska.6 This move was aided late in 1915 when a newspaper, *The Forty-Ninth Star*, was established in the senator's home town of Valdez for the express purpose of promoting the cause of statehood. The editor of this paper admonished his prospective readers: "If you are an Alaskan, then be a Forty-niner. Subscribe for this paper and stand by it until the 49th star is placed upon that banner of Freedom."7

Following the founding of the paper, the first statehood club in Alaska was also organized in Valdez. The fledgling group elected officers and adopted a twelve-paragraph constitution in which it committed itself to work for statehood. The organizers recognized the inherent and unavoidable imperfections of the territorial form of government. Long experience had shown, the statehood advocates declared, that full equality and the welfare of the people of Alaska could only be achieved by admission as a State.8

Wickersham, who was closely associated with the Valdez club, responded to their battle cries by drafting an enabling act for the proposed state of Alaska. He patterned his bill after the 1906 measure which had gained admission for Oklahoma. This particular bill, the Delegate reasoned, was recent, contained many new ideas, and was liberal in its grants of money and land to the new state. In addition, Oklahoma was a Democratic state, and, therefore, a similar enabling act should find favor with the Wilson administration.9

In the meantime, *The Forty-Ninth Star* continued to promote the statehood cause. Not only was the Territory entitled to statehood now, the editor asserted, but within five years Alaska would have a population of 100,000. In view of all of Alaska's potentialities, "... where is there a pessimist or politician who whines that we are not ready for Statehood?" he asked. But the editor had no illusions about the time it would take to achieve statehood. He thought it probably would be several years, but the important thing was to start the effort. Even under the most favorable conditions, he said, statehood could not be attained "until long after we deserve it."10

Delegate Wickersham finished his labors on the enabling act early in March, 1916. He sent advance copies of the bill to various Alaska newspapers and asked that the publication of them coincide with the official introduction of the measure on March 30, 1916. Wickersham had carefully chosen this date, which was the forty-ninth anniversary of the signing of the Treaty of Cession of Russian America, to emphasize Alaska's long apprenticeship as a possession of the United States.11 Even though he submitted the bill as planned, the Delegate was not convinced that Alaska was ready for statehood. His enabling act was intended to be a trial balloon. At a talk in Anchorage he pointed out to his listeners that all the costs of administration, now borne by the Federal Government, would have to be assumed by Alaska's taxpayers. These costs included law enforcement, the operation of the courts, and the expenses of the territorial legislature and the executive department. But since campaigns for statehood were historically lengthy affairs, he consoled his audience, Alaskans did not have to fear these added costs yet. By the time statehood was finally achieved the Territory would have the resources to meet the increased financial demands.12

As a more realistic goal, Wickersham also introduced two bills designed to enlarge the powers of the territorial legislature. The Delegate then teamed up with Senator Key Pitman of Nevada and together they presented identical measures which would have provided a modified commission form of government for the Territory. And to cap his efforts, he submitted a bill designed to provide "full territorial government" for Alaska.13 This measure was designed to correct the deficiencies, real or imagined, of the Organic Act of 1912. Wickersham, however, did not really think that it needed revamping. For, as he confided in his diary, "Am now preparing a fool bill entitled: A bill to establish a full territorial form of government in Alaska etc." Wickersham remarked that the *Alaska Daily Empire* (Juneau) and its editor, John W. Troy, had been "howling" for such a measure. Every time anything went wrong in Alaska, Wickersham complained, the supposed inadequacy of the 1912 act was blamed. "Now I am going to introduce a bill to cover everything they have urged as part of 'full territorial form of government'!" Wickersham was sure that the Democratic administration would reject his proposal. Then he could maintain that he had tried his best but had been foiled by the powers in Washington. The political benefits would be obvious.14

The statehood bill itself, the first in a long line of such measures, was simple and skeletal in nature. It contained a provision, standard in enabling acts, that the proposed new State be admitted on a basis of equality with the other States. Alaskans were to hold a constitutional convention and write a document acceptable both to the State and to Congress. The projected government was to be republican in form. There were the usual safeguards, such as those for religious toleration and for the franchise without regard to sex, creed, or color. Creditors were to be protected in that the State was to assume territorial debts. Elementary and higher education were made a State responsibility. The rights of Alaska's Indians, Eskimos, and Aleuts to lands claimed by them were protected. And the future state was to disclaim all rights and title to any unappropriated public areas which were claimed by the various indigenous groups until Congress extinguished those rights. The state was prohibited from selling the tidelands or banks or beds of waters within its boundaries, but instead would hold title to these areas in perpetuity for the public benefit.

The land grants to the new State generally followed those made to the public land States. There were land grants for public buildings and for the support of public schools, State universities, and charitable, penal, and reformatory institutions. In addition, the new State was encouraged to develop forests and forest reserves. Various sections dealt with the leasing of mineral and coal lands, including oil and gas, and for the disposition of funds derived from the sale and lease of such assets. As an ex-judge, Wickersham gave special attention to the section dealing with the judicial system. He carefully detailed the functions of the various courts, distinguishing between the jurisdictions of the State and Federal Government. Arrangements were also specified for the election of State officials. The Delegate was very generous when he proposed four representatives to Congress for Alaska, one from each of the four judicial districts into which Alaska was divided, and the usual two senators.[15]

As requested by Wickersham, many Alaska newspapers took notice of the first statehood bill, and some reprinted the text in full. *The Daily Alaska Dispatch* of Juneau remarked optimistically that "most of the western representatives and senators in other sections of the United States have pledged their support in behalf of the measure." The editor stated that the bill marked another epoch in the history of Alaska, for it meant an end to makeshift government and a firm desire of Alaskans for statehood. A few days later, the same paper summarized the views of those in opposition. "It will be claimed," it stated, "that statehood will cost too much; that Alaska is not ready ...; that there are too many isolated districts ...; [and that] the distances are too great." The paper maintained that the "reactionary press" approved of statehood in principle, but thought that Alaska was not ready just yet. The objections to statehood were the ones made by the same interests which had opposed the Organic Act of 1912. The paper identified these groups as the fishing industry, the Northern Commercial Company, an absentee-owned trading corporation, and all the other economic groups which preferred to maintain a cozy relationship with federal officials. The opponents always said that they wanted changes in the Organic Act instead of statehood. "There is a chance," the editor of *The Daily Alaska Dispatch* conceded, "to have the organic act amended in spots and to palce *[sic]* additional patches to the shabby territorial clothes." But in order to get an entire new organic act, the editor predicted, "will prove more difficult than to secure statehood." He concluded that "halfhearted support would not do. A person is either for statehood or else against it."[16]

Alaska statehood also received some attention in United States newspapers at this time. The publisher of the *San Francisco Chronicle* advised Alaskans to emulate the example of California, organize as a State, and apply to Congress for admission. Success, he told Alaskans, would be assured by following this procedure.[17] His advice was not taken. The *Portland Telegram* however, summed up the movement best when it stated: "We hear the first gentle rapping of Alaska at the door of statehood."[18] One of the reasons the first Alaska statehood movement failed was because "gentle rapping" was not enough. Historically, Territories had to pound at the door of Congress for a period of time in order to gain admission. In 1916, no one in Alaska was prepared for such a sustained effort.

In any event, the attention of Delegate Wickersham and his constituents was quickly diverted from the statehood issue to a fight to retain the measure of self-government the Territory had already gained under the Organic Act of 1912. The precipitating issue was a tax which the territorial legislature had imposed on the fisheries in 1915. Even though the assessment was nominal, the industry, joined by a number of the larger mining companies, took the subject to court and attempted to have the levy nullified. The federal court upheld the right of the Territory to tax, whereupon these groups turned to Congress and tried to obtain federal legislation which would have effectively taken away from the Alaska legislature what little authority it exercised over the fisheries. Wickersham narrowly prevented this attempt to curtail the powers of the territorial legislature. In exasperation, he warned that full territorial government would never be enacted into law "as long as the bureau [of Commerce] and Alaska Fish Trust can prevent it."[19]

Not until 1923 did the statehood idea come to life again, and then only for a short time. The occasion was the visit of President Warren G. Harding to Alaska. This was the first time a Chief Executive had visited the Territory during his term of office. The visit was of utmost importance to Alaskans and they looked upon it as an opportunity to present their views to the President on a variety of matters. Harding was interested, among other things, in finding a solution to the administrative tangle which existed in the Territory. Five cabinet officers and twenty-eight bureaus exercised authority over that northern land. Many of these agencies were in bitter conflict over how best to develop and utilize the vast resources of the area. Secretary of the Interior Albert B. Fall, for example, had consistently promoted a plan to concentrate the administration of Alaska into one department (presumably Interior), thus allowing private enterprise to exploit the natural resources as speedily as possible. Secretary of Agriculture Henry C. Wallace, in whose department the conservation-minded Forest Service was located, objected to Fall's plan. Harding was torn between these conflicting opinions and wanted to investigate on the spot before making any decisions. This was also an opportunity to draw attention to America's neglected northern Territory, and, in addition, the completion of the Federal Government's Alaska Railroad enabled the President to drive the official golden spike.[20]

The President and his party, traveling on the naval vessel *Henderson*, arrived in Metlakatla, Alaska, on July 8, 1923. There the Chief Executive was greeted by the town's Indian population and the territorial Governor, Scott C. Bone. From that village the party traveled on the *Henderson* along the southeastern Alaska coast, stopping at various towns, including Juneau, the capital, and Skagway of gold rush fame. The ship then crossed the Gulf of Alaska to Seward, the terminus of the recently completed Alaska Railroad. From that city the presidential entourage traveled to the new town of Anchorage and then to McKinley Park and Nenana on the railroad where the President drove the symbolic golden spike. From Nenana the party moved on to Fairbanks where Harding addressed most of that town's 1,500 citizens in the ball park. Then the President and his retinue turned south again and finally sailed for Vancouver and Seattle.[21]

During his fourteen days in the Territory, Harding had visited eleven different towns and made sixteen speeches. None of these talks was of any particular importance for Alaskan statehood, however, and the President's favorite expression was, " I did not come here to make you a speech. I have come to Alaska to learn and not to talk."[22] For the most part, he spoke in generalities and reserved his conclusions about Alaska for a speech in Seattle upon his return. A week after he gave this address the President died in San Francisco.

Harding's last major talk was delivered in the University of Washington Stadium on July 27, 1923. He spoke of the future of Alaska and indicated that he opposed radical changes in its administration. He rejected the idea of a sudden exploitation of Alaska's resources such as Secretary Fall had advocated, and, instead, endorsed the conservation policies of his predecessors. The President said that he favored a slow, planned evolution which would protect the Territory's natural resource endowments but yet permit their gradual use. Equally as important to Alaskans, Harding declared that the Territory was destined for ultimate statehood. "Few similar areas in the world present such natural invitations to make a state of widely varied industries and permanent character," he said. "As a matter of fact," he continued, "in a very few years we can well set off the Panhandle and a large block of the connecting southeastern part as a State." He concluded that he had great faith in Alaska's future.[23]

Alaskan reaction to the President's speech was overwhelmingly favorable. The *Ketchikan Chronicle* asserted that the President's speech "came as a tonic to every Alaskan who has taken off his coat, rolled up his sleeves, and worked for the betterment of the territory." *The Alaska Daily Empire* (Juneau) agreed that "there is nothing the Federal Government could do that would transform the Territory overnight into a populous and wealthy commonwealth." One of the few sour notes was injected by the *Anchorage Times* which insisted that "the impediments of bureaucracy" would have to be eliminated before Alaska could develop properly.[24]

Responses from newspapers in the continental United States to Harding's speech ranged from favorable to hostile. The Portland *Oregonian* applauded the idea of planned and gradual development, but insisted that governmental regulations over Alaska's resources needed to be relaxed in order to attract capital. The Philadelphia *Evening Public Ledger* favored statehood, as did the New York *Sun*, which stated: "The American ideal of a nation is not a territorial one; we have always been anxious to grant statehood when it is possible." The *Dearborn Independent* argued that Alaska existed under conditions of "taxation without representation," and that in the past Territories with less population than Alaska, among them Colorado, Indiana, and Michigan, had been admitted. Opposition to statehood was voiced by the Philadelphia *Record* on the basis that it would grant two Senate seats to a handful of Alaskans and would be patently unfair to the populous Eastern states.[25] As for the conservation forces, they strongly endorsed Harding's stand on Alaska's natural resources and welcomed him as one of their own. *Sunset Magazine*, a Western conservation voice, declared: "Almost with his last breath Warren Harding bequeathed to the Far West a priceless legacy, his support of the forces that desire to build wisely, soundly for the future."[26]

While Harding's Seattle speech and his subsequent death were still being discussed in the nation's press, the inhabitants of southeastern Alaska, the Territory's most populous and developed section, were taking steps to secede from the rest of Alaska. They had been encouraged by the late President's remark that their section would be the first to attain statehood. They wanted to speed that day by establishing a full-fledged territorial government for South Alaska. A straw vote taken on November 6, 1923, in various southeastern communities approved overwhelmingly of the plan. The people then memorialized Congress for action and included a proposed organic act for the political entity. To bolster their petition, they added a list of their region's impressive material resources and assets.[27] This move, however, was not merely one designed to bring statehood to South Alaska. The main reason, it appeared, was a desire to retain tax monies for specific use within that part of the Territory. Many in the Panhandle felt that they were supplying a disproportionate share of territorial revenue, and were in fact supporting the other sections of Alaska.[28] When the separationist movement in southeastern Alaska soon fizzled, the statehood issue became relatively quiescent, not to revive again with any strength until the early 1940's.

FOOTNOTES FOR CHAPTER IV

1. *Speech of Hon. James Wickersham, Delegate to Congress* (Juneau, Alaska [no publisher given], March 10, 1931).
2. *Cong. Record*, Appendix, 64 Cong., 1 Sess., p. 1518 (July 25, 1916).
3. *Ibid.*, pp. 1519, 1522.
4. James Wickersham, "The Forty-Ninth Star," *Collier's*, August 6, 1910, p. 17.
5. Senate Joint Memorial No. 2, 2nd Alaska Territorial Legislature, 1915, in Box 448, file 9-1-63, part 1, Records of the Office of Territories, Classified Files, 1907-1951, Record Group 126, National Archives; hereafter cited as R G, N A; *Ibid.*, Senate Joint Memorial No. 16, 2nd Alaska territorial legislature, 1915.
6. *The Forty-Ninth Star* (Valdez), December 18, 1915, p. 7.

7. *Ibid.*, December 4, 1915, p. 4.
8. *Ibid.*, March 4, 1916, p. 4.
9. Wickersham Diary, January 23, 1916.
10. Editorial, *The Forty-Ninth Star* (Valdez), January 8, 1916, p. 3; *Ibid.*, Editorial, p. 7.
11. Wickersham Diary, February 16, 1916.
12. *Alaska Daily Empire* (Juneau), March 31, 1916, p. 4.
13. *Cong. Record*, Index, 64 Cong., 1 Sess., H.R. 4648, p. 170; *Ibid.*, H.R. 6056, p. 189. This action on the part of Wickersham is difficult to understand in light of his vigorous campaign against the Taft proposal for such a form of government just a few years earlier. *Ibid.*, H.R. 232, p. 114, and S. 896, p. 14; *Ibid.*, H.R. 6887, p. 471. For a discussion of this bill, see *Cong. Record*, Appendix, 64 Cong., 1 Sess., pp. 1519-23 (July 25, 1916).
14. Wickersham Diary, December 27, 1915.
15. H.R. 13978, 64 Cong., 1 Sess., in bound volume, RG 233, NA.
16. Editorials, *The Daily Alaska Dispatch* (Juneau), March 30, 1916, p. 1; April 1, 1916, p. 3; April 8, 1916, p. 3; April 13, 1916, p. 3; April 15, 1916, p. 3.
17. Editorial, *San Francisco Chronicle*, quoted in *The Forty-Ninth Star* (Valdez), August 20, 1916, p. 2.
18. Editorial, *Portland Telegram*, quoted in *The Daily Alaska Dispatch* (Juneau), April 19, 1916, p. 3. See also, editorial, *Tacoma Daily News*, quoted in *The Daily Alaska Dispatch* (Juneau), April 22, 1916, p. 1; editorial, *Seattle Post-Intelligencer*, quoted in *The Daily Alaska Dispatch* (Juneau), April 27, 1916, p. 3.
19. For an account of this affair, see *Cong. Record*, Appendix, 64 Cong., 1 Sess., pp. 1520-22 (July 25, 1916). A pamphlet written to further the modern Alaska statehood movement colorfully describes Wickersham's fight to preserve the authority of the territorial legislature. See Evangeline B. Atwood, *Alaska's Struggle for Self-government . . . 83 Years of Neglect* (Anchorage, Alaska: Anchorage Daily Times, 1950), pp. 12-13.
20. See *New York Times*, July 17, 1921, Sec. VII, p. 2, for Secretary Albert B. Fall's plan for the development of Alaska. For the position of Secretary of Agriculture Henry C. Wallace, see "Secretary of Agriculture Wallace on President Harding's Views on Alaska," *The Commercial and Financial Chronicle*, September 1, 1923, pp. 959-60. See also Burl Noggle, *Teapot Dome: Oil and Politics in the 1920's* (Baton Rouge: Louisiana State University Press, 1962), pp. 15-31. The account of what motivated President Harding to visit Alaska is based on Robert K. Murray, *The Harding Era: Warren G. Harding and His Administration* (Minneapolis: University of Minnesota Press, 1969), pp. 439-40; and Francis Russell, *The Shadow of Blooming Grove: Warren G. Harding in His Times* (New York & Toronto: McGraw-Hill Book Company, 1968), pp. 572-73.
21. The account of Harding's visit is based on Murray, *The Harding Era* pp. 445-48; and Russell, *The Shadow of Blooming Grove*, pp. 581-89.
22. James W. Murphy, ed., *Speeches and Addresses of Warren G. Harding, President of the United States* (Washington: Government Printing Office, 1923), p. 307.
23. *Ibid.*, pp. 341-61; *New York Times*, July 28, pp. 1-2; Murray, *The Harding Era*, p. 448
24. "Alaska's Problem as President Harding Saw It," *The Literary Digest*, August 18, 1923, p. 18. Excerpts from both Alaska and continental United States newspapers are found in this article.
25. *Ibid.*
26. Walter V. Woehlke, "Warren Harding's Bequest: He Leaves to the Far West an Emphatic Endorsement of the Conservation Policy," *Sunset Magazine*, October 1923, p. 105.

27. *Memorial of the People of the First Judicial Division of Alaska* (Juneau, Alaska, n.d. [1923]), p. 9.

28. For a reapportionment bill which was debated in Congress, and which was criticized by Delegate Dan A. Sutherland, see U. S. Congress, House, Committee on Territories, *Reapportionment of the Alaska Legislature*, Hearings, 68 Cong., 1 Sess. (Washington: Government Printing Office, 1924). A typewritten note attached to the copy located in the University of Alaska Library states: "This plan to rob Northern Alaska of its share in the revenue of the Territory was instigated by Juneau politicians." Because of the regional differences and jealousies, this note was probably written by a disgruntled Alaskan from the interior of the Territory.

CHAPTER V

THE FEDERAL ROLE IN ALASKA

Former Governor and ex-United States Senator Ernest Gruening has characterized Alaskan history as being one of neglect by the Federal Government. He labels the period of 1867 to 1884 as "The Era of Total Neglect;" 1884 to 1898 as "The Era of Flagrant Neglect;" 1898 to 1912 "The Era of Mild but Unenlightened Interest;" and finally the period from 1912 to 1933 as "The Era of Indifference and Unconcern."[1] Alaskan historian Henry W. Clark also complained in 1930, "... the lack of government in Alaska is a blot upon our pretensions toward enlightened democracy." It was the gold rush which made government in Alaska a pressing problem, Clark continued, but not until the outbreak of the First World War did American colonial policy make a real start toward correcting some of the shortcomings.[2] J.A. Hellenthal, an Alaska author and lawyer, echoed the concerns of Gruening and Clark when he stated in 1936: "The government of Alaska is the worst possible under the American flag. The governments that are worse exist under other flags."[3]

It was Gruening, however, who most eloquently summed up the Territory's feeling toward the Federal Government in his keynote address to the Alaska constitutional convention in November, 1955. He defined a colony as "a geographic area held for political, strategic, and economic advantage." Alaska fitted this description precisely, he stated, and went on to say:

> The maintenance and exploitation of those political, strategic and economic advantages by the holding power is colonialism. The United States is that holding power.
>
> Inherent in colonialism is an inferior economic status. The inferior economic status is a consequence of the inferior political status.
>
> The inferior economic status results from discriminatory laws and practices imposed upon the colonials through the superior political strength of the colonial power in the interest of its own noncolonial citizens.

. . . .

We suffer taxation without representation. . . .

We are subject to military service for the Nation. . . yet have no voice in the making and ending of the wars into which our young men are drafted.

. . . .

The development of Alaska, the fulfillment of its great destiny, cannot be achieved under colonialism. The whole Nation will profit by an Alaska that is populous, prosperous, strong, self-reliant—a great northern and western citadel of the American idea.[4]

Unlike other colonial areas, Alaska was not inhabited by a large native population, militantly conscious of its cultural heritage and capable of developing a movement for freedom from colonialism. As a result, the Territory was slowly settled by white emigrants from the continental United States who were fully aware of their political freedoms and social privileges. As Alaskans they often felt that they had been relegated to second-class citizenship. This impression was sharpened by frustrating dealings with often indifferent and uninformed federal bureaucrats acting on some local matter. In addition, citizens of the Territory could not vote in national elections. Not surprisingly, many resented these conditions and were highly vocal in their criticisms of and attacks on the United States government, the most visible symbol of their real and imagined deprivations. For years, therefore, many territorial citizens were engaged in a two-pronged campaign to achieve relief from these circumstances. On the one hand, many Alaskans prodded Congress, through their delegate, to grant greater self-government to the territory, and, on the other, they goaded the local federal bureaucracy to rationalize and expedite its functions in Alaska.

Alaska's Delegate to Congress from 1921 to 1931, Dan A. Sutherland, unsuccessfully attempted to persuade Congress to make the office of territorial governor elective. Sutherland and many of his fellow citizens hoped that such a measure would give them not only an elected chief executive of their own choice, but also one who was a resident of Alaska and who would presumably understand its problems. Thus Sutherland introduced a bill for an elective governor in the first session of every Congress between 1923 and 1931.[5]

It was true, as Gruening pointed out, that the Federal Government was less than attentive to Alaska prior to 1898. The gold rush and its accompanying population influx, however, demanded that Washington take a more active role. By 1900 there were only a handful of federal representatives in Alaska, among them the governor, who was an employee of the Department of the Interior, internal revenue and customs collectors, a surveyor-general and his deputies, the staff of the agricultural experiment stations, and three United States district judges.6 The number of federal personnel, however, grew steadily, and many Alaskans began to view this phenomenon with alarm. For associated with this increase was a continued withdrawal of public lands and natural resources by various federal agencies.7 The rules and regulations of these various bureaus and agencies could, and did, invalidate those which had been made by the territorial legislature. Alaskans were soon complaining of too much government.

James Wickersham expressed this concern in 1923. He remarked that "the power of national bureaucracy" had found a home in Alaska. It was here, he stated, "that this autocratic enemy to free government is making its last stand for existence among a free people." It was a sad commentary, he insisted, "that there actually exists today a congressional government in Alaska more offensively bureaucratic in its basic principles and practices than that which existed here during the seventy years of Russian rule under the Czar." Comparing the government of Alaska under the Russians with that of the Americans "by executive proclamations and rules and regulations of more than thirty American bureaus," Wickersham concluded, one could not but admire "the comparative simplicity and reasonableness of the Russian system."8 Alaska author and lawyer J.A. Hellenthal blamed "the curse of conservation" for Alaska's stagnation. He angrily explained that "at the present rate of progress, it will not be long before an Alaskan will need a license signed by a cabinet officer to kill a mosquito."9 These and innumerable other expressions of dissatisfaction abounded.

The Federal Government tried to respond to such criticisms by meeting the increasing complexities of its Alaskan operations. It endeavored to streamline its administration and develop plans for the Territory's settlement and economic growth. President Wilson's Secretary of the Interior, Franklin K. Lane, for one, became highly critical of the Alaskan situation. His interest stemmed from the dominant role his department played in the Territory. After examining federal management procedures there, he concluded that Alaska had a number of interlocking, overlapping, cumbersome, and confusing governments. Each of these separate units, the Secretary stated, "is intent upon its own particular business, jealous of its own success and prerogative, and all are more or less unrelated in their operations." To correct this situation, Lane urged the creation of a development board of three members. It was to have complete control of the development and conservation of Alaska's resources, the promotion of industries, the development of transportation, and the settlement of the Territory.[10]

A Senate bill for such a board was introduced in 1914. It would have vested all federal authority in the development and management of the Territory's natural resources in a resident board whose members were to be appointed by the President, confirmed by the Senate, and responsible to the Secretary of the Interior.[11] Like other similar plans, this one was not enacted. In this particular instance, the Federal Government was too preoccupied with the deepening conflict in Europe.

While the First World War created a boom in the continental United States, Alaska did not share in it. Instead, the Territory's economic and population growth slowed down. Census statistics between 1910 and 1920 showed a drop of 9,320 in the population,[12] and many Alaskans as well as citizens in the states blamed the inept Washington bureaus as well as the conservation laws for this stagnation.

In 1921 Secretary of the Interior Albert B. Fall proposed the centralization of all responsibility for the management and development of Alaska's resources under a single, responsible head,[13] presumably himself. Fall, in essence, echoed previous proposals, and his successor, Secretary Hubert Work, also blamed the Federal Government for the lack of the Territory's development. He had no plan for a development board, but asserted that "without the inspiration of self-government and freedom, the country is now being retarded by unnecessary activity of government bureaus...."[14]

The nine major federal departments which controlled Alaskan affairs finally established an interdepartmental coordinating committee in Washington.[15] It consisted of one member from each of these departments. This group, in turn, delegated much of its authority to a similar body in Alaska, composed of the chief field representatives of the nine federal departments. This administrative streamlining did not function as expected. Sherman Rogers, the industrial correspondent for *Outlook*, visited Alaska in 1923 and reported that the attempt had failed. Instead of coordinating and expediting territorial affairs, he stated, it had added greatly to the confusion, red tape, and petty jealousies within the federal administration. Rogers recommended the elimination of the Washington committee and the transfer of executive powers to an Alaskan-based interdepartmental board. This recommendation was strongly endorsed by Secretary of Commerce Herbert Hoover and other federal officials. So far, Hoover remarked, the government had "made about as bad a job of it [Alaskan administration] as could have been done if we had set out to do our worst."[16]

After leaving office, Alaska Governor Scott C. Bone, writing in the *Saturday Evening Post*, reviewed Alaska's problems and concluded that governmental reorganization would do little for territorial growth. The remedy, he asserted, lay in full territorial government "preliminary to statehood at the earliest possible date. Then will Alaska grow as the Dakotas, Oklahoma, Colorado—indeed, all the continental Union—grew and thrived."[17]

It was not until 1927 that an act of Congress authorized the Secretaries of the Departments of the Interior, Agriculture, and Commerce each to appoint an ex-officio commissioner for Alaska to whom they could assign and delegate matters under the jurisdiction of that particular department.[18] These commissioners when chosen consisted of the governor of Alaska, representing the Secretary of the Interior, the head of the Bureau of Fisheries field force in Alaska, and the Department of Agriculture's chief territorial field representative in farming and forestry.[19] Little, however, was heard again of these commissioners. It was not surprising, for the strong departmental loyalties of the three members produced only ineffectiveness. After that, no serious attempts at coordinating, consolidating, and streamlining federal operations in the Territory were made for several years.

On October 24, 1929, stock market prices fell disastrously on the New York exchange and reached all-time lows in 1932. Nationwide economic activity slowed down in the wake of the crash, unemployment increased tremendously, and America began to experience its worst depression.

The effects of this economic misfortune were soon felt in Alaska. Governor George A. Parks euphemistically reported in 1930 that "during the early summer a surplus of laborers was reported in a few places...." In 1931 he observed that there was more unemployment than usual, and in 1932 that economic conditions had worsened. By 1933 unemployment in the Territory, as in the continental United States, had become the major problem.[20] The census of 1930 revealed that Alaska had gained 4,242 people over the census of 1920 which brought its population up to 59,278.[21] This influx was attributable to the unstable economic picture in the Pacific Coast states which led many to seek work in the north.

With the depression deepening, prices paid for fish and copper, the Territory's two chief commodities, declined. This drop, in turn, led to a curtailment of the production of these two items, and many of the new citizens Alaska had recently gained joined the army of the unemployed. The work force in the fishing industries dropped from 29,283 in 1929 to 12,695 in 1933, with an accompanying cut in wages. In the same time span, the value of fish products declined from $50,795,819 to $32,126,588. Likewise, imports of goods and supplies from the continental United States to Alaska dwindled from 350,193 tons in 1929 to 240,379 tons in 1933, while exports from Alaska for the same period, consisting mainly of fish products, minerals, and furs, shrank from 449,944 tons to 260,138 tons.[22] Government employment in the Territory was cut back proportionately.

The economic outlook was bleak in April of 1932 when Alaskans chose their delegates to the national party conventions and elected candidates for the delegateship. The Republican delegation left the Territory pledged to the renomination of President Herbert Hoover, while the Democrats favored the nomination of Governor Franklin D. Roosevelt of New York for President. The Democrats chose Anthony J. Dimond out of a field of three candidates for delegate to Congress, while Republican James Wickersham, who had returned from political retirement in 1930 to regain his old seat, was unopposed for a second term.[23]

Dimond was a topflight Alaskan lawyer from Valdez, a former prospector and miner, who had been repeatedly elected mayor of his city, and a one-time member of the territorial senate.[24] Although the *New York Times* described him as a man almost entirely lacking in political instinct, a Democrat of long standing who had never voluntarily sought office, he was rated as the most formidable candidate the Democrats had put into the field in years. Both Wickersham and Dimond campaigned vigorously, the seventy-five-year-old Wickersham fighting for his political life. Dimond electioneered by bush plane and suffered a mishap. He was struck by the plane's propeller on the shoulder and immediately rushed to the hospital in Fairbanks where he was treated for a deep flesh wound and a broken collar bone. Despite this interruption in his campaign, Dimond won by a substantial margin and Alaska Democrats gained large majorities in both houses of the territorial legislature.[25] The American public also voted for a national political change, and Dimond began his Washington career in an era of tremendous political ferment.

The tall, quiet, dignified Delegate quickly made an excellent impression on his colleagues in the House and his acquaintances in the Senate.[26] He worked ceaselessly to expand the powers of the territorial government. In particular, Dimond introduced measures to give Alaska control of the administration of its fish and game resources.[27] In 1938 his efforts were partially rewarded when Congress made a number of reforms which streamlined the administration of the territory's game laws and included many of his suggestions.[28]

During Dimond's six terms in Congress, he generally followed the example of his predecessors and submitted proposals which would have prevented the appointment of a nonresident as governor,[29] and which also provided for the election of a territorial chief executive.[30] He introduced measures which would have permitted the appointment of Alaska residents only to the positions of district court judges and United States attorneys and marshals.[31] All of these proposals were designed to overcome carpetbag charges which were often made against federal appointees and also to get personnel familiar with the Territory and its problems. None of the bills ever passed.

In 1934 Dimond joined forces with Hawaii's delegate and submitted legislation which would have given both Territories representation in the Senate comparable to that in the House, but without success.[32] His diligent attempts to persuade Congress to extend the Federal Aid Highway Act of 1916 to Alaska likewise were unsuccessful.[33]

Although Alaska failed to gain more self-government as a result of Dimond's efforts, it participated on a modest scale in some of the economic recovery programs of the New Deal. The National Reforestation Act of 1933 provided for the employment of several hundred men. Late in 1933, the Federal Government raised the price of gold from its fixed price of $20.67 to $35.00 per ounce. This action soon led to an increase in mining activity. The Territory also benefited from projects undertaken by the Public Works Administration and the Work Projects Administration as well as the Civilian Conservation Corps. Many programs of enduring worth were completed. These included waterworks, schools, playgrounds, fire stations, and the construction of roads, airfields, and a steel bridge across Gastineau Channel connecting Juneau on the mainland with Douglas on Douglas Island. In addition, trails and shelter cabins were built in the national forests. By 1936, PWA alone had allocated some $4,463,233 for the Territory.34

In 1935 the famous Matanuska Valley colonization scheme commenced. President Franklin D. Roosevelt envisioned this undertaking as an opportunity to take Americans from depressed agricultural areas and give them a chance to start life anew and become self-sustaining again. In addition, it was to demonstrate Alaska's agricultural possibilities and to stimulate population growth. Some 15,000 letters of application were received once final plans had been announced. The number of prospective settlers was finally limited to 202, who, together with their dependents, would number approximately 1,000 persons. The colonists were chosen from Michigan, Wisconsin, and Minnesota on the assumption that the climatic similarities of these areas to Alaska would best fit the pioneers for life in the Matanuska Valley. The final selection was haphazard. All unsolicited applications were disregarded and colonists were instead recruited and urged to go. Many mistakes were made and numerous people totally unsuited for such an undertaking were brought to Alaska.

In the spring of 1935, 202 families, amidst much fanfare, arrived in the town of Palmer in the center of the valley. They were sponsored by the Federal Emergency Relief Administration under its Rural Rehabilitation Division. Together with some 400 relief workers from the transient camps of California, they set about to clear land for the projected forty-acre tracts each settler was to receive. They also built living quarters, a school, trading post, cannery, creamery, and hospital.35

In the same year another settlement proposal was made by "The Alaska Colonization Branch of the United Congo Improvement Association" with headquarters in Cleveland, Ohio. The organization's letterhead proclaimed optimistically that "Alaska offers the American Negro full political rights." Dr. Joe Thomas, a medical practitioner and the group's head, represented some 2,000 members on relief. Many were farmers, heads of families and war veterans. Although the U.C.I.A., Inc. maintained that Alaska could eventually well support one million Negroes initial plans were very modest. It asked President Franklin D. Roosevelt to settle some 400 farmers in Alaska, 200 on the Kenai Peninsula and the rest at Iliamna Bay. With existing racial prejudices and prevailing beliefs that only people from the world's northern lands were suited for life in Alaska, Thomas' plan was foredoomed to failure. The proposal was shuttled from agency to agency in the Federal Government, until it landed on the desk of Ernest Gruening, head of the Division of Territories and Island Possessions, who turned it down.36

Although the New Deal quickened Alaska's economic pace, it brought no basic changes. In 1937 the National Resources Committee examined territorial conditions and found that Alaska's was still very small. There were only seven cities with a population of 1,000 or more, and from the beginning until 1937 less than 2,500 miles of public highways had been built in the whole of Alaska. This was equivalent to the mileage regarded as necessary in the continental United States to service an area of approximately thirty-six square miles. The committee reported that some fifty-two federal agencies operated in Alaska and that "often their authority and responsibility appear to be poorly defined. There is over-lapping of jurisdiction and divided responsibility, resulting in confusion, delay, and excessive 'red tape.'" The committee suggested maximum discretion for federal field officials and the establishment of a coordinating device outside the usual departmental loyalties. In addition, the committee outlined alternate avenues of development Alaska could follow. On the one hand, the Territory could simply serve as a source of raw materials for the continental United States. In that case, it soon would be destroyed as a future home for Americans. Another possibility was that Alaska could, with considerable government help, develop a diversified economy which would be conducive to population growth. The committee, however, expressed hope that a middle course would be followed.[37]

As a matter of fact, Alaska was soon to be rediscovered and rapidly developed, a circumstance which was neither foreseen nor planned by the Federal Government. As early as 1933, Delegate Dimond had recognized Japan as a threat to America's security and asked Congress for military airfields and planes, a highway to link the Territory with the continental United States, and army garrisons. In 1934 he cautioned that it was futile to fortify Hawaii and leave Alaska totally unguarded, because any attack from across the Pacific, he predicted, was bound to come by way of Alaska.[38] In 1935 he stated:

> Is it not obvious that an enemy moving across the Pacific would not come by way of Honolulu, or within 2,000 miles of it, but would rather strike, invade, and take Alaska at one gulp, for at the present time Alaska is absolutely undefended by any military force or installation of any kind... except... a force that is not sufficiently powerful to be of any use against a foreign attack.

He warned his House colleagues in 1937 that Japanese fishermen, ostensibly fishing off Alaska's coast, were actually disguised military personnel seeking information on the depth, defenses, and landmarks of Alaska's harbors. In the same year Delegate Dimond attempted to secure a $2,000,000 appropriation to begin construction of an air base near Fairbanks which had been authorized in 1935. He pleaded eloquently, pointing out that if Hawaii was one key to the Pacific, Alaska was the other. At the very least, he urged, Army Air Corps pilots should be trained in cold weather flying. The money was refused.[39] In time he made converts, most importantly General George C. Marshall, the Chief of Staff, and General Henry H. Arnold, head of the Army air force. Yet as late as 1938, Dimond reported that Alaska had only approximately 300 infantry troops, stationed at Chilkoot Barracks near Haines, and about six naval airplanes at Sitka, also in southeastern Alaska.[40]

Congress finally authorized $29,108,285 in 1940 for the construction of navy and army bases and a fort at locations ranging from Unalaska to Kodiak, and from Anchorage to Sitka. The construction of these facilities, however, was stretched in a leisurely fashion over several years.[41] It was not until the invasion of Denmark and Norway by the Nazis in the spring of 1940, Dimond stated later, that military building slowly commenced in the Territory. Many congressmen, Dimond believed, for the first time realized that the Scandinavian Peninsula was just over the top of the earth from Alaska, and that bombers which could fly such a distance existed. This sudden insight, the Delegate later commented, brought about a turning point in Alaska's fortunes and history.[42] Yet when the Japanese struck Pearl Harbor, none of the Alaskan bases were ready, although construction had been under way since 1940. Pearl Harbor immensely speeded the building of bases at Kodiak Island, Dutch Harbor, Anchorage, Sitka, and Fairbanks.

One contemporary journalist, Richard L. Neuberger, reported early in 1942 that Alaska had not been so conspicuous and prominent in the American press since its purchase in 1867. He anticipated that the war would speed Alaskan development and progress significantly.[43] A rash of articles appeared extolling the strategic importance of Alaska in the defense of the western shores of the continental United States.[44] Ernest K. Lindley of *Newsweek* reminded his readers early in 1942 that General "Billy" Mitchell in the mid-1930's had emphatically stated that Alaska was the most important strategic spot on the globe in the age of airpower. Nobody had listened at that time. For years there had been intermittent talk about a highway to the territory, Lindley related. Engineers had surveyed a route, but the project had remained at the talking stage. As late as 1940, Secretary of War Henry L. Stimson had thought that the defense value of such a road connection was at best negligible. But by October of 1941 the Secretary conceded that such a road would have a desirable long-range value as a defense measure.[45]

Then, on December 7, 1941, Japanese forces attacked the Pacific fleet at anchor in Pearl Harbor and practically destroyed it. America was at war. In the summer of 1942 enemy forces invaded and occupied Attu and Kiska on the Aleutian Chain. America's pride was hurt, and Secretary of the Interior Harold L. Ickes, who had been almost totally indifferent to Alaska thus far, suddenly declared that there was no question that the United States had to defend this "cherished" Territory. Indeed, all Americans were united in their desire to drive the Japanese out.[46] This attitude was far different from that expressed by retired Major General Smedley D. Butler, who, testifying in 1938 before Congress in connection with a naval construction bill, had recommended that the United States abandon Alaska in case of war.[47]

Far from abandoning its northern outpost, the United States quickly sent 10,000 soldiers, divided into seven Army Engineer regiments and supported by 6,000 civilian workers under the direction of the United States Public Road Administration, to start construction of the ALCAN (Alaska-Canadian Military Highway) in the spring of 1942. Work began simultaneously at three locations: Dawson Creek, the terminal of a railroad running northwest from Edmonton, Alberta; at Whitehorse, Yukon Territory, which was connected by the White Pass and Yukon Railway with Skagway at tidewater on the coast of southeastern Alaska; and at Big Delta in Alaska. The highway was completed with incredible speed, and in November of 1942 was formally opened for traffic. The construction of 1,671 miles of road over formidable terrain had been an engineering feat of the first order. It has been estimated that the cost of construction amounted to roughly $135,000,000 or $56,160 per mile, including the innumerable bridges which cost approximately $23,166,725 to build.[48]

While the ALCAN Highway rapidly took shape, thousands of other American soldiers came to Alaska to participate in its defense and prepare for the recapture of Kiska and Attu. Civilian workers toiled practically around the clock to build bases at various locations in Alaska. At the same time, between June 9 and September 13, 1942, Kiska was bombed by planes stationed on Umnak Island. Since these planes had to make a 1,200-mile round trip, they carried a small bomb load but much fuel. This situation improved in September, 1942, when the bombers began conducting their raids from the recently completed base on Adak Island, which cut the two-way trip to 500 miles. Next, an advance base was built on Amchitka Island, which was extensively used after February, 1943. Throughout the winter of 1942-43, American and Canadian bombers and fighters continued their missions against the Japanese preparatory for the May 11, 1943, amphibious assault on Attu. At the end of May, 1943, the island fell into American hands after fierce fighting. Subsequently, construction of airfields proceeded on Attu and Shemya, and on August 15, 1943, an amphibious landing was made on Kiska. The troops, however, discovered that the enemy had left the island at the end of July by submarines. Following this action, ground forces in Alaska were reduced. From a high of 150,000 men in November of 1943, military personnel of the Alaskan Department had been reduced to 50,000 by March, 1945. Forts were closed, bases dismantled, and airfields turned over to the Civil Aeronautics Administration.[49]

The impact of military activities had irrevocably altered the pace and tenor of Alaskan life, and the residual benefits to the civilian economy and the development of Alaska were tremendous. Between 1941 and 1945, the Federal Government spent well over one billion dollars in the Territory.[50] The modernization of the Alaska Railroad and the expansion of airfields and construction of roads benefited the civilian population. Many of the docks, wharves, and breakwaters built along the coast for the use of the Navy, Coast Guard, and the Army Transport Service were turned over to the Territory after the war. Thousands of soldiers and construction workers had come north. Many decided to make Alaska their home at the end of the hostilities, a fact reflected in the population statistics. Between 1940 and 1950, the territory's civilian population increased from roughly 74,000 to 112,000.[51] This influx put a tremendous strain on Alaska's social services, such as schools, hospitals, housing, and local government.

In short, the war was the biggest boom Alaska ever experienced, bigger than any of the gold rushes of the past. Alaskans themselves were forced into an awareness of the outside world. The Territory's isolation, partially self-imposed by the parochial outlook of many of its citizens, and partially caused by the lack of communication and transportation, had ended. The familiar economic pattern of primary resource extraction together with modest supporting services was disrupted and replaced by government and defense-related activities. Government employment rose from 12.1 per cent of the total employed labor force in September, 1939, to 53.7 per cent in April, 1950. Self-employment during the same time span dropped from 33.9 per cent to 13.7 per cent. The change in the commodity-producing industries, such as agriculture, forestry, fisheries, and mining, was even more pronounced. While 62.3 per cent of Alaska's total labor force was employed in these primary pursuits in September, 1939, it had shrunk to 26.5 per cent in April, 1950, and continued to fall.[52]

Meanwhile, Delegate Anthony Dimond utilized the attention Alaska enjoyed nationally. Between 1943 and 1945 he continued to press for an appointed governor to be chosen from among the Territory's residents, for making the governor elective, and for extending the Federal Highway Act of 1916 to Alaska—all to no avail.[53] His proposal to give Alaska proportional representation by electing one territorial senator and one territorial representative for every 4,000 persons was only partly successful. The Organic Act of 1912 had given the Territory a senate of eight members and a house of sixteen. Two senators and four representatives were allotted to each of the four judicial divisions. These geographic units, however, had gained population unequally. According to the 1940 census, the first judicial division showed a population of 25,241; the second, 11,877; the third, 19,312; and the fourth, 16,094. With more than twice as many people in the first than the second division, and the population in all, except the second, increasing, the territorial legislature had become less and less representative. As finally passed by Congress, the reform measure gave proportional representation in the house only. It increased the number of representatives to twenty-four and doubled that of the senators to sixteen.[54]

With the increase in population, talk about statehood for Alaska was heard again. As early as 1939, the Fairbanks-based "Alaska Home Rule Association" issued a statement in which it assailed "taxation without representation" and asked for future statehood.[55] A bill, defeated by the territorial senate in 1941, would have given Alaskans the opportunity of a statehood referendum.[56] A similar measure in the 1943 session met the same fate.[57] The modern statehood movement, however, was opened in April, 1943, when Senators William L. Langer and Pat McCarran, at Dimond's request, submitted the first statehood bill since Wickersham's measure in 1916.[58]

Dimond followed up with a discussion of the statehood question over radio station WWDC in Washington. Statehood for Alaska, he asserted, was a foregone conclusion. The Territory was ready economically and socially, and entitled to it, although the military might prefer to put off any change in the governmental structure until after the war. Opposition, he predicted, would come from the absentee-owned fishing and mining industries, "who usually cry out in agony at the thought that they may be obliged to pay more taxes." Further economic development and statehood, he concluded, were interdependent.[59]

Reactions to the proposal in Alaska varied. Robert B. Atwood, editor and publisher of the *Anchorage Daily Times*, was utterly surprised when he read the news of the Langer-McCarran bill in an

Associated Press dispatch. "I had never given statehood any thought or consideration," he recalled. "I wasn't in politics like Gruening, maybe he thought of it, but I hadn't." Atwood, however, quickly recognized the desirability of statehood and used his newspaper to disseminate this view.[60] The Wrangell Chamber of Commerce passed a resolution strongly urging passage of the measure, while the Juneau chamber thought that any action should be suspended until the end of the war. The Ketchikan Bar Association unanimously favored it, as did its Juneau counterpart.[61]

Secretary of the Interior Ickes stated that "statehood might be desirable as the ultimate political status for Alaska," but opposed it because of the Territory's seasonal economy and unstable population. The Secretary was emphatic in his opposition to section three of the bill which proposed to give the future state all vacant and unappropriated public lands. Such action, Ickes asserted, would give to one state the tremendous natural resources which belonged to all Americans. The Secretary recommended against passage of the bill.[62]

On December 2, 1943, Dimond crowned his years in Congress when he submitted a companion measure to the Langer-McCarran bill.[63] The political advantages of statehood, he asserted, were immense. Alaska no longer would be a beggar at the nation's capital, but instead would become a full-fledged member of the Union of States.[64]

FOOTNOTES FOR CHAPTER V

1. Gruening, *The State of Alaska*, Table of Contents.
2. Clark, *History of Alaska*, pp. 81, 129.
3. J. A. Hellenthal, *The Alaskan Melodrama* (New York: Liveright Publishing Corporation, 1936), p. 284.
4. Ernest Gruening, "Let Us End American Colonialism," Keynote Address, Alaska Constitutional Convention, University of Alaska, College, Alaska, November 9, 1955, in *Cong. Record*, 85 Cong., 1 Sess., pp. 470-71, 474 (January 14, 1957).
5. *Cong. Record*, Index, 68 Cong., 1 Sess., p. 606 (H.R. 6947 proposed to elect the governor and secretary of the territory); *Ibid.*, 69 Cong., 1 Sess., p. 669 (H.R. 7289 proposed to elect the governor and secretary of the Territory); *Ibid.*, 70 Cong., 1 Sess., p. 588 (H.R. 329 provided for the election of the governor only); *Ibid.*, 71 Cong., 1 Sess., p. 279 (H.R. 250 provided for the election of the governor only). None of the bills passed.
6. *Annual Report of the Governor of Alaska* (1904), pp. 15-16.
7. National Resources Committee, *Regional Planning—Part VII, Alaska—Its Resources and Development* (Washington: Government Printing Office, 1938), p. 11. The committee reported that most of

Alaska's resources were owned by the Federal Government. Their development was controlled and regulated under a policy of conservation. Coal lands were withdrawn from entry in 1906 under an executive order on November 12 of that year. A leasing law for coal lands was passed in 1913. Oil lands were withdrawn in 1910 and leasing regulations issued in 1920. An executive proclamation of February 16, 1909, created the Tongass National Forest, and the Chugach National Forest was created by a similar order on February 22, 1909. *Ibid.*

8. James Wickersham, quoted in Nichols, *Alaska*, p. 33.

9. Hellenthal, *Alaskan Melodrama*, pp. viii, 283.

10. "Red Tape Riddance for Alaska," *The Literary Digest*, June 27, 1914, p. 1530; Franklin K. Lane, "Red Tape in Alaska," *Outlook*, January 20, 1915, pp. 135-40; typewritten manuscript by Herman B. Walker, special inspector in the Office of the Secretary of the Interior, "Red Tape in the Government of Alaska: The Need for Centralized Responsibility and Accountability" (1914), pp. 1-67, in file 9-1-60, part 1, Central Classified files, 1907-1951, Office of Territories, Record Group 126, National Archives. Hereafter cited as RG,NA.

11. *Cong. Record*, 63 Cong., 2 Sess., p. 2722 (February 2, 1914).

12. Rogers and Cooley, *Alaska's Population and Economy*, vol. I, *Analysis*, p. 19. For an excellent study of Alaska's economic growth during the war years, see Joseph L. Fisher, "Alaska: The Development of Our Arctic Frontier" (unpublished Ph.D. dissertation, Harvard University, 1947). While a start toward a national highway network was made by the provisions of the Federal Highway Act of July 11, 1916 (39 U.S. *Stats. at Large* 212 [1916]), Alaska was specifically excluded from its benefits, although not from the collection of the Federal gasoline and other taxes to finance it. Puerto Rico, Hawaii, and the District of Columbia were included in the benefits. An act of Congress on June 29, 1956, included Alaska for the first time on a reduced basis, inasmuch as Alaska's share in the funds was to be calculated on only one-third of its area. See 70 U.S. *Stats. at Large* 374 (1956). For a full account of the story of highway construction, see Gruening, *The State of Alaska*, pp. 443-456.

13. *The New York Times*, July 17, 1921, Sec. VII, p. 2.

14. Hubert Work, "What Future Has Alaska," *National Spectator* in *Cong. Record*, 69 Cong., 1 Sess., p. 5126 (March 5, 1926).

15. In the 1930's, nine Federal departments were involved in Alaskan affairs. These were Interior, State, Justice, Commerce, Agriculture, War, Treasury, Post Office, and Labor. For the various bureaus operating under the departments, see *Annual Report of the Governor of Alaska* (1932), pp. 120-131; National Resources Committee, *Alaska: Its Resources and Development* (1938).

16. Sherman Rogers, "The Problem of Alaska's Government," *Outlook*, January 23, 1923, pp. 173-74. Assistant Secretary of Commerce C.H. Huston and Alaska Governor Scott C. Bone also endorsed the proposal. See *Ibid.*, p. 174. Governor Bone, in an article entitled "The Land That Uncle Sam Bought and Then Forgot," *Review of Reviews*, April, 1922, pp. 402-10, summarized the contributions Presidents and their administrations had made to Alaskan development, starting with President Benjamin Harrison. He also severely indicted Federal red tape in the Territory. He concluded that Alaska had been ignored at first, then had been granted a limited form of government, and subsequently had become a problem of conservation politics, only to be dealt with academically.

17. Scott C. Bone, "Alaska from the Inside," *Saturday Evening Post*, August 8, 1926, p. 130.

18. Alaska Law Compilation Commission, *Compiled Laws of Alaska, 1949, Containing the General Laws of the Territory of Alaska, Annotated with Decisions of the District Courts of Alaska, the Circuit*

Court of Appeals, and the Supreme Court of the United States (San Francisco: Bancroft-Whitney Co., 1948), title 10, chapter 4, sect. 1,5.

19. Ray Lyman Wilbur, "A New Alaska in the Making," *Current History*, XXXV (October, 1931), 84.

20. *Annual Report of the Governor of Alaska* (1930), p. 1; (1931), p. 1; (1932), p. 1; (1933), p. 2.

21. Rogers and Cooley, *Alaska's Population and Economy*, vol. I, *Analysis*, p. 16.

22. National Resources Committee, *Alaska—Its Resources and Development* (1938), pp. 62, 61, 150.

23. *New York Times*, April 27, 1932, p. 2, April 28, p. 3, and October 16, Sec. II, p. 6.

24. *Biographical Directory of the American Congress, 1774-1961*, p. 813.

25. *New York Times*, October 16, 1932, Sec. II, p. 6; *Ibid.*, November 11, 1932, p. 8.

26. Mary Lee Council, "Alaska Statehood" (unpublished manuscript, n.d.) in author's files; Richard L. Neuberger, "Anthony J. Dimond of Alaska," *Alaska Life*, September, 1943, in *Cong. Record*, Appendix, 78 Cong., 1 Sess., pp. 4282-90 (October 14, 1943).

27. *Cong. Record*, Index, 73 Cong., 1 Sess., H.R. 5205, H.R. 5209, p. 401; *Ibid.*, 74 Cong., 1 Sess. H.R. 161, H.R. 163, p. 712; *Ibid.*, 75 Cong., 1 Sess. H.R. 1562, H.R.1563, p. 720; *Ibid.*, 76 Cong.,1 Sess., H.R. 2411, p. 283; *Ibid.*, 77 Cong., 1 Sess., H.R. 79, p. 772.

28. H.R. 7844, which became Public Law 728, 75 Cong., 3 Sess., made some ten changes in Alaska's game laws which embraced many of the recommendations Dimond had made. For details see Public Law 728, *Cong. Record*, Appendix, 75 Cong., 3 Sess., p. 3177 (June 16, 1938).

29. *Ibid.*, Index, 76 Cong., 3 Sess., H.R. 9112, p. 765; *Ibid.*, 78 Cong., 1 Sess., H.R. 344, p. 692.

30. *Ibid.*, 78 Cong., 1 Sess., S. 1436, p. 670, provided for the election of a governor and was introduced by Senator William L. Langer at Dimond's request; *Ibid.*, H.R. 2462, p. 742.

31. *Ibid.*, 78 Cong., 1 Sess., H.R. 2977, p. 757.

32. *Ibid.*, 73 Cong., 2 Sess., H.R. 6378, p. 540; H.R. 6617, p. 545.

33. *Ibid.*, 73 Cong., 2 Sess., H.R. 8679, p. 589; *Ibid.*, 74 Cong., 1 Sess., H.R. 6861, p. 840; *Ibid.*, 75 Cong., 1 Sess., H.R. 1554, p. 719; *Ibid.*, 76 Cong., 1 Sess., H.R. 1955, p. 155.

34. *Annual Report of the Governor of Alaska* (1933), p. 2, (1935), p. 1; Gruening, *The State of Alaska*, p. 300; *Cong. Record*, 74 Cong., 2 Sess., p. 10876 (June 20, 1936).

35. Gruening, *The State of Alaska*, p. 299; *Annual Report of the Governor of Alaska* (1935), p. 36. For an excellent account and evaluation of this experiment in subsistence farming, see Orlando Wesley Miller, "The Frontier in Alaska and the Matanuska Valley Colony" (unpublished Ph.D. dissertation, Columbia University, 1965).

36. Dr. Joe Thomas, The Alaskan Colonization Branch of the United Congo Improvement Association, to C. E. Pynchon, General Manager, Federal Subsistence Homesteads Corporation, Department of the Interior, March 20, 1936, file 9-1-60, Alaska, Development of Resources, Office of Territories, RG 126, NA; Dr. Joe Thomas to President Franklin D. Roosevelt, February 18, 1935, file 9-1-60, part 1, Alaska, Development of Resources, Office of Territories, RG 126, NA. For an account of this project see Claus-M. Naske, "A Study in Frustration; Blacks Blocked by Bureaucracy," *The Alaska Journal*, Autumn, 1971, pp. 8-10.

37. National Resources Committee, *Alaska—Its Resources and Development* (1938), pp. 11-14.

38. *Cong. Record*, 73 Cong., 2 Sess., p. 8257 (May 7, 1934). See also Arthur R. Robinson, "Will Japan Seize Alaska?" *Liberty Magazine*, March 24, 1934, in *Cong. Record*, 73 Cong., 2 Sess., pp. 8257-59 (May 7, 1934).

39. *Cong. Record*, 74 Cong., 1 Sess., p. 2343 (February 20, 1935); Richard L. Neuberger, "Anthony J. Dimond of Alaska," *Alaska Life*, September, 1943, in *Cong. Record* Appendix, 78 Cong., 1 Sess., pp. 4288-90 (October 14, 1943); *Cong. Record*, 75 Cong., 1 Sess., pp. 4014-15, 4056 (April 29, 30, 1937).

40. *Cong. Record*, 75 Cong., 3 Sess., p. 1949 (May 11, 1938).

41. *Ibid.*, 76 Cong., 3 Sess., p. 4599 (July 25, 1940). The appropriations covered the two fiscal years beginning on July 1, 1939, and ending on July 1, 1941.

42. Richard L. Neuberger, "Anthony J. Dimond of Alaska," *Alaska Life*, September, 1943, in *Cong. Record*, Appendix, 78 Cong., 1 Sess., p. 4289 (October 14, 1943).

43. Richard L. Neuberger, "Alaska—Northern Front," *Survey Graphic*, February, 1942, pp. 57-62.

44. "U.S. Strengthens Defenses in Alaska and Bering Straits to Meet Twin Threat of Russian and Japanese Action," *The China Weekly Review*, January 11, 1941, pp. 186-87; "Alaska to be Fortified Against Japanese Invasion: New Northern Airplane Route Envisaged,"*Ibid.*, May 10, 1941, pp. 318-19; Vilhjalmur Stefansson, "Alaska, American Outpost No. 4," *Harper's*, June, 1941, pp. 83-92; "Alaska's Future is the Responsibility of the U.S.," *Fortune*, March, 1942, p. 114; Bella Doherty and Arthur Hepner, "Alaska: Last American Frontier," *Foreign Policy Reports*, December 1, 1942, pp. 328-47.

45. Ernest K. Lindley, "Alaska: Strategic Stepchild of the Continent," *Newsweek*, March 16, 1942, p. 28.

46. Harold L. Ickes, "Bastion and Last Frontier," *New York Times*, July 26, 1942, Sec. IV, p. 7.

47. *Ibid.*, April 9, 1938, p. 10.

48. United States Army, Alaska, *The Army's Role in the Building of Alaska*, pp. 81-85. See also Joseph Driscoll, *War Discovers Alaska* (Philadelphia: J.B. Lippincott Company, 1943); Jean Potter, *Alaska Under Arms* (New York: The Macmillan Company, 1943).

49. United States Army, Alaska, *The Army's Role in the Building of Alaska*, pp. 88-95.

50. *Ibid.*, p. 96.

51. Rogers, *The Future of Alaska*, p. 95.

52. Rogers and Cooley, *Alaska's Population and Economy*, vol. II, *Statistical Handbook*, pp. 120-23.

53. *Cong. Record*, Index, 78 Cong., 1 Sess., H.R. 344, p. 692; *Ibid.*, H.R. 2462, p. 742. For a companion bill in the Senate introduced by William L. Langer, see S. 1436, *Ibid.*, p. 670; *Ibid.*, 78 Cong., 2 Sess., H.R. 4648, p. 524.

54. *Ibid.*, Appendix, 77 Cong., 2 Sess., p. 4445 (December 16, 1942); Gruening, *The State of Alaska*, pp. 461-63.

55. *New York Times*, March 17, 1939, p. 9.

56. "The Statehood Referendum," *Alaska Frontier*, May-June, 1941, p. 3.

57. William R. Carter, "The Sixteenth Alaska Legislature—A Report to the People," in *Cong. Record*, 78 Cong., 1 Sess., p. 8228 (October 12, 1943).

58. *Ibid.*, 78 Cong., 2 Sess., S. 951, p. 2835 (April 2, 1943).

59. "Notes on a Radio Broadcast, Richard Eaton and Anthony J. Dimond," Personal Correspondence, Statehood Committee—X, Y, Z—General-Folder Statehood for Alaska, speeches and statements,

Box 39, Anthony J. Dimond Papers, University of Alaska Archives, College, Alaska.

60. Interview with Robert B. Atwood, August 26, 1969, Anchorage, Alaska.

61. *Cong. Record*, 78 Cong., 1 Sess., p. 8223 (October 12, 1943); Walter B. King, Ketchikan, to Senator Millard Tydings, June 14, 1943, S. 78A-E1, papers accompanying S.B. 951, April 2, 1943, Senate Committee on Interior and Insular Affairs, RG 46, NA; mimeographed manuscript, Ralph E. Robertson, "Statehood for Alaska: Don't Measure Political Rights by Money Cost," Juneau, September 10, 1943, pp. 1-10, Folder Statehood for Alaska, speeches and statements, Box 39, Anthony J. Dimond Papers, University of Alaska Archives, College, Alaska.

62. Secretary Harold L. Ickes to Senator Millard Tydings, September 2, 1943, S. 78A-E1, papers accompanying S.B. 951, Senate Committee on Interior and Insular Affairs, RG 46, NA.

63. *Cong. Record*, 78 Cong., 1 Sess., H.R. 3768, p. 10261 (December 2, 1943). For Dimond's explanation on the principal differences between H.R. 3768 and S. 951, see "Statement by Anthony J. Dimond," December 6, 1943, file 9-1-44, part 2, Alaska-Legal-Statehood, Records of the Office of Territories, RG 126, NA.

64. Anthony J. Dimond, "Statehood for Alaska," December 1, 1943, file 9-1-44, part 2, Alaska-Legal-Statehood, Records of the Office of Territories, RG 126, NA.

CHAPTER VI

BARTLETT AND GRUENING: CRUSADERS FOR STATEHOOD

Late in the summer of 1939 war clouds were hanging heavy over Europe. Hitler's armies had invaded Poland, and many Americans kept close to their radios to follow the latest developments. Among the many avid listeners were Ernest and Dorothy Gruening, on a vacation in New England from Washington where he headed the Division of Territories and Island Possessions in the Department of the Interior. While driving through Rockport, Massachusetts, they heard on the automobile radio that President Franklin D. Roosevelt had appointed him governor of Alaska. The date was September 3, 1939.[1]

Gruening brought an impressive background to his new job. He had received an M.D. from Harvard in 1912, but instead of practicing medicine, he had pursued a career in journalism. He moved from reporter with the *Boston American* to editor and managing editor of *The Nation*.[2] In his capacity as newspaperman, Gruening became acquainted with various New Deal personalities, including President Roosevelt. He caught the President's eye and in 1933 was appointed to serve as an adviser to the United States delegation at the Seventh Inter-American Conference at Montevideo. There he had a hand in fashioning the New Deal's policy toward Latin America.[3] While director of the Division of Territories and Island Possessions, Gruening had come into conflict, not only with his superior, Secretary of the Interior Harold L. Ickes, but also with Rexford G. Tugwell, who was setting up Puerto Rican development programs. Gruening attempted to do the same thing in his division.[4] At that point, the President apparently decided to "kick" Gruening upstairs and make him governor of Alaska.

It was not suprising that Gruening, with his background and ambition, came to Alaska determined to make something out of the Territory, to demonstrate to the President his capabilities. All his frustrated ambitions he now poured into Alaska. And with a man of his talent, ability, determination, and ego, it was a foregone conclusion that he would have a great impact on the Territory.[5]

A contemporary of Gruening's, although considerably younger in years, and a man who also had a great influence on Alaska, was Edward Lewis "Bob" Bartlett. The son of Klondike pioneers, he was born in Seattle and grew up in Fairbanks. He attended the Universities of Alaska and Washington for a time and then, in 1927, became a reporter for the *Fairbanks Daily News-Miner* where he remained until 1933. He then became secretary to Delegate Anthony J. Dimond, remaining in Washington until 1934. After his return to Alaska he served briefly as assistant territorial director of the Federal Housing Administration and operated a placer gold mine until he was appointed secretary of Alaska, a position comparable to lieutenant governor, by President Roosevelt in January, 1939. Bartlett resigned in February, 1944, to become a candidate for the delegateship.[6]

Gruening and Bartlett, two very dissimilar personalities, the former aggressive and determined, the latter quiet and persuasive, nevertheless developed a lasting working relationship. But while the Governor soon polarized Alaskan politics into pro- and anti-Gruening camps by the sheer force of his personality, Bartlett continued to widen his acquaintances among all elements of the Territory's population and to build political goodwill. Gruening antagonized many Alaskans, prominent among them territorial legislators, when he unsuccessfully recommended to the 1941 and 1943 sessions of the Alaska legislature a complete revision of the antiquated tax laws. Many territorial senators and representatives went so far as to oppose automatically anything that had the backing of the Governor.[7]

The statehood movement soon developed into a crusade under the leadership of these two men. They did not invent the movement, to be sure, because it already had been ebbing and flowing in the Territory for a long time. They did, however, give it a vitality and dynamism which it had not possessed before.

Gruening promoted statehood on a broad front. When he went on lecture tours in the states, he insisted on advertising the issue. He utilized his connections with the nation's press to advantage. He clearly defined the devils, the "Outside" interests, including Seattle's monopolistic control of Alaskan shipping. The people of the Territory had known all along that their freight rates were high. Gruening explained that this was due to a provision in the Maritime Act of 1920 (sponsored by Washington's Senator Wesley Jones and known as the Jones Act in the Territory) which foreclosed the alternatives of shipment through the Canadian ports of Vancouver and Prince Rupert, both far more economical, and made Seattle the port through which Alaska trade had to pass. The salmon fisheries had been declining for a number of years. The Governor maintained that the White Act of 1924, a measure which had been hailed as the Magna Carta of fishery conservation by both federal officials and industry spokesmen, worked to the detriment of the small operator in Alaska and protected the large companies and their fish traps.[8] In short, Gruening set up the targets and called upon Alaskans to join the movement. He organized the statehood cause within the Territory and barnstormed the United States in the service of it.

Bartlett operated in a far different fashion, but just as effectively. He was not as flamboyant as Gruening, although every inch as tenacious. His greatest service for the statehood movement was performed in the halls of Congress. In his 1944 primary fight for the Democratic nomination to replace Delegate Dimond, he faced H. Ziegler and Henry Roden, both well-known, old-time political figures. Against the advice of amateur and professional politicians alike, Bartlett ran on a statehood platform. Despite gloomy predictions, he not only defeated his two opponents but went on to win in the general election by 7,255 to 3,763 votes over his Republican adversary, John E. Manders.[9]

After six terms in Congress, Delegate Dimond had decided to retire and return to Alaska. In addition, there was the prospect of appointment to a federal judgeship in the Territory. When taking leave of his colleagues in the House of Representatives late in 1944, he introduced his successor and recommended him highly to the House membership. Bartlett, he told them, felt as strongly about statehood for the Territory as he did.[10] Not surprisingly, then, Bartlett followed in his mentor's footsteps and attempted to have the Organic Act of 1912 amended and revised. To this end, he introduced measures for an elective as well as resident governor and secretary of Alaska in almost every session between 1945 and 1955.[11] By 1955, however, he realized the futility of these actions and discontinued submitting such bills. But Bartlett continued to tell his colleagues about Alaska, its promise and problems. He appeared before every committee of the Senate and House which had anything to do with the Territory. In addition, he and his Congressional friends began to bombard Congress with statehood bills in almost every session.[12]

World War II ended, at least in Europe, in May of 1945. As previously mentioned, Alaska had profited enormously from the publicity and development it had received thus far in the war.[13] The territorial legislature took advantage of the prevailing idealistic mood, and early in 1945 the house of representatives sent a memorial to Congress. This document pleaded dramatically for the extension to Alaska of the "Four Freedoms" proclaimed in the Atlantic Charter, which supported the right of small nations and minorities to choose their own form of government and to have control over their own destinies.[14] The memorial was followed shortly by a request to admit Alaska as the forty-ninth State.[15] In the same session Governor Gruening asked the lawmakers to establish provisions for a referendum on the statehood question. The legislature complied, with the vote to be taken in the 1946 general election. Gruening knew that an educational program had to be undertaken at once to assure a large turnout of voters. Congress could not be expected to act on Alaskan statehood without a loud and positive expression from the territorial citizenry. The Governor toyed with the idea of engaging either the Library of Congress or the Brookings Institution to make a study of the pros and cons of statehood, but could not find the necessary funds. He decided that George Sundborg, an old friend then working for the Bonneville Power Administration, might be employed to undertake such an analysis for a more modest fee.[16]

At that point a group of Anchorage statehood enthusiasts, led by Mrs. Evangeline Atwood, the wife of the editor and publisher of the *Anchorage Daily Times*, organized a nonpartisan, nonprofit, territory-wide Alaska Statehood Association. Invitations were sent out to many of the Territory's citizens which stated:

> Every Alaskan interested in the progress and welfare of the Territory should want his name on this membership list. In the years to come this . . . list will be a directory of Alaskans who had the foresight, vision and generosity to pioneer this study of statehood.

A membership fee of five dollars was charged, and soon chapters had been established in Anchorage, Fairbanks, Juneau, Ketchikan, Sitka, Wrangell, Palmer, Valdez, Kodiak, and Seward.[17] The Alaska Statehood Association hired Sundborg to make the proposed study, which was published in pamphlet form and as a tabloid supplement which was provided free of charge to all Alaskan newspapers for the widest possible distribution. For many years this booklet was the authoritative reference work for the statehood forces. As might be expected, it clearly showed the sympathies of its author and the sponsoring group, because out of fifty-six pages, only five were devoted to arguments against statehood.[18]

During most of the war period, statehood had not been a subject of serious consideration. By mid-1945, however, even the federal departments most concerned with Alaska's administration had to take an official stand. Secretary of the Interior Ickes had voiced his opposition in 1943. One of his objections was what he considered the excessive land grants proposed for the new state. In 1945, Jack B. Fahy, Acting Director of the Division of Territories and Island Possessions, took the lead. He drafted a memorandum in which he enumerated the reasons why Alaska should become a State and cited the activities of Interior designed to further this end. Fahy circulated his position paper among the policy-making personnel of the department where it was approved by most except the Fish and Wildlife Service. Also, the Geological Survey expressed some doubts. He next sent it to Ickes, mentioning that it had already gained wide departmental acceptance. Fahy sought to reassure the Secretary when he pointed out that statehood did not mean that ownership of all the public lands would be vested in the State. As a matter of fact, he reminded Ickes, past enabling acts had granted certain acreages for schools, roads, and other public purposes, but title to the bulk of the lands had always remained with the Federal Government. Perhaps this argument was convincing enough to win over the "Old Curmodgeon;" perhaps it was the influence of wartime idealism. Whatever the reasons, Acting Secretary of the Interior Abe Fortas announced on August 11, 1945 that statehood was now a part of the department's policy for Alaska and had been approved by Secretary Ickes. [19]

While Interior had been formulating a policy, two Congressional groups had traveled to Alaska to investigate conditions on the spot and hold informal statehood hearings. The House Subcommittee on Appropriations reported that, although the majority of Alaskans favored statehood, the members seriously doubted the Territory's ability to assume the burdens connected with it. The reasons mentioned were the absence of an adequate tax law as well as inadequate social legislation.[20] Representative John Rooney, a member of this committee, amplified these views in a newspaper interview. Any people, he remarked, who allowed a major industry like fishing to take out some $60,000,000 annually and retained only $1,000,000 in taxes obviously were not ready for the responsibilities of statehood.[21] The House Committee on Territories heard statehood widely discussed but found no agreement as to how soon the Territory should seek admission. Opponents of statehood, they reported, generally feared increased taxes, while proponents argued that representation in Congress would offset any disadvantages, such as increased costs. The committee members agreed to consider carefully a suggestion by territorial Attorney General Ralph J. Rivers. He proposed that for a five-year period prior to statehood the Federal Government return a certain portion of the corporate and individual income taxes collected in the Territory every year. These funds then could be used to establish a territorial judicial system, to pay the legislature and executive branches of government, and to construct the physical facilities necessary to operate a state. After five years, federal aid could be withdrawn, Rivers believed, and Alaska made a state.[22]

In his State of the Union message in January, 1946, President Harry S. Truman gave Alaskan statehood a boost when he recommended that the Territory be promptly admitted as soon as the wishes of its citizens had been determined.[23] This presidential endorsement helped to keep national attention focused on the Territory. Secretary of the Interior Julius A. Krug visited Alaska in the fall of 1946 to determine, among other things, the extent of the statehood movement; and *U.S. News and World Report* predicted that Alaska would soon become the forty-ninth State. The news magazine expected the territory to be America's most important defense frontier in the age of long-range planes and guided missiles.[24] Pollster George Gallup reported in September that 64 per cent of American voters favored the admission of Alaska, 12 per cent were opposed, and 24 per cent were undecided. Gallup went on to say that Americans favored admission mainly because the Territory was vital to the defense of the nation, and, in addition, its citizens deserved equal representation.[25]

Those Alaskans who went to the polls in the general election in October, 1946 were acutely aware of the national attention focused on the Territory. Amidst much campaigning and publicity,[26] they reelected Delegate Bartlett by a vote of 11,516 to 4,868 over his

Republican opponent Almer Peterson. The statehood referendum was approved by a margin of three to two, or 9,630 to 6,822 votes.[27]

Alaskans, like Americans everywhere, desired equality, representation in Congress, and full participation in their government. The referendum results in each judicial division also told much about the old and the new Alaska, about the transformation the Territory was undergoing as a result of the war and the new emphasis on defense. In the first judicial division (southeastern Alaska) the vote was 66 per cent in favor and 34 per cent against statehood (3,872 to 1,953). Sentiment in this, the Territory's most economically advanced part, ran high on the statehood issue, because whatever else statehood might do, it promised to transfer the control of the fishery resources to Alaska. The strength of this sentiment is indicated by the votes in the various towns in this region as shown in Table 1.[28]

TABLE 1

VOTES IN SOUTHEASTERN ALASKA IN THE 1946 STATEHOOD REFERENDUM

Town	For Statehood	Against Statehood
Ketchikan	765	253
Juneau	783	558
Sitka	213	160
Wrangell	152	61
Petersburg	249	57
Skagway	152	67

The third judicial division approved statehood by 60 per cent to 40 per cent (3,427 to 2,257).[29] Anchorage, a town of 4,229 inhabitants in 1940 and of 11,254 in 1950,[30] approved 66 per cent to 34 per cent (1,424 to 707).[31] Anchorage was a new town by Alaskan standards. It got its start in 1915 with the construction of the Alaska Railroad. It was the Territory's only planned city, and unlike other communities, had not developed around the exploitation of one of the Territory's natural resources, such as fish, minerals, or forest products. Instead, its location had become a defense resource. During the Second World War the two largest military bases in the Territory had been installed there. Consequently, Anchorage had become a boom town which attracted many newcomers who sought the high wages and opportunities offered by military construction and other government spending. It also quickly became the busiest community in Alaska and contained more new arrivals than any of the other territorial towns or settlements. Many of these war and postwar emigrants from the lower forty-eight States were determined to make Anchorage a modern community. They soon felt the limitations of the Organic Act of 1912. Victor Fischer, one such new resident, recalls, "... it was just a preposterous situation; the municipalities were in effect governed by the United States Congress which couldn't care less about Alaska or municipal problems."[32] Thus the city soon became the center for the modern statehood movement.

In the second judicial division 56 per cent voted against statehood and 44 per cent voted for it (742 to 933). Nome, the largest city in this division, voted affirmatively by 256 to 235. In the fourth judicial division, the story was similar. Here 49 per cent voted for statehood and 51 per cent against (1,589 to 1,679). Fairbanks, the largest city in this division, went on record in favor of statehood by 737 to 584 votes.[33] Geographically, these two divisions were remote and climatically harsh. The second division embraced the northern areas of Alaska while the fourth division constituted the interior. Nome depended on gold mining and government employment for its livelihood. This helps explain the fairly even division of the vote, because, for instance, the mining interests opposed statehood out of fear of higher taxes. Fairbanks had some gold mining, but the military was becoming the most important economic factor. It therefore was experiencing, although on a much smaller scale, the same influx of newcomers that Anchorage was undergoing. Both Nome and Fairbanks were supply centers for a vast "bush area" inhabited by Indians, Eskimos, and sourdoughs. The first two groups did not participate to any extent in political life. Delegate Bartlett explained the vote of the sourdoughs when he stated that they disliked "all the change and commotion that came about in 1940 when the Army started to arm Alaska ...; they would rather go back to ... the good old days." George Sundborg, manager of the Alaska Development Board, explained that the negative vote was due to "the sourpuss branch of the sourdough family."[34]

The total vote in the Territory had not been large. But taking as a base the 1940 census, which listed a population of 72,524 for Alaska, a turnout of 16,384 voters amounted to a respectable 23 per cent of the total population. This compared with a high of 47 per cent for New Mexico and a low of 2 per cent and 1 per cent for Mississippi and South Carolina, respectively.35

The statehood referendum had reaffirmed the leadership of Gruening and Bartlett. After the October elections, the movement gathered momentum. The Department of the Interior not only pledged to support the movement but also to work closely with Bartlett; and President Truman continued to back Alaska's aspirations.36 In March of 1947, the Ketchikan Central Labor Council and the American Federation of Labor unions and councils of Alaska sponsored a special Alaska statehood and international development edition prepared by the *Ketchikan Alaska Chronicle*. Statehood and self-government, the sponsors stated, were not debatable. Among the many other benefits to be derived would be lower freight rates, because two Senators and one Representative could have the objectionable and discriminatory Maritime Act of 1920 amended. British Columbia, which stood to gain from such a change, also approved of Alaska statehood and showed it by contributing heavily to the special edition.37

At the same time other Alaska statehood proponents were also at work. They presented admission to the Union as a panacea which would cure the various social and economic ills of the Territory, such as a sparse population, inadequate social services, deficient venture and development capital, and poor transportation and communications. Support from the continental United States stressed Alaska's key position in the American defensive system. The Japanese invasion of Kiska and Attu during the Second World War was vividly recalled. The possibility of an Alaskan Pearl Harbor with far more serious consequences was to be avoided at all costs.38

Although three statehood bills had been submitted to Congress between 1943 and 1946, the exigencies of war had helped prevent their consideration. By 1947, however, Alaska's role in that conflict and in the Cold War generated some support for statehood among Americans in the continental United States and members of Congress. Delegate Bartlett therefore introduced a statehood bill on January 3, 1947. This measure was substantially identical to the one he had introduced in 1945 and to the Dimond bill of 1943. However, Bartlett now enlarged the public land grant to the prospective state. He proposed to withdraw from reserve and give to Alaska the Aleutian

Islands west of the 172nd meridian west longitude, the Pribilof Islands and all the lands with adjacent waters, and other property set aside or reserved for the use or benefit of the Indians, Eskimos, and Aleuts.39

Public hearings on the Bartlett bill before the House Subcommittee on Territorial and Insular Possessions were held in Washington between April 16, and 24, 1947. On the first day of the proceedings, Acting Secretary of the Interior Warner W. Gardner recommended the enactment of the statehood measure. He objected, however, to sections 3, 4, and 5 which, with few exceptions, would have transferred to the new State title to practically all public lands. This, he stated, was contrary to the traditional practice which had been followed throughout the American West. Lands had always been granted for schools and internal improvements, but the bulk had been retained by the Federal Government. Gardner proposed to grant to Alaska about 21,000,000 acres for schools, about 438,000 acres for the University, and another 500,000 acres for various internal improvements.40 These generous land grants were mainly opposed by the various federal departments as well as by conservation groups in the continental United States.

Numerous Alaskans flew to Washington to testify in the hearings, and the majority of them spoke in favor of the statehood bill. There were representatives from chambers of commerce, small businessmen, editors and publishers of newspapers, sourdoughs, and federal and territorial officials. Also, some non-Alaskans who supported the movement appeared before the subcommittee. Bartlett, as a member of the subcommittee, made full use of his privilege of questioning the witnesses. He skillfully used the friendly ones to strengthen the statehood case. Among the less friendly witnesses there were some who approved statehood in principle but said that Alaska was not yet ready. One of these was Herbert L. Faulkner, an attorney and a long-time resident of Juneau. He praised the Bartlett bill, but then introduced a formidable array of statistics and detailed information, all designed to totally demolish the case for statehood. The gist of his argument was that Alaska simply would be financially unable to afford statehood. On being pressed by Bartlett, Faulkner admitted that as a lawyer he represented some of the canneries, the largest mining company, a few lumber concerns, and a bank and a telephone business, but he asserted that on this occasion he was representing only himself.41

The House Subcommittee on Territories and Insular Possessions went to Alaska in the early fall of 1947 to gather more information. The members stopped at Anchorage, where they found the sentiment for statehood overwhelmingly favorable. In Seward, the ocean terminus of the Alaska Railroad, they heard relatively little about statehood as such; instead the witnesses concentrated on denouncing the Seattle shipping monopoly and the outrageous prevailing freight rates. In Fairbanks, Al Anderson, secretary of the Alaska Miner's Association, stated his opposition to statehood in terms of the added costs involved. Norman Stines, a Fairbanks resident, complained that the hearing seemed to be packed with statehood advocates. These people, he continued, always claimed to be objective about the issue. Statehood opponents, he concluded, were always labeled as paid agents of the "absentee" owners by these same disinterested and objective individuals.[42] Mrs. Alaska Linck, a pioneer resident of the city as well as a past member of the territorial house, was perhaps typical of the "sourdough opposition" to statehood. She said that Delegate Dimond had submitted his statehood bill in 1943 to create new bureaus and agencies, curb individual freedom, and stifle free enterprise and individual industry. She told subcommittee members how she had watched the movement spread, in part through the efforts of the Alaska Statehood Association, but that she had not participated. To be opposed to the movement, Mrs. Linck stated, was not easy because the "anti-statehood" label had become a derogatory one. She maintained that newcomers did not understand what Alaska needed, and that veterans had been won over by rosy promises of what statehood would accomplish for them. The "New Dealers," she declared in conclusion, were for statehood because they believed in spending now and burdening future generations with unpaid bills.[43]

It was also at Fairbanks that the most formidable witness against statehood was heard. He was Winton C. Arnold, managing director of the Alaska Salmon Industry, Inc. (a trade organization) and representative of the powerful Alaskan fishing interests. Arnold had gained the appellation of "Judge" in the 1920's in Hyder, a small silver boom town at the southeastern tip of Alaska. In 1933, the redoubtable Judge became the Alaska attorney for the cannery operators and shortly thereafter moved his offices and residence to Seattle. Although he still lived in Seattle, Arnold was reputedly the most powerful man in Alaska because of his influence on the territorial legislature. In Juneau, where he scrupulously paid his ten-dollar lobbying fee, he supposedly exerted so much pressure that he was credited with killing basic tax reforms from 1939 until 1949, when the legislature finally enacted a basic property and income tax. Arnold reputedly also used his influence on legislation which dealt with fishing methods and controls over the fishing industry.[44]

Arnold appeared briefly at Fairbanks and again in Juneau and Ketchikan. His approach in each instance was disarming; never did he come out publicly against statehood. He contended that it was a logical and laudable ambition for Alaskans to aspire to statehood. But he disagreed with those who advertised it as a panacea for all of Alaska's problems. Throughout his testimony he hammered at the Territory's inability to pay for the increased burdens of statehood. He pointed out that land grants to the new state would overlap aboriginal claims and come into conflict with the reservation policies inaugurated by the Department of the Interior. Whatever the legal complexities, he advised the subcommittee, the Native land issue should be settled once and for all by the Federal Government before any steps were taken on statehood.[45]

The 1947 hearings on the statehood bill were important because they placed the issue squarely before Congress. Most of the arguments on both sides were brought into the open. Perhaps most important, the opposition had been ably represented by Al Anderson and Judge Arnold. But also the pro-statehood cause had gained new strength and dimension. By 1948 the increased vigor and enthusiasm for statehood were apparent. The *Anchorage Daily Times* and the *Ketchikan Alaska Chronicle*, as well as *The Alaska Weekly* of Seattle, were lending their editorial voices in support of the cause. Many private citizens were at work as well. Mildred Hermann, president of the Alaska Women's Club, the first woman lawyer in Alaska and an ardent feminist of the old school, assumed a role of leadership in Juneau. Ralph J. Rivers of Fairbanks and William A. Egan, territorial senator from Valdez, spent even more time and effort than before. Several prominent Tlingit families in southeastern Alaska and many other respected Alaskans, too numerous to mention, joined the movement.[46]

With the voluminous hearings closed, the House Subcommittee on Territories and Insular Possessions met in Washington in February, 1948, to discuss Alaska statehood. It soon became apparent that the subcommittee did not agree with the Departments of the Interior and

Agriculture on land grants to the new State in support of its schools. Interior insisted on two sections in each township, while the subcommittee and Delegate Bartlett held out for four. An impasse developed, and the Delegate was instructed to meet with Interior and Agriculture officials and work out a compromise, which, together with subcommittee amendments, would be incorporated into a new bill. On March 2, 1948, Bartlett submitted such a statehood bill.[47] Two days later the subcommittee approved the new measure, and in April the House Committee on Public Lands unanimously approved the Delegate's bill, reporting it with amendments. The committee report briefly discussed the history of Alaska and the Territory's inadequate governmental structure and discounted the argument that Alaska could not support statehood. Instead, the committee members suggested a number of new revenue sources, expressed the conviction that statehood would attract new settlers, and disposed of the argument of noncontiguity as of little importance in the age of modern transportation.[48]

On April 14, 1948, the new statehood bill was reported to the House but was then bottled up in the Rules Committee.[49] Despite a special message from President Truman[50] and a resolution introduced by California's Senator William F. Knowland on behalf of Hawaii,[51] Senator Hugh Butler, chairman of the Senate Interior and Insular Affairs Committee, refused to allow either the Alaska or Hawaii statehood bills to come up for discussion and debate.

As a result, Alaska statehood died as far as that particular session of Congress was concerned. But the defeat was not decisive or even a major one. For while the Bartlett bill had been debated in the various committees, it was given wide circulation in Alaska newspapers and through Delegate Bartlett's newsletter to his territorial constituents. Bartlett had traveled widely in Alaska and discussed the details of his efforts. In addition, the national press had given considerable attention to the issue. There were many reasons to be optimistic, among them the fact that hearings on Alaska statehood had been held for the first time and that a statehood measure had been approved unanimously by a committee of Congress.

FOOTNOTES FOR CHAPTER VI

1. Sherwood Ross, *Gruening of Alaska* (New York: Best Books, Inc., 1968), pp. 112-13.

2. *New York Times*, September 3, 1939, p. 5.

3. Ross, *Gruening of Alaska*, pp. 77-89.

4. Rexford Guy Tugwell, *The Srticken Land: The Story of Puerto Rico* (New York: Greenwood Press, Publishers, 1968), pp. 5, 71.

5. Interview with Dr. George W. Rogers, January 19, 1970, College, Alaska. Dr. Rogers was a research economist on the staff of Governor Gruening in the 1940's. Later he became chairman of the Federal Field Committee in Alaska, and subsequently was employed by Resources for the Future, Inc. and the Arctic Institute of North America. He now is a research professor of economics at the University of Alaska.

6. *Biographical Directory of the American Congress*, pp. 522-23.

7. *Annual Report of the Governor of Alaska* (1943), pp. 1-5; William R. Carter, "The Sixteenth Alaska Legislature: A Report to the People," in *Cong. Record*, 78 Cong., 1 Sess., pp. 8226-27 (October 12, 1943).

8. Gruening, *The State of Alaska*, pp. 409, 382-85.

9. Interview with Mary Lee Council, July 20, 1969, Washington D.C. She stated that even "Ernest Gruening was bitterly opposed [and] did everything he could to get Bob not to mention statehood." Gruening told Bartlett that the people of Alaska were not ready for statehood, Miss Council recalled. Election returns were found in "Alaska General Election, September 12, 1944," in the Office of the Secretary of State, Juneau, Alaska.

10. Dimond, Hon. Anthony J., Exercises in Honor of, Original Proceedings on, November 30, 1944, rough draft, House Committee on the Territories, H.R. 78A-F36.1, RG 233, NA.

11. *Cong. Record*, Index, 79 Cong., 1 Sess., p. 889, H.R. 3323 (election of governor) and H.R. 3324 (resident for governor); *Ibid.*, 80 Cong., 1 Sess., p. 721, H.R. 181 (election of governor) and H.R. 179 (resident for governor); *Ibid.*, 80 Cong., 2 Sess., p. 630, H.R. 6851 (election of governor) and a companion bill in the Senate, S. 2839, introduced by Senator Malone, in *Ibid.*, 80 Cong., 2 Sess., p. 548; *Ibid.*, 81 Cong., 1 Sess., p. 792, H.R. 218 (resident for governor) and in the Senate, S. 727 (election of governor in Alaska and Hawaii, introduced by Senator Hugh Butler), in *Ibid.*, 81 Cong., 1 Sess., p. 725; *Ibid.*, 83 Cong., 1 Sess., p. 781, H.R. 1916 (election of governor and lieutenant governor) and a companion bill in the Senate, S. 224, introduced by Senator Hugh Butler, in *Ibid.*, 84 Cong., 1 Sess., p. 672.

12. Senate Bill 41, introduced by William L. Langer, January 11, 1945, 79 Cong., 1 Sess., RG 46, NA; H.R. 1807, introduced by Sam Ervin, January 29, 1945, 79 Cong., 1 Sess., RG 233, NA; H.R. 3898, introduced by E. L. Bartlett, July 21, 1945, 79 Cong., 1 Sess., RG 233, NA.

13. See Richard L. Neuberger, "Alaska—Our Spearhead in the Pacific," *New York Times Magazine*, April 12, 1942, in *Cong. Record*, Appendix, 77 Cong., 2 Sess., pp. 1736-37 (May 7, 1942); Richard L. Neuberger, "Gruening of Alaska," *Common Sense*, May, 1942, in *Cong. Record*, Appendix, 77 Cong., 1 Sess., pp. 1682-84 (May 11, 1942); Richard L. Neuberger, "Yukon Country Described as Beckoning Mecca for Warriors Imbued with Spirit of the Pioneers who Settled the West," *Sunday Oregonian*, October 15, 1944, in *Cong. Record*, Appendix, 78 Cong., 2 Sess., pp. 4432-33 (November 14, 1944); Richard L. Neuberger, "Go North, Young Man!" *Collier's*, December 23, 1944, in *Cong. Record*, Appendix, 78 Cong., 2 Sess., pp. 4776-79 (December 15, 1944).

14. *New York Times*, January 27, 1945, p. 12.

15. *Cong. Record*, 79 Cong., 1 Sess., p. 2519 (March 21, 1945).

16. Governor Ernest Gruening to Edwin G. Arnold, Director, Division of Territories and Island Possessions, September 5, 1945 and

September 26, 1945, file 9-1-44, part 2, Alaska-Legal-Statehood, Records of the Office of Territories, RG 126, NA.

17. Robert B. Atwood, "Alaska's Struggle for Statehood," *State Government*, Autumn, 1958, p. 205; "Invitation to Join the Alaska Statehood Association," in Personal Correspondence, Statehood Committee—X,Y,Z—General, folder Statehood Committee, Box 39, Anthony J. Dimond Papers, University of Alaska Archives, College, Alaska.

18. George Sundborg, *Statehood for Alaska: The Issues Involved and the Facts About the Issues* (Anchorage, Alaska: Alaska Statehood Association, August, 1946). Sundborg worked closely with Governor Gruening, Mrs. Evangeline Atwood, territorial Attorney General Ralph J. Rivers and Dimond, then a federal district judge in Anchorage, in the preparation of the pamphlet. Judge Dimond received one of the unfinished copies and commented on it in detail, drawing on his long experience as a lawyer and as Alaska's delegate to Congress. See Anthony J. Dimond to George Sundborg, July 4, 1946, folder of correspondence with George Sundborg, Box 39, Anthony J. Dimond Papers, University of Alaska Archives, College, Alaska.

19. Jack B. Fahy, Acting Director, Division of Territories and Island Possessions, to Secretary of the Interior Harold L. Ickes, July 26, 1945, file 9-1-13, part 3, Records of the Secretary of the Interior, RG 48, NA; News Release, Department of the Interior, August 11, 1945, file 9-1-44, Alaska, Self-Government, General, Classified Files, 1907-51, Records of the Department of the Interior, Box 327, RG 48, NA.

20. U.S., Congress, House, Subcommittee of the Committee on Appropriations, *Official Trip of Examination of Federal Activities in Alaska and the Pacific Coast States*, 79 Cong., 1 Sess. (Washington: Government Printing Office, 1945), p. 11.

21. *Washington Post*, August 14, 1945, clipping in file 9-1-13, part 3, Records of the Office of the Secretary of the Interior, RG 48, NA.

22. U.S., Congress, House, Committee on the Territories, *Official Trip to Conduct a Study and Investigation of the Various Questions and Problems Relating to the Territory of Alaska*, H. Rept. 1583 pursuant to H. Res. 236, 79 Cong., 2 Sess. (Washington: Government Printing Office, 1946), pp. 28-30. For a full account of this plan, as well as an enumeration of the restrictions of the Organic Act of 1912, see Ralph J. Rivers, "Alaska—the 49th State?" *Alaska Life*, December 1945, pp. 8-11.

23. Excerpt from the Message of the President on the State of the Union and Transmitting the Budget, January 21, 1946, file 9-1-44, part 2, Alaska-Legal-Statehood, Records of the Office of Territories, RG 126, NA.

24. Memorandum on Secretary Krug's visit to Alaska, August 11-22, 1946, file 9-1-34, part 3, Records of the Office of Territories, RG 126, NA; "Alaska: Our Next State; Bolstering Arctic Frontier," *U.S. News and World Report*, September 13, 1946, pp. 19-20.

25. U.S., Congress, House, *Statehood for Alaska*, Hearings before the Subcommittee on Territories and Insular Possessions of the Committee on Public Lands, Committee Hearing No. 9, 80 Cong., 1 Sess. (Washington: Government Printing Office, 1947), pp. 349-50. Hereafter cited as *Statehood for Alaska* (1947).

26. "What Alaskans Say About Statehood," *Alaska Life*, September, 1946, p. 9; clipping from *Ketchikan Alaska Chronicle*, September 14, 1946, asking Alaskans to buy one dollar statehood buttons. This money was to be used to pay the costs of printing the Sundborg report as a newspaper supplement and in permanent pamphlet form. Any money left over, the advertisement stated, would be used to persuade Congressmen to enact statehood for Alaska. The Office of Territories attached the following comment to the clipping:

"??How much is the price for Congressmen??" File 9-1-44, part 2, Alaska-Legal-Statehood, Records of the Office of Territories, RG 126, NA. See also John L. Manders, "Statehood for Alaska," *Alaska Life*, September, 1946, pp. 8-9.

27. The election returns are found in "Official Returns—Territorial Canvassing Board, General Election, October 8, 1946," Office of the Secretary of State, Juneau, Alaska.

28. *Statehood for Alaska* (1947), p. 425; Mary Lee Council, "Alaska Statehood" (unpublished manuscript, n.d.), p. 4, copy in author's files; George W. Rogers, *Alaska in Transition: The Southeastern Region*, A Study Sponsored by the Arctic Institute of North America and Resources for the Future, Inc. (Baltimore: The Johns Hopkins Press, 1960), pp. 3-17; Gruening, *The State of Alaska* pp. 382-407.

29. *Statehood for Alaska* (1947), p. 425.

30. Rogers and Cooley, *Alaska's Population and Economy*, vol. I, *Analysis*, p. 46.

31. *Statehood for Alaska* (1947), p. 425; Mary Lee Council, "Alaska Statehood" (unpublished manuscript, n.d.), p. 4, copy in author's files.

32. Interview with Victor Fischer, March 22, 1970, College, Alaska.

33. *Statehood for Alaska* (1947), p. 425.

34. *Ibid.*, p. 275.

35. *Ibid.*, p. 273.

36. Secretary of the Interior Julius A. Krug to Wayne Henrickson, February 7, 1947, file 9-1-34, part 3, Alaska, Secretary's trip to Alaska, Records of the Office of Territories, RG 126, NA; President Harry S. Truman to Secretary Krug, February 8, 1947, file 9-1-13, part 4, Alaska, Administrative, General Records of the Office of the Secretary of the Interior, RG 48, NA.

37. *Ketchikan Alaska Chronicle (Alaska Statehood and International Development Edition)*, March 29, 1947.

38. Bob Sikes, "A Congressman's View of Alaska," *Alaska Life*, May 1947, p.5. See Melvin Price, "Statehood for Alaska, Hawaii, and Puerto Rico," *Cong. Record*, Appendix, 80 Cong., 1 Sess., pp. 1654-58 (April 4, 1947); Wilbur Forrest, "Alaska—a Bastion Unfortified, and an Easy Pearl Harbor No. 2 . . .," *New York Herald Tribune*, December 1, 1947, in *Cong. Record*, Appendix, 80 Cong., 1 Sess., p. 4458 (December 2, 1947); Richard L. Neuberger, "Alaska Now Last Frontier—Call to New Pioneers—Thousands of Soldiers are Looking Northward to Land that Offers Great Opportunities Along with its Hardships," *St. Louis Post-Dispatch*, February 18, 1945, in *Cong. Record*, Appendix, 79 Cong., 1 Sess., pp. 927-29 (March 1, 1945).

39. H.R. 206, introduced by Bartlett, January 3, 1947, RG 233, NA; S. 56, introduced by Senator William L. Langer, January 6, 1947, RG 46, NA; and H.R. 1808, submitted by Representative Homer Angell, February 10, 1947, RG 233, NA.

40. *Statehood for Alaska* (1947), pp. 5-13.

41. *Ibid.*, pp. 73-78, 121-74; interview with Herbert L. Faulkner, August 11, 1969, Juneau, Alaska. Faulkner stated that his attitude toward statehood had in no way been influenced by his clients. He simply felt that Alaska could not afford it financially. Salmon fishing was in decline, he recalled, mining had been going downhill for a number of years, and there were no prospects of any new industries which could take the place of these two. He told the author that he talked to Senator Ernest Gruening at the Seattle airport in 1968, and Gruening told him that if oil had not been discovered, the state would have gone bankrupt. Faulkner felt vindicated in his stand, particularly since nobody could foresee the impact oil would have on Alaska.

42. U.S., Congress, House, *Alaska*, Hearings before the Subcommittee on Territories and Insular Possessions of the Committee on Public Land pursuant to H. Res. 93, Committee Hearing No. 31, 80 Cong., 1 Sess. (Washington: Government Printing Office, 1948), p. 120. Hearafter cited as *Alaska* (1948).

43. *Ibid.*, p. 132.

44. Herbert H. Hilscher, *Alaska Now* (rev. ed.; Boston: Little, Brown and Company, 1950), pp. 277, 274.

45. Alaska (1948), pp. 156, 162-63. However, before a subcommittee of the Senate Public Lands Committee in Anchorage in August, 1947, Arnold stated: "The Alaska Salmon Industry is opposed to statehood. We're paying most of the cost of running the Territory now. We don't propose to pick up the check for the additional cost of statehood." Ernest Gruening, *The Battle for Alaska Statehood* (College, Alaska: University of Alaska Press in cooperation with the Alaska Purchase Centennial Commission, 1967), p. 21.

46. Interview with Dr. George W. Rogers, January 19, 1970, College, Alaska.

47. Memorandum on the chronology of Alaska statehood legislation with reference to public lands, April 28, 1950, file Persons Leaving Alaska, Box 795, Records of the Office of the Governor of Alaska, 1884-1958, Federal Records Center, Seattle, Washington.

48. U.S., Congress, House, *Providing for the Admission of Alaska Into the Union*, H. Rept. 1731 to accompany H.R. 5666, 80 Cong., 2 Sess. (Washington: Government Printing Office, 1948), pp. 3-6.

49. *Congressional Quarterly Almanac*, 80 Cong., 2 Sess. (Washington: Washington Congressional Quarterly News Features, 1948), p. 290.

50. *Message from the President of the United States to the Congress of the United States Relative to Enactment of Necessary Legislation to Admit Alaska to Statehood at the Earliest Possible Date*, 80 Cong., 2 Sess. (Washington: Government Printing Office, 1948).

51. *Cong. Record*, 80 Cong., 2 Sess., p. 6123 (May 20, 1948). S. 232, the motion to discharge the bill from the Senate Interior and Insular Affairs Committee, mustered only twenty votes.

CHAPTER VII

CONTROLLING THE SPECIAL INTERESTS

Time and again since the first territorial legislature met in 1913 attempts were made to establish a basic and adequate tax system to meet the needs of Alaska, but always without success. Instead, the Territory limped along with the inadequate system of license fees and levies which had been established in 1899. Yet, the modern statehood movement could not expect success until Alaska set its own house in order. It must break the influence of the special interests, which, as primary taxpayers, had worked strenuously against anything which would bring self-determination for Alaska a step closer or increase the tax level.

Spurred on by the financial needs of the New Deal period, Governor John W. Troy asked the territorial planning council to make a tax study in the late 1930's. The research was not completed until Troy was replaced by Governor Ernest Gruening. The authors of the report concluded that an annual revenue of $10,000,000 was entirely feasible. They recommended the adoption of a modern tax system, and urged that the revenue obtained be invested in a soundly planned and economically executed program of permanent improvements such as roads, schools, hospitals, and public buildings.[1]

It was this tax reform plan which Governor Gruening presented to the 1941 session of the territorial legislature. The study proposed to abolish all obsolete mercantile and license fees, to establish a very modest income and profits tax, and, in addition, to place a nominal levy on property outside of incorporated towns. The legislature not only soundly defeated the Governor's proposal, but also abolished the territorial planning council which had formulated this plan. The defeat was blamed on the mining and canning lobbyists, led by Winton C. Arnold.[2] The legislature, and indirectly the people, were not yet ready to bite the hand that seemed to feed them. The exploitative resource industries still held the threat of total withdrawal of livelihood over many Alaskans.

In the meantime, the estimated value of the combined physical properties of these industries had grown to more than a half billion dollars by the 1940's. Even a modest tax of one per cent on these assets would have produced five million dollars annually.[3] In addition, the Federal Government spent an estimated three billion dollars in Alaska during the war. A small levy on the profits of the contractors and a modest income tax on the salaries of defense workers would have produced a great deal of revenue.[4] But instead, territorial appropriations barely took care of the most pressing needs. Biennial expenditures between 1933 and 1947 were exceedingly small when compared with the potentially available financial resources:

>   1933-1935 — $2,133,662.67
>   1935-1937 — $2,563,500.00
>   1937-1939 — $3,074,930.00
>   1939-1941 — $3,511,510.00
>   1941-1943 — $4,496,932.00
>   1943-1945 — $4,335,861.39
>   1945-1947 — $5,631,822.00[5]

In 1947, journalist Richard L. Neuberger described Alaska as a feudal barony where the absentee-owned mining and fishing corporations took out millions in natural resources and left next to nothing behind in the form of social and economic benefits.[6] The following year he referred to the Territory as the "looted land." Of the 434 fish traps licensed by the Department of the Interior, Neuberger stated, only 38 belonged to Alaskan residents, while 245 were owned and operated by 8 large canning companies. In 1946, a representative year, the value of the fish pack amounted to $56,571,000, on which the industry paid a territorial tax of $630,000, or approximately 24 cents on each case of salmon (one case contained 48 one pound cans). The same year the fishing industry hired 10,956 Alaskans, to whom it paid $3,729,000 in wages. A work force of 12,484 was brought north from the lower forty-eight states. These workers were paid $7,206,000 in wages, which, however, were not distributed to the laborers in Alaska but rather at the end of the season in a lump sum at the point of hire. Territorial merchants, therefore, did not derive any multiplying benefits from these wage dollars. In addition, two Seattle steamship lines, the Alaska Steamship Company and the Northland Transportation Company, both owned by the Skinner family of that city, monopolized the Alaskan trade. These same interests also operated a salmon brokerage. The fishing industry, preferred customers of the shipping monopoly, paid an average of $14.23 a ton for cannery supplies, while other Alaskan customers were charged $28.12 a ton for transporting of food, staples, and general merchandise north.7

It was to the advantage of these interests to keep territorial government and the tax structure at a minimum. The same applied to many established Alaskan businessmen who turned the status quo to their profit. Among such individuals was Austin E. "Cap" Lathrop, Alaska's lone millionaire, and the Lomen brothers, Ralph and Carl, of Nome. Congressman Preston E. Peden of Oklahoma, a member of the Subcommittee on Territorial and Insular Possessions of the Committee on Public Lands, told journalist Frank L. Kluckhohn of the *American Mercury* in 1949 that he had recently dropped in on Lathrop. Peden stated to "Cap" that he favored statehood, whereupon Lathrop replied that if a statehood bill passed, he would immediately sell out for fifty cents on the dollar. When Kluckhohn related this information to Gruening, the Governor declared to Kluckhohn that Lathrop's opposition was determined by his economic stake in territorial status. Lathrop paid no territorial taxes on his movie theatres in Fairbanks, Anchorage, and Cordova, but merely a $100 license fee to the municipalities in which they were located. The same was true of the two banks he owned, for which he paid only $250 each. There were no territorial taxes on his two newspapers, two radio stations, and assorted apartment houses, Gruening stated. Lathrop operated a coal company, and there he paid an assessment of less than one cent per ton, which he passed on to his customers. The same advantages were enjoyed by the Lomen brothers, the Governor continued, who had a monopoly on the lighterage business and paid no taxes whatsoever. These persons and others, according to Gruening, had all lobbied against the basic tax program and statehood because they feared that their privileged position would be destroyed.8

The general aim of this combined special interest lobby was a negative one, designed to defeat all measures which would increase governmental costs and to kill any moves which would allow Alaska more control over its natural resources. All that was needed to achieve this objective was a tie vote in one of the two houses of the territorial legislature. The senate was perfect for this strategy with its sixteen members, four from each one of the four judicial divisions regardless of population. The lobby had to control only eight votes out of a total of forty in both houses. Four of the senators were elected from the sparsely settled second judicial division by fewer than 1,000 voters around Nome who depended for a living upon the United States Smelting and Refining Company.9 The task of the lobby was not a very difficult one under such conditions.

Governor Gruening, who battled these forces, later stated that the long standing paralysis of the territorial legislature reached its climax in the 1947 session. In the face of Alaska's mounting needs for schools, hospitals, a new physical plant for the University of Alaska, expanded health services, more assistance for the aged, and legislation to make airport contruction possible, the legislature provided revenues of $6,500,000 as against a budget request of $10,500,000. The 1947 legislature, the Governor declared, was the worst in his experience.10 As a result, the incensed chief executive made a special report to the people of Alaska on the events which transpired during the 1947 session. At issue, he asserted, was whether the Territory should be run for its citizens or continue to be governed for and by the large economic interests whose sole concern was the profit motive. He appealed to his fellow Alaskans to elect a legislature which would move the Territory forward, presumably toward statehood.11

The territorial electorate responded by sending "the Republicans, who in the halls of the Territorial Legislature . . . had shown what they would do, what they could do, and what they did do . . . back to the sidelines."12 The Governor was unfair in this assessment, because obstruction was not the monopoly of the Republicans alone. Many Democratic legislators had played the same game. In any event, in the 1948 general election the Democrats won control of both houses, and Bartlett was returned to Congress by the decisive margin of 17,520 to 4,789 votes over his Republican opponent R. H. Stock. For the Delegate this was an affirmation of his statehood leadership. There also was a referendum on the ballot to determine whether or not Alaskans favored the continued use of fish traps, the symbol of absentee economic control. The vote was advisory in nature only, because these devices were regulated by the Federal Government. However, Alaskans answered with a resounding "no" of 19,712 to 2,624 "yes" votes. The highly emotional nature of this issue becomes apparent when the votes are broken down by judicial divisions. In the first judicial division, southeastern Alaska, where the working force was heavily dependent on fishing, the vote was 7,179 against and 1,113 for. In the second judicial division, along the Arctic and Bering Seas, and in the fourth judicial division, the interior of Alaska—both areas where few people had ever seen traps—the tabulations were 1,151 against and 521 for, and 3,665 against and 438 for, respectively. In the third judicial division, which included Anchorage and Kodiak and which had a large and flourishing fishing industry, the vote was 7,727 against and 552 for.13

The 1948 election was a turning point for Alaska, because it indicated to the special interests that they would confront a totally different situation in the 1949 territorial legislative session. It signaled the onset of changes and reform. In effect, the legislature which met in Juneau early in 1949 set the territorial house in order and prepared Alaska for statehood.

This legislature adopted a comprehensive but moderate tax program which reached out to include businesses and individuals deriving their income from Alaska but who had not been paying any taxes, or at best negligible ones. A territorial income tax was based on ten percent of the federal tax, which made computation of this levy fairly simple. A property tax of one per cent was credited against the municipal and school district assessments, and thus duplication was avoided. At the same time the territorial legislature took over and streamlined the old system of license fees from the Federal Government. For each separate business an initial application fee of $25 was charged. Beyond the initial fee, a sum equal to one-half per cent of gross receipts in excess of $20,000 and one-fourth per cent above $100,000 received during the income year were to be remitted to the Territory. This levy applied to those concerns which, so far, had paid no monies whatever to the Alaska territorial government. These included steamship companies, air and bus lines, lighterage companies, banks and motion picture theatres, oil and construction companies, garages and service stations, newspapers, radio stations, and logging operations. Professional registration, examination, and insurance levies were to be collected by the various professional boards. The tax on the fishing industry was changed from a case tax to one based on the wholesale value of the pack, amounting to four per cent of the value of raw fish processed for salmon canneries to one per cent of the value of raw material for herring processing plants. The territorial legislature increased fishermen's licenses from $1 to $5 for residents and from

$25 to $50 for nonresidents. Fishing gear, such as traps, gill nets, and seines also were taxed. Excise taxes on liquor were raised, and establishments serving alcohol were regulated by fees which varied from $75 to $5,000, according to type of business, the size of the town, or the volume of the business. In addition, the usual motor fuel taxes, vehicle and drivers' licenses, and tobacco and various miscellaneous taxes were modernized.[14]

Still another important achievement of the 1949 legislative session, in recognition of the popular demand for statehood, was the creation of the official Alaska Statehood Committee. The measure, Senate Bill 49, the number a symbol of the hope that the Territory would become the forty-ninth state, was introduced by Senators Frank Peratrovich of Klawock, the Territory's outstanding Tlingit legislator, and Victor C. Rivers of Anchorage. The language of the bill was more indicative of hope than of existing reality at that time:

> In recognition of near attainment of Statehood for Alaska and the responsibility that will devolve upon the people of Alaska in framing a fundamentally sound and workable state constitution embodying the best provisions that have evolved in the interest of better government in the several states, and in recognition of the many problems that will attend the transition from Territorial status to Statehood, it is deemed necessary in the public interest to establish a Committee, non-governmental in character, to assemble applicable material, make studies and provide recommendations in a timely manner. [15]

The Alaska Statehood Committee was to consist of eleven Alaskans, nominated by the governor and approved by the legislature. As an indication of its bipartisan character, not more than six of the members could belong to the same party. In addition, Governor Gruening, Delegate Bartlett, and his immediate predecessor, ex-Delegate Anthony J. Dimond, were to be ex-officio members. For operating expenses, the legislature voted an appropriation of $80,000 for the committee.

Governor Gruening had the task of selecting at least two members from each of Alaska's four judicial divisions, to satisfy regional pride and desire for recognition. Gruening also was determined to appoint one Indian and one Eskimo as well as one woman. He nominated from the first judicial division William L. Baker, a Democrat and the editor and publisher of the *Ketchikan Alaska Chronicle*; Mildred R. Hermann of Juneau, a Republican, one of Alaska's two women lawyers, a feminist, and former president of the territorial Federation of Women's Clubs; and Frank Peratrovich, a Democrat and Tlingit legislator from Klawock. From the second judicial division, he chose Howard Lyng of Nome, a Democrat, miner, and Democratic National Committeeman; and Percy Ipalook, a Republican and an Eskimo Presbyterian minister from Wales. Both were members of the territorial legislature. Gruening selected from the third judicial division Victor C. Rivers, a Democrat from Anchorage, an engineer and architect, and a member of the territorial senate; Robert B. Atwood, a Republican of the same city and the editor and publisher of the *Anchorage Daily Times*; Stanley J. McCutcheon, a Democrat, also from Anchorage, an attorney, president of Alaska Airlines, and speaker of the house in the 1949 session; and Lee C. Bettinger, a Republican, mayor of Kodiak, and a businessman. From the fourth judicial division, he named Andrew Nerland, a Republican, a businessman from Fairbanks, and a member of the legislature; and Warren A. Taylor, a Democrat from the same city, an attorney, and a legislator who had served several sessions in the house.[16]

Governor Gruening was also obligated to call a meeting of the Alaska Statehood Committee, but since the prospects for the passage of an enabling act looked so promising early in 1949, the Governor postponed doing so. Only when it became apparent late in the summer of 1949 that no Congressional action on a statehood measure would be forthcoming did he summon the members of the committee. One of the first obstacles to this new statehood strategy arose when the territorial board of administration froze the $80,000 appropriation for the committee, along with other funds. This action was made necessary because the 1947 legislature had failed to provide the necessary revenue to meet the expenditures it had approved. Undeterred, the members of the committee advanced their own expenses and met in Juneau late in August of 1949 to organize and plan strategy.[17]

It soon became apparent that the road to statehood was still a tedious one. The main task of the Alaska Statehood Committee, it quickly developed, would consist of publicizing and educating the public on statehood both in Alaska and in the continental United States. In addition, the committee would have to mobilize expert witnesses for Congressional statehood hearings. One committee member, William L. Baker of Ketchikan, expressed the opinion that

Alaska's strategic importance to the defense of the United States would have to be stressed to advance the cause of statehood. In order to generate widespread public support in the states, Baker continued, national labor and fraternal organizations, as well as prominent Americans, would have to be won over to the cause. He concluded that it might be useful to send Alaskan Natives to Washington to plead the Territory's case.[18] Other members of the committee disapproved of sending Indians, Eskimos, or Aleuts to Washington in the belief that such action would only stir up additional opposition among racially biased members of Congress and perpetuate the belief that Alaska was still living in Jack London's era.[19]

At its first meeting, the committee elected as its chairman Robert B. Atwood and named Mildred R. Hermann as secretary. It also appointed four subcommittees, for education and public relations, legislation, constitution, and state organization. Governor Gruening recommended the employment of a public relations firm in Washington to do lobbying on behalf of statehood, and suggested the names of a number of available firms. Delegate Bartlett informed the members that the statehood bill, then buried in the House Rules Committee, had an excellent chance of passage in the House in 1950, but cautioned that the four leaders of the House were adamantly opposed to Alaskan statehood and would have to be won over. These four were Sam Rayburn of Texas, Joseph W. Martin and John McCormack of Massachusetts, and Charles Halleck of Indiana. Bartlett urged the committee to organize letter writing campaigns in the home states of those members of Congress who were opposed to statehood.[20]

After 1949 the Alaska Statehood Committee worked diligently at its task. Individual members also utilized their association with national organizations to advertise Alaskan statehood. For instance, Mrs. Hermann gained the support of Mrs. Leslie B. Wright, legislative chairman of the General Federation of Women's Clubs, who promised to put her organization squarely behind the Alaskan campaign.[21] The success of these efforts became evident at the 1950 Senate hearings when numerous national groups, fraternal organizations, labor unions, newspaper editors, and even state governors testified in favor of the cause.[22] It was Governor Gruening who developed the suggestion of establishing a committee of distinguished Americans who would support the movement. The Governor capitalized on his experience, first as a newspaper man and later as a government official in Washington. Through a letter writing campaign, he recruited a "committtee of one-hundred" prominent Americans who supported Alaska's aspirations. This national committee consisted of citizens from all walks of life. They included famous personalities such as Eleanor Roosevelt, Rear Admiral Richard E. Byrd, Arctic explorer Vilhjalmur Stefansson, actor James Cagney, novelists Rex Beach and Pearl S. Buck, author John Gunther, General Douglas MacArthur, philosopher Reinhold Niebuhr, and historians Arthur M. Schlesinger, Jr. and Jeannette Paddock Nichols.[23]

1949 was an important year in the Alaska statehood movement. The adoption of tax reform and the establishment of the Alaska Statehood Committee signified that the voting population, and with it the legislature, was at last determined to break the stranglehold of the special interests. From that time on attempts to gain statehood shifted increasingly to the national level and to Washington.

FOOTNOTES FOR CHAPTER VII

1. Hilscher, *Alaska Now*, pp. 275-77.
2. *Ibid.*
3. *Ibid.*, p. 278.
4. Interview with Ernest Gruening, July 16, 1969, Washington, D.C.
5. *Statehood for Alaska*, (1947), p. 140.
6. Richard L. Neuberger, "Gruening of Alaska," *Survey Graphic*, October, 1947, p. 513.
7. Richard L. Neuberger, "The State of Alaska," *Survey Graphic*, October, 1947, p. 513.
8. Frank L. Kluckhohn, "Alaska Fights for Statehood," *American Mercury*, May, 1949, pp. 55-62. For a brief biography of Austin E. Lathrop, see Driscoll, *War Discovers Alaska*, pp. 214-28.
9. George W. Rogers, *Alaska in Transition: The Southeast Region*, A Study sponsored by the Arctic Institute of North America and Resources for the Future, Inc. (Baltimore: The Johns Hopkins Press, 1960), p. 164.
10. "A Record of Achievement," Address by Governor Ernest Gruening, Jefferson-Jackson Day Dinner, Fairbanks, Alaska, March 4, 1950, file 37-9, No. 3, Box 442, Records of the Office of the Governor of Alaska, 1884-1958, Federal Records Center, Seattle, Washington.
11. Neuberger, "Gruening of Alaska," p. 513.
12. "A Record of Achievement," Address by Governor Ernest Gruening, March 4, 1950.
13. "Official Returns, Territorial Canvassing Board, General Election, October 12, 1948," in Office of the Secretary of State, Juneau, Alaska. For a full discussion of the trap issue, see Rogers, *Alaska in Transition*, pp. 3-15.

14. Alaska Statehood Committee, *Alaska Statehood: Analysis and Refutation of Minority Views on S. 50* (Juneau, Alaska, January, 1952), pp. 47-55; Gruening, *The State of Alaska*, pp. 317-18. This pamphlet was actually written by Dr. George W. Rogers.

15. *Session Laws of Alaska,*, Chapter 108, Sects. 1, 2, 3, and 8.

16. Gruening, *The Battle for Alaska Statehood*, p. 11.

17. Ernest Gruening to Victor C. Rivers, July 25, 1949, file 35-45, Box 436, Records of the Office of Governor of Alaska,1884-1958, Federal Records Center, Seattle, Washington; Minutes of Organizational Meeting of Alaska Statehood Committee, Juneau, Alaska, August 29-31, 1949, file 68, folder Statehood Committee, Personal Correspondence, Statehood Committee—X,Y,Z—Gen'l., Box 39, Anthony J. Dimond Papers, University of Alaska Archives, College, Alaska. A brief history of the Alaska Statehood Committee is found in Alaska Statehood Committee, *Statehood for Alaska: A Report on Four Years of Achievement* (Juneau, Alaska: Alaska Statehood Committee, 1953).

18. Position Paper by William L. Baker, July 20, 1949, folder Statehood for Alaska, Personal Correspondence, Statehood Committee—X,Y,Z—Gen'l., Correspondence with Gruening, Box 39, Anthony J. Dimond papers, University of Alaska Archives, College, Alaska.

19. Telegram, Lee C. Bettinger to Governor Gruening, August 28, 1949, file 35-45, Box 436, Records of the Office of The Governor of Alaska, 1884-1958, Federal Records Center, Seattle, Washington.

20. Minutes of Organizational Meeting of Alaska Statehood Committee, Juneau, Alaska, August 29-31, 1949, file 68, folder Statehood Committee, Personal Correspondence, Statehood Committee—X,Y,Z,—Gen'l., Box 39, Anthony J. Dimond Papers, University of Alaska Archives, College, Alaska.

21. Mildred R. Hermann to all members of the Alaska Statehood Committee, October 26, 1949, Personal Correspondence, Statehood Committee—X,Y,Z—Gen'l., Box 39, Anthony J. Dimond Papers, University of Alaska Archives, College, Alaska.

22. See U.S., Congress, Senate, *Alaska Statehood*, Hearings before the Committee on Interior and Insular Affairs on H.R. 331 and S. 2036, 81 Cong., 2 Sess. (Washington: Government Printing Office, 1950).

23. Alaska Statehood Committee, letterhead, in the file of the author. The national committee was completed by February, 1950, and the names of its members were announced by Robert B. Atwood in a formal news release which was sent to various news services around the country. A direct mailing was made from Juneau to 718 papers. A copy was addressed to all the newspapers in the hometown of every member of Congress. Along with the release went a separate brief story for each state, pointing out the people who were on the committee from that area. Biographies of the ninety-six members were prepared, printed by the *Ketchikan Alaska Chronicle*, and mailed to every member of the House of Representatives. George Sundborg designed the letterhead which included the names of the "committee of one-hundred" for the official use of the Alaska Statehood Committee. See George Sundborg to Mildred R. Hermann, February 4, 1950, Personal Correspondence, Statehood Committee—X,Y,Z—Gen'l., folder Statehood Committee, Box 39, Anthony J. Dimond Papers, University of Alaska Archives, College, Alaska.

CHAPTER VIII

THE FIGHT FOR STATEHOOD BECOMES NATIONAL

While the territorial legislature was working out long-needed tax reforms in Alaska, Delegate Bartlett and his friends in the House and Senate again submitted some statehood bills in January of 1949.[1] Bartlett's measure differed from his previous bills mainly in its scaled-down land grants. Instead of the 200,000,000 acres asked for in prior measures, he now proposed to transfer sections 2, 16, 32, and 36 in each township for the support of common schools, and section 33 in certain townships in the Tanana Valley for the support of the University of Alaska. In addition, 1,000,000 acres of vacant, unappropriated, and unreserved public lands were to pass to the new state for public buildings, asylums, penitentiaries, reformatories, and other such purposes. In case the particular sections allotted were subject to homestead or aboriginal claims, the state would be given the right of lien selection, that is, the right to choose land elsewhere. Perfunctory hearings before the Subcommittee on Territorial and Insular Affairs of the House Committee on Public Lands were held in Washington on March 4 and 8, 1949. At that time the Secretaries of the Interior and Agriculture and a representative of the Department of Defense gave favorable testimony. Winton C. Arnold of the Alaska Salmon Industry, Inc., and Al Anderson, executive secretary of the Alaska Miners Association, submitted written statements in which their objections, oddly enough, centered on the inadequacy of the land provisions in Bartlett's 1949 statehood bill. They also pointed out that aboriginal claims to Alaskan lands clouded any future title by the State.[2]

Despite these objections, the subcommittee reported the Bartlett measure favorably, and on March 10, the full Public Lands Committee recommended that the statehood bill be passed by the House. The brief report concluded that Alaska was ready for statehood and should be admitted immediately.[3] With that action, the bill went to the House Rules Committee where it remained bottled up for the rest of 1949. Early in 1950, the House Public Lands Committee voted to bypass the Rules Committee and instructed its chairman, J. Hardin Peterson, to take the necessary steps. This procedure for circumventing the Rules Committee was possible because the previous year, in the organization of the House, a reform was approved which barred the Rules Committee from holding for more than twenty-one days a measure which had been approved by one of the other committees. After the specified time period, the chairman of such a committee could move for a bill's consideration on the floor. Speaker Sam Rayburn of Texas granted Hardin's request, and the Alaska statehood bill as well as the one for Hawaii came to the floor of the House. The former passed on March 3, 1950 by a vote of 186 to 146, and the latter on March 7 by a margin of 262 to 110.[4]

Hawaii's statehood movement went back to 1903 when the territorial legislature had requested Congress to pass an enabling act and make it possible for the islands to adopt a state constitution and be admitted to the Union. It was not until 1935, however, that Congress gave serious consideration to Hawaiian statehood. At that time, the House Committee on Territories held hearings in Washington, and a subcommittee conducted an investigation in Hawaii. The committee, in its report, came to no definite conclusions. Hearings were also held in 1937 and 1946, again in Hawaii. In 1947, the focus shifted to Washington and after still another inquiry into the matter, the House passed the Hawaiian measure in June of that year by a vote of 195 to 133.[5] From that time until 1958, the Hawaii and Alaska statehood struggles were intertwined. Ernest Gruening asserts that partisanship in relation to statehood for both territories began in 1947 when House Speaker Joseph W. Martin of Massachusetts decided that Hawaii was likely to send a Republican Congressional delegation to Washington upon statehood, whereas Alaska probably would select Democrats. Hawaii's ambitions, therefore, received the Speaker's blessing, but the Alaska measure languished in the House Rules Committee.[6] In subsequent years, arguments based on noncontiguity, racial diversity, disproportionate Senatorial representation, and the precedent which might be set for other noncontiguous possessions were used against both Alaska and Hawaii.

In 1950, however, there was a great deal of optimism in Alaska because for the first time a statehood measure had passed in one house of Congress. Senate hearings on the Alaska measure were scheduled to begin in April before the Interior and Insular Affairs

Committee in Washington. Governor Gruening lost no time in beginning his efforts to sway opinions and change attitudes. Early in April he wrote to Governor Vail Pittman of Nevada and asked him to use his influence with Senator George W. Malone, a Nevada Republican and an ardent opponent of statehood. Gruening argued that Malone, as a Westerner, should consider it an honor to help bring not only Alaska into the Union but Hawaii as well. If words alone were not enough, Gruening suggested, Governor Pittman should "build a fire behind him [Malone] and get various organizations in Nevada to communicate with him." Pittman speedily complied with Gruening's request when he pointed out to Malone that the addition of one Representative and two Senators from Alaska would be highly advantageous to the Western bloc of states.[7] At the same time Governor Gruening and other members of the Alaska Statehood Committee were working to obtain a favorable press for the Alaskan effort. Newspaper support ranged from New York to Texas and from Louisiana to Michigan. The *New York Journal-American* probably summed up the situation best in stating:

Alaska wants statehood with the fervor men and women give to a transcendent cause. An overwhelming number of men and women voters in the United States want statehood for Alaska. This Nation needs Alaskan statehood to advance her defense, sustain her security, and discharge her deep moral obligation.[8]

Opponents of statehood also organized for the upcoming hearings. Delegate Bartlett advised Secretary of the Interior Oscar L. Chapman that the Alaska Salmon Industry, Inc., would be represented at the hearing by Winton C. Arnold, who was "a smooth operator, intelligent and with a pleasing personality." Bartlett cautioned the Secretary that Arnold was the industry's "chief lobbyist," and that he had "fought and is fighting against every liberal and progressive proposal ever made [for Alaska]." Bartlett concluded that a couple of publicity men from McWilkins, Weber and Cole, a Seattle advertising firm handling the salmon industry account, would be in Washington to smooth press relations for Arnold.[9]

When the Senate hearings opened in Washington in April, not only Arnold but also a planeload of Alaskans, mobilized by the Alaska Statehood Committee, appeared as witnesses. The territorial group consisted of mostly older, established residents, including lawyers, businessmen, ministers, representatives of labor, spokesmen for chambers of commerce, officials from veterans' groups, and newspaper editors.

On the first day of the hearings, April 24, Secretary Chapman made a very strong and impassioned plea for Alaska statehood. He summarized the arguments in favor of admission and disposed of the case against statehood. The Secretary also cautioned the Senate committee to beware of the economic interests represented by various witnesses. Glancing around the hearing room, the Secretary noted the presence of Judge Arnold, whom he described as "a registered lobbyist in Alaska for the salmon-packing industry." Governor Earl Warren of California spoke eloquently for admission, and General Nathan F. Twining of the air force, then Commander-in-Chief of the Alaskan Command, testified that statehood for the Territory would strengthen the defenses of America. However, the Reverend Bernard R. Hubbard of Santa Clara, California, well-known for his studies of Alaskan glaciers, expressed doubt that the Territory could bear the added costs of statehood.[10]

Several Alaskans appeared before the committee on April 25 in support of the territory's cause. The most effective pro-statehood testimony was given by Mildred R. Hermann. In commenting on the added costs a State government would entail, she stated that $4,242,000 per year above current expenditures would suffice. This amount, she concluded, could be raised from Alaska's resources.[11] On the third day representatives from various national organizations, such as the Veterans of Foreign Wars and the Order of Railway Conductors of America, presented resolutions in favor of statehood. Delegate Bartlett asserted that the salmon industry did not care how much or how little land the state received, but simply opposed statehood. It was inconceivable he said, that:

> this committee or this Senate is going to allow a single industry, no matter how powerful, to dictate in fields outside its proper boundaries. The plea of that industry in a matter of no direct concern to it at all—namely the amount of land to be conveyed to the new State—is proof that the statehood opposition is reduced to a truly desperate expedient in its attempt to block this bill.[12]

Judge Arnold appeared before the committee on the fourth day with an elaborate exhibit of charts and graphs, maps and tables, all designed to demonstrate the inadequacy of the statehood bill under discussion. His arguments ranged widely from impairment of international treaties and noncontiguity to questions concerned with Federal land policies in Alaska and their relationship to the transfer of public lands to the proposed State. Arnold reminded the Senators of his earlier warnings about the confusion which would result from the aboriginal land claims. He criticized the Department of the Interior for the erratic policies it had pursued in the Territory for years. He asserted that less than one per cent of Alaska's land area had been surveyed between 1867 and 1950. At that rate, he continued, it would take thousands of years before enough land had been measured to transfer title of the acreage granted in the statehood bill.13

On April 28, the second day of his testimony, Arnold introduced two witnesses whom he had brought at industry expense to Washington. The first, retired Rear Admiral Ralph Wood, had served in Alaskan waters during the Second World War. Wood denied that statehood, as claimed by General Twining, would enhance the national security or help substantially in the defense of Alaska. The second witness, Edward W. Allen, was a Seattle attorney and chairman of the International Fisheries Commission. He opposed giving the new State control over its fisheries and other sea resources. Allen insisted that such a transfer would be detrimental to international treaty obligations because of uncertain jurisdiction and dual responsibility which would arise as a result of federal and state participation in the management of this resource. In addition, he pointed to the possibility of imprudent exploitation of these assets under a lax state administration.14

The response to Arnold's thorough presentation varied. But his testimony raised questions in the minds of many Senators about the adequacy of the statehood bill under discussion and the applicability of the Western land state model in the case of Alaska. This latter concern was expressed by Senator Ernest McFarland of Arizona, who asserted ominously that the committee wanted to write a good bill and would carefully consider all the criticisms.15

Many pro-statehood Alaskans blamed Arnold for the delays and difficulties the movement had encountered in Congress. To them he appeared as an obstructionist giant with tremendous forces behind him which were able to thwart the desire of a majority of the Territory's citizens. Although this was an oversimplification, Arnold was a very dedicated and skillful advocate for the industry he represented. Dr. George W. Rogers, then an economist on the staff of Governor Gruening, later stated:

> [W. C. Arnold] . . . spearheaded the anti-statehood forces, and he was very effective, because he was very intelligent, and very energetic, and very ruthless. His testimony before statehood committees was always done very cleverly. He didn't come out and say very bluntly, "I'm against statehood." [Instead, he would say,] "I'm for statehood, but not statehood now." This was his opening remark generally. Then he'd give a devastating case against statehood which ended up to statehood never.[16]

Ralph J. Rivers, long-time resident of Alaska, erstwhile Attorney General of the Territory, and later the new State's first elected Representative to Congress, recalled that Arnold was loyal to the people he represented and expressed their viewpoint vigorously. "We used to say that we wished we had a W. C. Arnold on our side," Rivers declared. Although the Judge was a good Alaskan, Rivers asserted, he was the "fly in the ointment of the statehood movement." Not until the industry which Arnold represented had practically ruined the salmon runs, Rivers concluded, did the canners begin to relax their opposition to statehood.[17]

Judge Arnold, "the fly in the ointment," later stated that he personally had felt that statehood was inevitable after the first Congressional hearing in 1947, but was unable to persuade his employers of this belief. Placed in a difficult position, Arnold asserted, he had fashioned a policy which would serve both the salmon industry and Alaska.[18] This statement might be interpreted to mean that Arnold actually desired immediate statehood and that his actions and testimony were designed to achieve that goal. Mary Lee Council, Delegate Bartlett's administrative assistant for many years, did not see Arnold in the role of a statehood "angel." His testimony, she stated, was designed to defeat the measures. Thus he insidiously and cleverly clouded the real issue as far as the salmon industry was concerned. The industry's opposition, she said, and Arnold's as its spokesman, was based on the knowledge that the new State would take over control of the fisheries and immediately abolish the hated and deadly efficient fish traps. Nevertheless, Ms. Council stated, Arnold inadvertently showed the Senators the way to write a decent statehood bill. Apparently Arnold had been convinced that no such measure could be written because the Senators would adhere to the Western land state model with its small land grants and specific township-section requirements, which were totally inapplicable in Alaska due to its size and peculiar physical characteristics. Much to Arnold's surprise, she maintained, his testimony provided the basis for a unique and generous land selection formula which, even though enlarged in subsequent years, did not change in concept.[19]

It matters little what motivated Judge Arnold. The fact is that he made a significant contribution to Alaska statehood. He educated his Congressional audience on Alaska's problems and potential, and his arguments stimulated positive discussion and action.

The Senate hearings ended on April 29, 1950. Early in May, President Truman again gave his support to Alaska and Hawaii statehood and urged the speedy admission of both. Very few of the existing States, the President said, had possessed such great human and natural resources at the time of their admission. Truman asserted that he was disturbed by objections to Alaska and Hawaii statehood because they would be entitled to equal representation in the Senate. This argument was not only entirely without merit, but also belied "a basic tenet of the constitutional system under which this nation had grown and prospered." Without equal representation in the upper house for large and small states alike, the Chief Executive concluded, "there probably would have been no United States."[20] On June 29, the Senate Interior and Insular Affairs Committee completed its revision of the Alaska statehood bill and reported it favorably, stating that refusal to admit Alaska would break the historic mold in which the United States had grown great. In addition, Alaskans desired and merited statehood, and were willing and able to support it. Statehood, the Senators concluded, would be in the best interest of both the United States and Alaska.[21] The most important achievement of the committee, however, was the changed land selection formula. Instead of requiring the new state to select sections, 2, 16, 32, and 36 in each township regardless of where they happened to be located, whether on mountain tops or in valleys, the proposed new state was granted the right to select 20,000,000 acres of vacant, unappropriated, and unreserved lands from the public domain best suited to its particular needs.[22]

The minority report, written by Senator Hugh Butler of Nebraska, asserted that statehood would bring financial chaos and the quick collapse of Alaska. In essence, Senator Butler reiterated Judge

Arnold's criticisms, and maintained that Alaska was not yet ready to assume the burdens of statehood. He was willing, Butler stated, to sponsor legislation which would enable Alaskans to elect their own governor and other territorial officials, and thus prepare the Territory for eventual statehood.[23] Obviously this was only a sop. Butler failed to explain how an elected governor would be able to overcome the Territory's economic handicaps. Despite the improvements in the Alaska measure, the outlook for getting either it or the Hawaii bill before the Senate for a vote appeared rather dim at the end of June, 1950. On June 20, President Truman still insisted that there was time for the Senate to act on the bills. At Bartlett's prompting, the President promised early in July to do all he could to get administration leaders in the Senate to push the statehood measure onto the floor.[24] Editorials in leading national newspapers also urged the Senate to act on both the Alaska and Hawaii bills.[25]

In a brief speech in the Senate on August 8, Senate Democratic leader Scott Lucas of Illinois strongly supported the Alaska measure. He revealed, however, that the Democratic leadership had been told by Senator James Eastland of Mississippi that if either statehood bill were brought up, Eastland would try to displace it by promoting the Mundt-Ferguson anti-communist bill. If that happened, Lucas stated, one of the Senators might try to attach a civil rights amendment to the anti-communist measure. Such action, according to the Majority Leader, held the prospect of a prolonged debate on the Mundt-Ferguson bill and a filibuster on the civil rights amendment which would indefinitely delay the recess of Congress before the elections in the fall.[26] On August 24, Senator Warren G. Magnuson of Washington demanded that the Senate leadership inform the nation of what had happened to the statehood bills. The Senate was stalling because, he said, there were some Senators who did not want to add four members to the upper house and dilute a "voting bloc," namely the Southern Democratic-conservative Republican coalition.[27]

Presidential prodding finally prompted the Senate Democratic Policy Committee to put the statehood bills on the list of "essential legislation." This move, however, brought no corresponding promise to push it through the Senate. At that point, a bipartisan group, led by Democratic Senator Richard B. Russell of Georgia, decided to prevent any action on the Alaska and Hawaii bills before the recess of Congress. A few days later, Senate Majority Leader Lucas, anxious to return home to campaign, buckled under and announced that he would have to drop consideration of the measures if the opposition threatened a filibuster which would postpone the pre-election recess.[28] And this is exactly what happened.

When Congress reconvened late in November of 1950, Senator Lucas, who had been defeated in Illinois by Everett McKinley Dirksen, proposed to bring up the Alaska bill. This action touched off a lengthy debate on the merits of statehood for both Territories. Senator Hugh Butler stated that he did not want to "thrust statehood upon the helpless Alaskans." The political immaturity of the Territory and its citizens, he declared, was amply demonstrated by the fact that the Gruening administration "ruthlessly" controlled the voters of Alaska and perpetuated its own powers. The Territory could not afford statehood because its two major industries, gold mining and salmon fishing, were declining. This left only the gigantic defense expenditures which one day would have to come to an end and upon which a stable society could not be built. Senator John L. McClellan, Democrat of Arkansas, opposed the two statehood bills because of the "communist influence" on Harry Bridges and his International Longshoremen's and Warehousemen's Union in Hawaii, and because Bridges now had "his men working in all the fishery towns in Alaska, trying to put under his thumb every union in Alaska...." Democratic Senator John Stennis of Mississippi was shocked to learn that of the 580,000 square miles in Alaska, the Federal Government owned 99.7 per cent. Privately owned land amounted to roughly 1,500 square miles, he said, the equivalent of one large county in Minnesota or two in Mississippi. Yet, such a small area was to be represented by two Senators. The real danger, Stennis remarked, was that the addition of four Senators might curtail the privilege of unlimited debate. In addition, those four new Senators would come from areas not "attached geographically [to the continental United States] and to which in many ways they are not attached in culture, ideals, and ideas." Once Alaska was admitted, it would lead to the admission of Hawaii as well. Then, what would stop the admission of the Virgin Islands, Puerto Rico, Guam, and Okinawa?[29]

On December 1, Republican Senator Guy Cordon of Oregon made a speech on the Senate floor in which he dismissed such arguments as noncontiguity, lack of population, inadequate political maturity, and, in the case of Alaska, meager financial resources. "If taxation without representation was tyranny in 1776," he stated, "it is tyranny today." Cordon asserted that the threat of a filibuster had prevented action on the statehood bills. "I feel," he remarked, "that my friends in the South have perhaps, as we say in the West, been too close to the trees for a long time to evaluate the forest." Nobody could predict what the views of four new Senators would be on civil rights or on any other issue. In addition, Cordon said, public sentiment was overwhelmingly in favor of the admission of both Territories. This was a valid point. In 1949, as cited by Cordon, a Gallup poll had revealed that only 68 per cent of the American voters favored Alaska's admission, while one year later it had risen to 81 per cent. A similar trend was discernible for Hawaii. In 1949, 58 per cent of the American people favored Hawaiian statehood, while late in 1950 this percentage had risen to 76.[30]

But the Southern Democratic-conservative Republican coalition prevented both the Alaska and the Hawaii bills from coming to the floor of the Senate.[31] As a result, this meant, of course, that the whole tedious process of getting a new bill through the House and then through the Senate had to be repeated. But there had been gains. The House had passed an Alaska statehood bill, and the Senate, for the first time, had considered such a measure. In addition, the Senate Interior and Insular Affairs Committee had departed from the traditional Western land grant formula.

On January 8, 1951 Senator Joseph C. O'Mahoney, Democrat of Wyoming, submitted an Alaska statehood measure for himself and eighteen of his colleagues from both parties.[32] With the introduction of three companion bills in the House, the statehood struggle was rolling again.[33] Late in January of 1951, the Senate Interior and Insular Affairs Committee began its study of the Alaska measure.[34] Since extensive hearings had been held in the preceding year and there was little that could be added, committee consideration of the Alaska bill was very cursory. In May, the committee reported the measure favorably by a very narrow margin of 7 to 6.[35] A substitute bill offered by Senator Hugh Butler, which would have allowed Alaskans to elect their own governor, was rejected as an obvious device to defeat statehood.

With the outbreak of the Korean War in June of 1950, national priorities shifted rapidly; and as American forces became more deeply involved, Alaska statehood took a backseat. The years 1951 and 1952 were lean ones for the statehood forces. Even the Alaska Statehood Committee slumped into a moribund condition.[36] Some citizens of the Territory, however, were becoming increasingly impatient with Congressional delays. In the 1951 territorial legislative session, a house memorial, although later withdrawn, reflected this dissatisfaction. Its authors requested that Alaska be granted statehood. If it could not be done, the memorialists asked that Alaska be given the right to declare its independence of and from the government of the United States and to form a "Republic of Alaska."[37]

Early in 1952, Delegate Bartlett told members of the Alaska Statehood Committee that he had received firm assurances that the Alaska bill would receive favorable consideration in the Senate. The Hearst papers and the Scripps-Howard chain had promised editorial support, Bartlett stated, and all the national organizations which so far had supported the cause had promised to do so again. Bartlett surmised that if the Alaska bill came to a vote in the Senate, it would gain a safe, although small, margin of victory. The Delegate accurately predicted that the anti-statehood forces in Congress would try to prevent such a vote so that they would not be forced to go on record against a popular measure. One way they could accomplish this objective, he concluded, would be to send the bill back to committee for further study or filibuster it to death.[38]

Debate on the Alaska bill resumed early in 1952 and continued intermittently throughout February. As early as February 5, however, a poll of Senators showed that a majority of Republicans and Democrats would vote to send the Alaska bill back to committee for further study.[39] Senator Hugh Butler, as much a foe of Alaska statehood as ever, confessed that he had great emotional feeling for Alaska, as a great northern frontier. But, he said, his desire to help the citizens of the Territory prompted him to reject statehood at that time. He asked his colleagues how they could think of burdening 108,000 Alaskans with the costs of statehood until it had been ascertained beyond any doubt that this was what the citizens of the Territory really wanted. Butler asserted that up to that time, Congress had only heard testimony from a small group of Alaskans who had come to Washington "at the taxpayer's expense to present us with their reasons for desiring statehood." In addition, the Senator introduced voluminous documents, all designed to show that Alaska was totally unprepared to assume the responsibilities of statehood.[40]

When Senator Stennis asked Senator Magnuson how he explained the large vote of approximately 6,000 against statehood in the 1946 territorial referendum, Magnuson replied that he could explain it, although it would not be politically popular for him to do so.

> Most of the votes in opposition to the granting of statehood to Alaska came from my own home town of Seattle, and were stirred up by a very small group of people who for a long time have been able to go to Alaska, make fortunes, help to develop Alaska—and I do not blame them—and who would like to have things remain as they are, in the status quo, without change. That is the source of the opposition. I do not say anything is wrong about that; some of those persons have been very good citizens of my State and have also been very helpful in connection with the development of Alaska. But, because it has been so profitable for some of them in connection with mining, fishing, and other commercial activities, they would prefer to preserve the status quo. They live in Seattle, go to Alaska in the summer time, and then return to Seattle. I could discuss the matter of the manipulation of that campaign [the 1946 territorial referendum] in great detail.

A few days later, Senator Magnuson presented editorials from leading newspapers across the nation which urged the Senate to do its duty and pass the Alaska and Hawaii statehood bills.[41]

Both Delegates Bartlett of Alaska and J. R. Farrington of Hawaii wrote to Senator Joseph C. O'Mahoney, chairman of the Senate Interior and Insular Affairs Committee, supporting each other's cause. Bartlett stated that he wanted Hawaii to be admitted in 1952. "I should hope for that result even if by some mischance Alaska's hope were not to be realized. We Alaskans want statehood for ourselves," he stated, "but we want it for Hawaii too." Delegate Farrington echoed these sentiments when he said, "I hope the Senate will adopt the bill reported by your committee for the admission of Alaska to the Union as a state without regard to what may be done with the bill to give statehood to Hawaii."[42]

On February 20, Republican Senator Fred R. Seaton of Nebraska, a newspaper publisher and radio station owner who had been appointed to fill the vacancy created by the death of Senator Kenneth Wherry, delivered his maiden speech in support of Alaska statehood. Seaton had been persuaded to support Alaska's cause by Gruening, who also wrote the speech for him.[43] On the same day, Senator

George Smathers of Florida introduced a motion to recommit the Alaska bill to the Committee on Interior and Insular Affairs with instructions to hold hearings on the measure. Senator A. S. "Mike" Monroney of Oklahoma requested and received permission from Smathers to include directions which asked the committee also to consider commonwealth status for Alaska and Hawaii. On February 27, the Alaska measure was returned to committee by a vote of 45 to 44.[44] As in 1950, a coalition of conservative Republicans and Southern Democrats had successfully killed Alaskan statehood for another session of Congress. The House, under these circumstances, saw no need to act at all.

FOOTNOTES FOR CHAPTER VIII

1. *Cong. Record*, Index, 81 Cong., 1 Sess., pp. 787, 844, 759 (H.R. 331, introduced by Delegate Bartlett; H.R. 25, submitted by Representative Homer Angell; H.R. 2300, introduced by Representative Mike Mansfield; and S. 2036, submitted by Senator Estes Kefauver).

2. U.S., Congress, House, *Statehood for Alaska*, Hearings before the Subcommittee on Territories and Insular Possessions of the Committee on Public Lands on H.R. 331 and related bills, Committee Hearing Serial No. 3, 81 Cong., 1 Sess. (Washington: Government Printing Office, 1949), pp. 2-3, 14-25, 7-8.

3. U.S., Congress, House, *Providing for the Admission of Alaska Into the Union*, H. Rept. 255 to accompany H.R. 331, 81 Cong., 1 Sess. (Washington: Government Printing Office, 1949), pp. 36-52.

4. George B. Galloway, *The Legislative Process in Congress* (New York: Thomas Y. Crowell Company, 1955), pp. 343-45; *Cong. Record*, 81 Cong., 2 Sess., pp. 2780-81 (March 3, 1950). In this instance, 125 Democrats and 61 Republicans voted for and 66 Democrats and 80 Republicans against passage. The Rules Committee bypass reform was repealed in 1951.

5. "The Question of Granting Statehood to Hawaii: Pro & Con," *Congressional Digest*, January, 1959, p. 9.

6. Gruening, *The State of Alaska*, p. 471.

7. Gruening to Governor Vail Pittman, April 4, 1950, and Pittman to Senator George W. Malone, April 14, 1950, file Persons Leaving Alaska, Box 795, Records of the Office of the Governor of Alaska, 1884-1958, Federal Records Center, Seattle, Washington.

8. Editorial, *New York Journal-American*, March, 1950, in *Cong. Record*, Appendix, 81 Cong., 2 Sess., p. 1840 (March 13, 1950). For a sampling of some 300 editorials in favor of Alaska statehood, see *Ibid., pp. 2506-07 (March 29, 1950).*

9. Bartlett to Secretary of the Interior Oscar L. Chapman, April 14, 1950, file Alaska Statehood, Records of the Office of the Secretary of the Interior, Office Files of the Secretary of the Interior, Oscar Chapman, Box 33, RG 48, NA.

10. U.S., Congress, Senate, *Alaska Statehood*, Hearings before the Committee on Interior and Insular Affairs on H.R. 331 and S. 2036, 81 Cong., 2 Sess. (Washington: Government Printing Office, 1950), pp. 30, 1-108.

11. *Ibid.*, p. 124.
12. *Ibid.*, pp. 204-05.
13. *Ibid.*, pp. 317-18. The anti-statehood *The Daily Alaska Empire* (Juneau) faithfully mirrored the Arnold testimony in its editorial pages. It also had a feature series by Robert DeArmond with a decidedly anti-statehood slant which ran from April 24 to May 2, 1950.
14. *Ibid.*, pp. 369-438.
15. *Ibid.*, p. 500.
16. Interview with Dr. George W. Rogers, January 27, 1970, College, Alaska.
17. Interview with Ralph J. Rivers, December 31, 1969, Fairbanks, Alaska.
18. Interview with Winton C. Arnold, August 25, 1969, Anchorage, Alaska.
19. Interview with Mary Lee Council, July 20, 1969, Washington, D.C.
20. President Harry S. Truman to Senator Joseph C. O'Mahoney, Chairman, Committee on Interior and Insular Affairs, May 15, 1950, in U.S., Congress, Senate, *Providing for the Admission of Alaska Into the Union*, S. Rept. 1929 to accompany H.R. 331, 81 Cong., 2 Sess. (Washington: Government Printing Office, 1950), p. 9.
21. *Providing for the Admission of Alaska Into the Union*, S. Rept. 1929 (1950), pp. 11-12.
22. *Ibid.*, p. 11.
23. *Ibid.*, pp. 31-42.
24. *The New York Times*, July 7, 1950, p. 7; July 8, 1950, p. 4.
25. See editorials, *The New York Times*, June 30, 1950, in *Cong. Record*, Appendix, 81 Cong., 2 Sess., pp. 4890-91 (July 3, 1950); *St. Louis Post-Dispatch*, July 5, 1950, in *Ibid.*, p. 4958 (July 7, 1950); *Washington Post*, July 19, 1950, in *Ibid.*, pp. 5232-33 (July 19, 1950).
26. Editorial, *Washington Daily News*, August 10, 1950, in *Cong. Record*, Appendix, 81 Cong., 2 Sess., p. 5802 (August 11, 1950).
27. *Ibid.*, p. 13512 (August 24, 1950).
28. *The New York Times*, September 8, 1950, p. 21; September 13, 1950.
29. *Cong. Record*, 81 Cong., 2 Sess., pp. 15924-39 (November 28, 1950).
30. *Ibid.*, pp. 16028-31 (December 1, 1950).
31. For the debate, see *Ibid.*, pp. 15919-16035 (November 28 to December 1, 1950).
32. *Cong. Record*, Index, 82 Cong., 1 Sess., p. 658.
33. *Ibid.*, H.R. 1493, introduced by Bartlett, p. 763; H.R. 1510, submitted by Representative Sam Yorty, p. 764; and H.R. 1863, introduced by Representative Homer Angell, p. 773.
34. *The New York Times*, January 24, 1951, p. 31.
35. U.S., Congress, Senate, *Providing for the Admission of Alaska Into the Union*, S. Rept. 315 to accompany S. 50, 82 Cong., 1 Sess. (Washington: Government Printing Office, 1951). In content this report was very similar to the one of 1950. See U.S., Congress, Senate, *Providing for the Admission of Alaska Into the Union*, S. Rept. 1929 (1950). The latest report had a more extensive minority view and a more complete appendix. This time Senator Butler was supported by Republicans George W. Malone of Nevada and Arthur L. Watkins of Utah, and Democrats Russell B. Long of Louisiana and George A. Smathers of Florida. The minority objected to the specific provisions in the statehood bill and criticized inadequacies, such as insufficient land, no curbs on the "whim of bureaucrats," and the "faulty methods" for selecting delegates to the constitutional convention. The Senators opposed the admission of Alaska in principle because it was

noncontiguous and failed to meet the "requirements" for statehood. The minority report contained a list of what was called "instances of the extremely poor leadership in Territorial affairs." These, and other criticisms made by Senator Butler and his colleagues, were answered by Dr. George W. Rogers in Alaska Statehood Committee, *Alaska Statehood: Analysis and Refutation of Minority Views on S. 50* (Juneau, Alaska, January 1952). Dr. Rogers stated that the citations of alleged "failures of the Territorial administration" were based "upon smear literature produced by the malicious fringe campaigns and recognized at the outset by most Alaskans of all political affiliations as a low form of partisan slander, since amply answered and refuted." Dr. Rogers concluded that it was a deplorable practice to introduce "such maliciously false propaganda into what is represented to be an objective study." *Ibid.*, pp. 15-16.

36. Howard Lyng to Robert B. Atwood, December 19, 1951, Personal Correspondence, Statehood Committee—X,Y,Z—Gen'l., folder Statehood Committee, Box 39, Anthony J. Dimond Papers, University of Alaska Archives, College, Alaska.

37. John R. Noyes, Commissioner of Roads, to Joe T. Flakne, Chief, Alaska Division, Office of Territories, May 7, 1951, file 9-1-63, Territorial Legislative—General, Classified Files, 1907-51, Box 449, Records of the Office of Territories, RG 126, NA.

38. Memorandum, Bartlett to all members of the Alaska Statehood Committee, January 16, 1952, Personal Correspondence, Statehood Committee—X,Y,Z—Gen'l., folder Statehood Committee, Box 39, Anthony J. Dimond Papers, University of Alaska Archives, College, Alaska.

39. *The New York Times*, February 5, 1952, p.1. For the full debate, see *Cong. Record*, 82 Cong., 2 Sess., pp. 751-68, 869-70, 953-55, 1066-67, 1077-82, 1115-28, 1131-39, 1185-91, 1194-98, 1237-39, 1241-50, 1253-56, 1324-29, 1378-96, 1409-11, 1498-1537 (February 4 to 27, 1952).

40. *Ibid.*, pp. 1501, 1504-15 (February 27, 1952).

41. *Ibid.*, p. 768 (February 4, 1952); pp. 1247-50 (February 21, 1952).

42. Bartlett to Senator Joseph C. O'Mahoney, Chairman, Senate Interior and Insular Affairs Committee, February 4, 1952, and Delegate J.R. Farrington to O'Mahoney, February 2, 1952, in *Cong. Record*, 82 Cong., 2 Sess., p. 1066 (February 18, 1952).

43. *Ibid.*, pp. 1194-97 (February 20, 1952); Gruening, *The Battle For Alaska Statehood*, pp. 57-58.

44. *Cong. Record*, 82 Cong., 2 Sess., pp. 1183, 1537 (February 27, 1952).

CHAPTER IX

ALASKANS DEMAND "STATEHOOD NOW"

The Republicans chose Dwight D. Eisenhower as their standard bearer in 1952. With his wide grin, military reputation, and fatherly image, he made an extremely attractive candidate to a nation dominated politically by the Democrats for two decades and tired of the continuing war in Korea. The Democrats nominated Adlai Stevenson, a man who brought considerable intellectual stature and subtle wit into national politics. A plank in the Democratic platform again urged immediate statehood for Alaska and Hawaii, and the party's national convention for the first time gave both Territories their alphabetical place in the roll of the States. This lifted them from the bottom of the list as Territories, and Alaska became second, right after Alabama. A plank in the 1948 Republican platform had referred to "eventual statehood" for Hawaii and Alaska; it was now changed to read "immediate statehood for Hawaii" and "statehood for Alaska under an equitable enabling act."[1]

Alaska's Delegate Bartlett did not intend to take any chances on his reelection in view of the strong Republican Presidential candidate. He returned to Alaska late in July to open his campaign.[2] His Republican opponent was Robert Reeve, owner and operator of the Anchorage-based Reeve Aleutian Airlines, who, according to *The New York Times*, belonged to the "statehood in the future" camp. Reeve thought that the Territory's population was too small, its financial needs too great to be met locally, and the statehood bills so far considered entirely unsatisfactory.[3] Governor Gruening, in a less charitable frame of mind, referred to Reeve as

> ... a gentleman growling around the Territory now rattling the bogey of "creeping or leaping socialism" as part of his Republican campaign. He says we must get away from all government subsidy or assistance. However, this loud-voiced campaigner ... has not mentioned that to his success as a private enterprise the federal government in the last four years has contributed—not loaned, but paid—over half a million dollars in air mail subsidies. That isn't creeping or even leaping socialism.... That would be "flying socialism." Yet I haven't

heard that he's refused any of this dough, or offered to turn it back! Why doesn't he practice what he preaches? The fact is, he's just another fellow, who down at heels and out at elbows when he came to Alaska at the end of the Republican era twenty years ago, has been made prosperous by Democratic policies.4

Bartlett won a fifth term by beating his opponent 14,219 to 10,893 votes. A referendum on whether or not the Federal Government should turn over complete control and operation of the fisheries to the Territory was overwhelmingly approved by a vote of 20,544 to 3,479. The territorial Republicans, however, brought Democratic dominance to an end and won control of the Alaska legislature.5 This was the party's first revival since the advent of the New Deal in 1933, and *The New York Times* asked curiously, "As Alaska Goes—?"6 The November national elections furnished the answer—"As Alaska Goes, So Goes the Nation"—because nationally the Republicans elected their first White House occupant in twenty years, although their control of Congress brought only a tenuous majority of one in the Senate.

With the change in administration, statehood proponents were immediately concerned regarding the President-elect's attitude. Some encouragement could be derived from a speech which Eisenhower delivered in Denver, Colorado, on September 17, 1950 as president of Columbia University. On that occasion he stated that the quick admission of Alaska and Hawaii would show the world that the United States practiced what it preached, namely self-determination for all peoples.7

Delegate Bartlett expressed his conviction that Alaska's statehood chances looked dim for the next four years of Republican rule. Senator Hugh Butler of Nebraska, soon to be chairman of the Senate Interior and Insular Affairs Committee, had already told the Delegate that he did not favor the admission of the Territory because of its narrow economic base. As a matter of fact, Butler did not think that the issue would even come up. Hawaii, on the other hand, would be dealt with, although the Senator told Bartlett that he was not personally committed to the island Territory's cause.8 Despite these dire predictions, half a dozen Alaskan statehood measures were submitted in the new Congress early in 1953.9

It soon became apparent that statehood had become a partisan issue. The Republican leadership quickly recognized that the admission of Republican-leaning Hawaii would bolster their weak hold on Capitol Hill. If traditionally Democratic Alaska were admitted at the same time, however, Republican gains would be neutralized. President Eisenhower reflected this attitude in his first State of the Union message on February 2, 1953. The President urged that Hawaii be granted statehood "promptly with the first election in 1954," but failed to mention Alaska.[10] The House of Representatives speedily complied with Eisenhower's request and passed a Hawaii bill on March 10, 1953.[11] On the same day, Representative A.L. "Doc" Miller, Republican of Nebraska, the new chairman of the House Interior and Insular Affairs Committee, attempted to placate Alaska statehood advocates in the House when he announced that hearings on an Alaska measure would start on April 14, 1953.[12]

As the date of these hearings approached, Douglas McKay, the new Secretary of the Interior, and an ex-automobile dealer from Salem, Oregon, expressed his reluctance to appear before the committee. He seemed to reason that since statehood for Alaska was not a part of the administration's plan, the committee hearings would only be a waste of time. Early in April, Chairman Miller warned McKay that failure to appear might be fatal politically. "If you can't do anything but take a neutral stand that should be done," Miller advised. If all else failed, McKay could state that he was "studying the problem." Miller concluded by reminding the Secretary that it was "absolutely necessary" to promise hearings on Alaska if the Republicans were to get the Hawaii bill out of the House committee.[13] The political nature of the statehood issue was further emphasized by a political skit performed at the 1953 Washington Gridiron Club Dinner, which the President attended. "Miss Hawaii" and "Miss Alaska Eskimo" appeared, with the latter singing to the tune of "Sweet Lielani":

> *Sweet Hawaii, G.O.P. flower*
> *Leaders smile on statehood just*
> *for you*
> *They say you'll give them extra power*
> *While I have votes so few*
> *Poor Alaska, we are forsaken*
> *We have no Wai-Ki-Ki like you*
> *No hula girls to charm the senate*
> *You are their dreams come true.*[14]

The House hearings opened on April 14, 1953, as scheduled.[15] The usual cast of witnesses attended, including the Alaska Statehood Committee and its friends. The military was represented by Undersecretary of the Air Force James H. Douglas. In his testimony, Douglas mirrored the administration's attitude toward the admission of Alaska. He told the committee that while the Department of Defense felt statehood might have long-range military advantages, there would be no immediate benefits. Secretary McKay appeared on April 15, and was predictably noncommittal. The Secretary stated that Alaska should be admitted "when it is ready and under a proper bill so that it can develop, pay its taxes and support itself."[16] Since hearings and investigations into the matter of Alaska statehood had occurred with regularity since 1947, and not much new material was added on this occasion, the committee reported the measure favorably in June, 1953, along with a number of amendments. The most important of the amendments increased the proposed land grant from 40,000,000 to 100,000,000 acres and reduced a projected Federal transitional grant from $50,000,000 to $15,000,000. The committee felt that the State should construct its own mental, charitable, penal, and reformatory institutions and build many of its roads and harbors without federal assistance. Most importantly, the committee report characterized the amended statehood bill as the "equitable enabling act" called for in the 1952 Republican platform.[17] After this favorable treatment, the Alaska measure promptly disappeared into the House Rules Committee.

In the meantime, the House-passed Hawaii measure was considered by the Senate Interior and Insular Affairs Committee. It soon became apparent to the Democratic committee members that the Senate's Alaska bill would not even be reported out. To force action, the seven Democrats, led by Clinton P. Anderson of New Mexico, proposed to add the Alaska measure to the Hawaii bill. The motion passed 8 to 7 on a straight party-line vote, except that Senator George W. Malone, a Republican from Nevada who opposed statehood for either territory, but believed both should get the same chance, voted with the Democrats.[18] The Democrats were simply telling the administration that there would be no admission of Hawaii without reciprocal action for Alaska. Realizing the futility of getting combined bills passed, the Senate Interior and Insular Affairs Committee refused to report the twin measures.

In the spring of the same year, Senator Hugh Butler, now chairman of the Senate Interior and Insular Affairs Committee, had announced his intention of holding hearings in Alaska on a statehood bill. "We are going where we can get the reaction of the little people—not just a few aspiring politicians who want to be Senators and Representatives," Butler stated. In August of 1953, therefore, Butler and five committee members journeyed to the Territory. Before the hearings opened he requested that only those who had not yet testified do so now.[19]

Butler's hearings in Alaska were the catalyst which started the "populist" phase of the Alaska statehood movement. His emphasis on wanting to hear the "little people" mobilized a large number of those who had come to Alaska during and shortly after the Second World War. Victor Fischer, then planning director of the city of Anchorage, and Niilo Koponen, a homesteader and surveyor at the time, were typical of this new group of territorial citizens. They had been sympathetic to statehood, but had not been directly involved in it. The indigenous movement so far had been propelled mostly by resolutions from the territorial legislature, formal reports and actions taken by the Alaska Statehood Committee, and editorials in the *Anchorage Daily Times* and other territorial papers. The people who had actively participated were the old-time, established, and yet politically progressive professionals and businessmen who, regardless of party affiliation, had followed the leadership of Gruening and Bartlett generally and on the statehood issue in particular. The "little people" who turned out in great numbers for the Butler hearings included many young lawyers, public officials, small businessmen, housewives, nurses, and homesteaders.[20]

As late as mid-August these statehood forces in Anchorage and Fairbanks had begun to prepare for the upcoming hearings. In Anchorage, the "Little Men for Statehood" movement was formed by two young lawyers, Barrie White and Cliff Groh, and that city's Republican club and its chamber of commerce. In Fairbanks, the local Democrats primarily took the initiative.[21] Victor Fischer, a leader in Anchorage, later recalled the formation of the movement there:

> I remember there were a few phone calls, a few people got together, and we sort of said, what are we going to do. Here the committee is coming, Butler is coming. Somebody said we must have a name for our group. So the natural thing was the

LITTLE MEN FOR STATEHOOD. And it happened that one of our little signs that we made up at that point read, "I am a little man for statehood." And we made up these little signs, we made up big posters, and they were plastered all over Anchorage. And we tried to contact the "little men" we knew in other places, and again, it wasn't done through any formal organization. It was just a bunch of citizens acting together. And we found an empty office somewhere on Fourth Avenue in Anchorage and we painted signs and posters and each of us threw in a couple of dollars. And we got a little printing done. We never had a letterhead or a formal organization. We never had a chairman or an executive director.

The Butler committee heard testimony at Ketchikan, Juneau, Fairbanks, and Anchorage. Of the approximately 140 witnesses, fewer than 20 opposed statehood, and most of the latter spoke in Ketchikan and Juneau. Probably typical of those against statehood was Allen Shattuck of Juneau, a successful insurance agency owner and a resident of Alaska since 1897. Shattuck did not favor statehood because he was convinced that the territory could not pay for the added costs of a state government. Carl Heinmiller of Haines belonged to the post-World War II group of Alaskans. He had come to the territory in 1947 as a war veteran to homestead. He wholeheartedly supported statehood, and remarked that he was annoyed with Alaska's old aristocracy who were against statehood because they obviously did not want to pay their share of the added expenses. Nineteen-year-old Jerry Wade of Juneau thought it pathetic that "American citizens had to come here and get down on their knees and plead for the right of complete citizenship." Niilo Koponen told the Senators in Fairbanks that without statehood, Alaska would be unable to provide the stable political environment needed to build solid communities and retain population.[23]

Butler and his fellow Senators arrived in Anchorage on a gray, rainy day in late August. The "Little Men for Statehood" group met them at the railroad depot, uncertain as to how many people would turn out for the occasion. Victor Fischer remembered that he and his friends were concerned because they were so unorganized. They did not know if there would be five or fifty people. As it turned out, there were literally hundreds who met the train, waving banners and placards proclaiming "Statehood Now."[24]

Of the nearly sixty witnesses in Anchorage, only one opposed statehood. There were some dramatic moments, when, for example, Mitchell Abood presented the Senators with the signatures of 3,129 individuals who demanded statehood. There was also the testimony of Margaret Rutledge, Republican committeewoman from the third judicial division. She told the Senators of having received an invitation to attend the inaugural ceremonies for the first Republican President in twenty years. But under the McCarran Act, which had become effective late in 1952, persons arriving from Alaska in the continental United States were required to pass through immigration to establish their legal citizenship before being granted entry. Mrs. Rutledge described her feelings as she had to stand in line and wait her turn to be cleared before being admitted to the main floor of SEA-TAC air terminal in Seattle-Tacoma. "[As I]...stood in line I was profoundly and unjustly humiliated. I was—and still am—seething with indignation." Mrs. Rutledge concluded that "some degrading influence had robbed me of the thing I value most—my birthright as an American, my freedom in my own country."[25] Thereupon, she broke down in front of the committee and cried. Victor Fischer, also a witness, later stated that the tears of a mature woman, a Republican, a pillar of the establishment, impressed the Senators profoundly.[26]

When the hearings concluded on August 27, Senator Butler remarked that the prospects for Alaskan statehood had been improved by the visit. Butler said that he supported a generous land grant for the future state. Then, in his typically ambiguous fashion, he stated that the Territory could afford to wait for statehood, but should not be asked to wait too long.[27] Thereupon, the Senators left Alaska, except for the tireless Butler, who remained for another three days to investigate the areas where the most economic development was taking place. After his private inquiry, Butler concluded that the Federal Government should provide the Territory with, above all else, an adequate road network, a complete survey of all federal land withdrawals, and, to make the acquisition of land titles easier, a complete revision of the land laws applying to Alaska. These measures, Butler remarked, would be far more important than any inadequate statehood bill.[28]

The visit of Butler and his colleagues brought together those Alaskans sympathetic to the statehood cause. Many of those who had before been standing on the sidelines decided, in the words of Victor

Fischer, "Hell, this is our fight and not just an official one. We, the people, have to participate." Out of the "Little Men for Statehood" forces there soon evolved another group which dubbed itself "Operation Statehood." In those days the military had made the term "operation" fashionable, and "Operation Statehood" quickly became popular. It had a small executive committee and a series of small committees for special assignments. One committee mounted a campaign to encourage as many newcomers as possible to write to their homestate Congressional delegations and, through their families and friends in the continental United States, to exert pressure in Congress for Alaska statehood. A "gimmicks" committee devised unique ways to popularize statehood in Congress. On one occasion, the "gimmick" involved the Forget-Me-Not, Alaska's official flower. A group of women made artificial bouquets and mailed them to members of Congress just before an Alaska statehood vote. They included a message which went something like this: "We the people of Alaska, say forget-us-not."[29] In addition, the organization prepared informational packets for wide distribution which included a concise summarization of the reasons why statehood should be granted. Alaskans were urged to send Christmas cards to friends in the continental United States which stated:

> *A merry merry Christmas*
> *With happiness and cheer*
> *And in your Christmas greetings*
> *Give a thought to us up here*
>
> *Only you can give us statehood*
> *With a short card or a note*
> *to your elected Senator*
> *For we don't have a vote*
>
> *So for us Alaskans*
> *to make our future bright*
> *Ask your Senator for statehood*
> *And start the New Year right.*[30]

Such activities indicated that statehood had become a popular cause, and especially so in the most populous third judicial division. Moreover, many proponents were no longer asking for statehood, but demanding it as a right. Victor Fischer, in 1954 the vice-president of Operation Statehood, later said that most people realized by then that the legal precedents for statehood were inconsequential, and that it was simply a political issue. Fischer likened the fight for statehood to the process of

> rolling a boulder up the hill and you keep sliding back, and you push it up and it rolls back, and you keep wondering how long you can persevere, pushing that boulder to the top until it stays at the top and rolls down the other side.[31]

Popular participation on a large scale had not come a minute too soon. Senator Butler, upon his return to Omaha, Nebraska, stated that he thought he had convinced "the rank and file in Alaska that statehood should not come at this time." Most of "the clamor for statehood," he said, was coming from those "politicians who want to run for office."[32] Democratic Senators Clinton P. Anderson and Earle C. Clements, who had accompanied Butler to Alaska for the hearings, took sharp exception to Butler's statements, accusing him of having completely misread the signs of the times in Alaska. Almost every Alaskan who had testified, the Senators stated, had demanded "statehood . . . now."[33]

In his 1954 State of the Union message, President Eisenhower renewed his request for the immediate admission of Hawaii, but again he did not mention Alaska.[34] *The Washington Post* commented editorially that "a murky cloud of politics" hovered over Eisenhower's request for Hawaiian statehood. A number of legislators were supporting statehood for both Territories, while some Southern Democrats were anxious to kill any statehood action by adding Alaska to the Hawaii bill. "Much of the politics of statehood," the editor stated the obvious, "lies in the assumption that Hawaii would send Republican Senators to Congress, whereas Alaska would elect Democrats." But with Congress almost evenly divided, the editor observed, "this conjecture assumes disproportionate importance."[35]

It was under this "murky cloud of politics" that a subcommittee of the Senate Committee on Interior and Insular Affairs finally drafted an equitable Alaska statehood bill early in 1954. Senator Guy Cordon of Oregon was the subcommittee chairman. The hearings, which lasted from January 20 to February 24, produced yet another thick volume of information on the Territory as well as the statehood bill.[36] This measure proposed to give Alaska 100,000,000 acres of its own choice from the unreserved public lands. In addition, 400,000 acres within the Tongass National Forest in southeastern Alaska and another 400,000 acres from public lands elsewhere were bestowed on the new

State to allow room for the expansion of the municipalities in that area and in other localities. A grant of 500,000 acres was made to finance the construction of legislative, executive, and judicial buildings, and 200,000 acres were allocated to aid schools and asylums for the deaf, dumb, and blind. For the partial support of the University of Alaska, the subcommittee granted 500,000 acres. It also provided for a federal grant of $42,000,000 for road construction spread over a six-year period, $30,000,000 for road maintenance over a period of fifteen years, and a $15,000,000 appropriation for land surveys and the improvement and construction of harbors.[37] This was a generous bill and very similar to the House measure of the previous year.

In order to move the Hawaii bill, Senator Butler had come out for Alaska statehood as early as January 25, 1954. The committee thereupon favorably reported the Hawaii bill two days later.[38] Despite such seemingly encouraging signs, the administration had no intention of seeing Alaska admitted. Reports on the Alaska measure had been requested from the Bureau of the Budget, the agency which determined whether or not a piece of legislation was consistent with the President's program, and from the Departments of the Interior, State, and Commerce as early as January, 1953. No replies had been received by March 11, 1954. Several Alaska statehood proponents in the Senate were afraid that the President would veto a separate Alaska statehood bill. To add to these fears, the House Committee on Interior and Insular Affairs had favorably reported its Alaska bill in June of 1953, and the House Rules Committee had not acted upon it. Senator Clinton P. Anderson spoke for many of his Senate colleagues when he remarked that the only chance the House would have to vote on Alaska statehood would be in the event the Senate passed a combined Hawaii-Alaska measure. On March 11, 1954, the Senate agreed to Senator Anderson's proposal to join the two statehood bills by a vote of 46 to 43; and on April 1, it passed the twin measures by 57 to 28 votes.[39] This was the first time the Senate had passed the two statehood measures, which was viewed as a good omen by some supporters.

The Senate-passed bill next went to the House, where its fate became fairly certain when House Speaker Joseph W. Martin of Massachusetts announced that he did not see much hope for the combined measure.[40] At this critical juncture, Alaska's Governor B.

Frank Heintzleman wrote a letter to the Speaker in which he suggested that Alaska be partitioned, with only the populated areas to be incorporated within the boundaries of the new state. The Governor's plan would have made a state out of the roughly 250,000 square miles which contained the larger population centers and approximately 85 per cent of the people. Northern and western Alaska would have remained a Territory, to be called "Frontier Alaska" or "Alaska Outpost," until it could be absorbed into the new State.[41] The excluded area was rich in natural resources, such as tin, gold, copper, coal, mercury, uranium, undetermined amounts of oil, and various other valuable resources.[42] This suggestion elicited a heated debate among Alaskans, and was vigorously opposed by the majority.[43] Delegate Bartlett commented that the Governor's suggestion was "a nicely calculated effort to hurt the statehood cause." Leaders of both parties in Anchorage were dismayed at the Governor's proposal, but President Eisenhower, while reiterating that he considered Alaska unready for statehood, conceded that he might modify his opposition in view of the partition proposal, since it would safeguard the needs of military defense.[44]

Not only partition, but also commonwealth status for Alaska, had been mentioned from time to time. As early as 1952, Senator A.S. "Mike" Monroney, Democrat of Oklahoma, had instructed the Senate Interior and Insular Affairs Committee to consider the commonwealth arrangement for both Alaska and Hawaii. In March of 1954, Monroney introduced an amendment, in the form of a substitute bill for the tandem Alaska-Hawaii measure, which would have granted commonwealth status to both Territories. The plan was defeated by a vote of 60 to 24.[45] Essentially, commonwealth advocates proposed to grant all the rights and responsibilities, except national representation, to Alaska and Hawaii. To sweeten the bait, the two Territories were to be granted exemption from federal income taxes, and all the revenues gathered within their borders were to be used locally. Residents of Alaska and Hawaii were to enjoy the complete protection of the Constitution and the Bill of Rights. They would share in the benefits of social security, unemployment compensation, federal housing, and similar legislation. At the same time they would have the full obligations of selective service, but could not participate in Presidential elections. Commonwealth status, Senator Monroney observed, was the "best way to give justice to the distant areas and at the same time protect the political unity and the present political stature of our 48 contiguous sister states."[46]

Soon commonwealth organizations sprang up in Alaska. One such group explained that under a status similar to that of Puerto Rico, Alaska would have self-government, freedom from federal taxation, and control of its lands and natural resources. Another organization distributed some 25,000 pamphlets stating that as a commonwealth the Territory would become a completely autonomous state, voluntarily associated with the United States, and yet would keep the opportunity to choose statehood at a later date. In addition, commonwealth status would exempt Alaska from federal income and excise levies, and thus enable it to offer tax incentives to new industries.[47] John Manders, Anchorage attorney and a member of this group, Commonwealth for Alaska, Inc., probably best explained what these Alaskan advocates expected:

> ... whether you call it commonwealth, territorial status, protectorate or state or home rule the main object of the so-called movement for commonwealth status for Alaska is to take off the backs of the people the burdensome taxation that is now plaguing each and every one of them. It makes little difference what you call it. The main purpose is the elimination of federal taxation and then whatever you are taxed by your own legislature is your own fault as to whether or not you are taxed heavily or lightly.[48]

There were other favorable interpretations of this new approach. Richard Strout, writing in *The New Republic*, drew a parallel with the dominion status enjoyed by several members of the British Commonwealth of Nations. Strout maintained that a similar arrangement would be an excellent solution for America's non-contiguous Territories. He also asserted that an area with only 129,000 inhabitants was scarcely entitled to two United States Senators, when New York State, with a population of 14,800,000 had only two. Additionally, Strout expressed concern about the precedent the admission of Alaska and Hawaii would set. Could statehood be denied to Guam or the Virgin Islands, he asked? Many of the Senate's most important decisions, he pointed out, were reached by a two-thirds vote. This being the case, Alaska's Senators could conceivably neutralize the votes of Senators from large populous states.[49] The same argument, of course, could be made with regard to Hawaii's prospective Congressional delegation.

Columnist Walter Lippmann also became a convert to the commonwealth cause. He asserted that the admission of outlying Territories would constitute a radical change in the structure of the Union and its external relations. Lippmann did not explain how or why whis would happen, nor did he point out that denying statehood to incorporated Territories and transforming them into commonwealths would constitute a departure from American historical experience. Lippmann doubted that the interests of Alaska and Hawaii were identical to those of Americans in the continental United States and, therefore, whether these outlying areas could be successfully assimilated. Like others, he was worried lest Guam, the Carolines, and even Formosa might someday take advantage of the precedent set by the admission of Hawaii and Alaska.[50] Senator Monroney was similarly bothered by the precedent which would be established, and asked, "Must we forever continue . . . the proposition that all States . . . [can] come in, no matter where they . . . [are] located beyond our land mass, with influence in the upper chamber equal to the contiguous States . . . . ?"[51]

Douglas Smith of the *Washington Daily News* ridiculed such views, and especially Lippmann's argument. Alaska and Hawaii, he asserted, were the only two incorporated Territories left, and the Supreme Court had repeatedly held that such a Territory was in a state of tutelage in preparation for statehood. The admission of Hawaii and Alaska would mean no more and no less than the addition of two stars to the flag and of four new Senators and an appropriate number of Representatives. Each time a Territory had been admitted to statehood, Smith observed, "the Republic survived. . .despite the warnings of alarmists. . . ."[52] Delegate Bartlett and Robert B. Atwood of the Alaska Statehood Committee evaluated the Alaska commonwealth movement in testimony before a Congressional Committee in 1955. They stated that the subject seemed to come up in the Territory only when statehood was being discussed before Congress and there was a possibility of success. Once statehood legislation failed in a particular session, talk of commonwealth status also quickly subsided.[53]

The commonwealth proposals for Alaska and Hawaii actually were flimsy and ill-defined. During a 1954 Senate debate, Clinton P. Anderson pointed out that time and again the Supreme Court had designated Alaska and Hawaii as incorporated Territories. This implied that both were embryonic States and that all the provisions of the Constitution applied to them. Such was not the case, of course, with unincorporated areas such as Puerto Rico, Guam, and the Virgin Islands. Also, as pointed out by Senator Guy Cordon, once incorporated status had been conferred, all applicable court decisions bore out the conviction that Congress could not change such status except to statehood.[54]

It was true, as proponents asserted, that Puerto Rico had acquired commonwealth status in 1952 and did not pay federal taxes. The core of the commonwealth plans for Alaska and Hawaii promised similar privileges. Delegate Bartlett reported in 1956 that he had made extensive inquiries about the possibility of such freedom from federal taxation. The replies he received had all been negative. Typical was that of Representative Wilbur D. Mills, Democrat of Arkansas and chairman of the House Ways and Means Committee:

> ... it would appear that the uniformity clause of the Constitution requires that all Federal tax laws apply uniformly to Alaska, just as to any other part of the United States. It has also been argued that Congress' power to enact legislation governing the Territories is derived from article IV, section 3, clause 2 of the Constitution, and that this power is independent of the prohibition contained in the uniformity clause. This question has never been decided by the courts. However, I am inclined to think that if and when it arises, the courts will decide that the mandate of the uniformity clause must prevail.[55]

Secretary of the Interior Douglas McKay bluntly stated in 1955 that a federal tax moratorium for Alaska might "be a fine thing," but that it had about as much of a chance of passing Congress as a bill "to replace the stars and stripes on the American flag with the hammer and sickle."[56] Without federal tax exemption, the commonwealth scheme lost its main appeal. But despite the obvious inapplicability of commonwealth status to incorporated Territories, the idea did not die easily. As late as 1957, Representative Thomas M. Pelly of Washington proposed it as an alternative to Alaska's admission. In April of that year, the Ketchikan Commonwealth Club requested information on the subject from the Department of the Interior, only to be told that the meaning and implications of commonwealth were entirely unclear.[57]

While the possibilities of commonwealth status were being explored, the tandem Alaska-Hawaii statehood bill had become thoroughly ensnarled in partisan politics. In the middle of April, 1954, an objection from Sam Rayburn of Texas, the House Democratic leader, blocked the twin measures from going to conference with the Senate.[58] This move further dimmed the chances of a vote in the House on Alaska and Hawaii statehood. As a last ditch effort to try to rescue the tandem measure from the House Rules Committee, members of the Alaska Statehood Committee and Operation Statehood planned to fly to Washington. The suggestion had been made by a Hawaiian statehood group to go to Washington in force and attempt to persuade House Speaker Joseph W. Martin to move the twin bills to the floor of the House. The combined Alaskan group chartered an Alaska Airlines plane. One participant recalled that the majority of the Alaskans on the flight consisted of young statehood activists of both political parties from Anchorage and other communities. These were the people who had been brought into the fold by the "Little Men for Statehood" movement. Many had continued in Operation Statehood. On May 10, 1954, they, and members of the Alaska Statehood Committee, in addition to the Hawaiian group, descended upon Congress.[59]

Alaskans were told by A. L. Miller, chairman of the House Interior and Insular Affairs Committee, that statehood chances for the Territory would be immeasurably improved if partition of Alaska was accepted. Such a division of Alaska, Miller observed, would permit the establishment of military reservations in case of need. But this plan, he warned, would preclude any chance for future annexation by the State of these areas. Chairman Miller felt confident that such a partition proposal would overcome President Eisenhower's objections to Alaska statehood. If Alaskans rejected this proposal, Miller pointed out to his audience, there would be no statehood for the Territory.[60]

The Alaskan group also met with President Eisenhower. They found the President perched on his desk when they lined up before him. John Butrovich, a Republican from Fairbanks, told Eisenhower:

> We feel that you are a great American. But we are shocked to come down here and find that a bill which concerns the rights of American citizens is bottled up in a committee when you have the power to bring it out on the House floor.[61]

For emphasis, Butrovich banged his fists on the President's desk as he spoke. Eisenhower is said to have reddened. He replied that he wanted to extend full citizenship to as many Americans as possible, but that Alaska statehood posed many problems which would first have to be resolved. The President obviously referred to the Territory's military importance and the safeguarding of these interests through the partition plan. The political ramifications of the issue, Eisenhower told his audience, had only recently come to his attention. He denied, however, that partisanship played any role in the Alaska statehood issue.[62]

After a week of making the rounds in Washington, the weary Alaskans returned home, expressing the belief that their visit, if nothing else, had added to the pressure for statehood. The members of the flight, however, were thoroughly confused by the partition proposal. Ray Plummer, Democratic National Committeeman from Alaska, reflected the feeling of the group:

> No one told us that even if we divide Alaska six ways we would have a better chance of getting statehood than if we stand firm ... No one made a firm commitment that "if you accept partition you will get statehood."[63]

In any event, another statehood effort had failed for that session of Congress. Between 1953 and 1955, the role of President Eisenhower had been important in delaying statehood for Alaska. With Republican control of Congress, the Chief Executive might well have exerted the necessary pressure to force a House vote on the issue. Instead, Eisenhower, with an eye on the narrow Republican edge in the Senate, attempted to gain admission for Hawaii alone.

In his 1955 State of the Union message, the President again strongly recommended the admission of Hawaii. For the first time in such an address, Eisenhower mentioned the possibility of Alaska statehood, but only dubiously. He expressed hope that "as the complex problems of Alaska are resolved ... [it] should be expected to achieve statehood."[64] Then, after the Democratic victory in the 1954 election, Alaska once more became an issue in Congress. Many citizens in the Territory, deeply frustrated, began to consider a new statehood strategy. They started to talk seriously about holding a constitutional convention on their own.[65]

FOOTNOTES FOR CHAPTER IX

1. Kirk H. Porter and Donald Bruce Johnson, compilers, *National Party Platforms, 1840-1956* (Urbana: The University of Illinois Press, 1956), pp. 486, 453.

2. *The Daily Alaska Empire* (Juneau), July 31, 1952, p. 1.
3. *The New York Times*, September 2, 1952, p. 23.
4. "The American Way of Life: A Democratic Achievement—Let's Preserve It!" Address by Governor Ernest Gruening, Jefferson-Jackson Day Dinner, April 24, 1952, Anchorage, Alaska, file 37-9, No. 5, Box 442, Records of the Office of the Governor of Alaska, 1884-1958, Federal Records Center, Seattle, Washington.
5. "Official Canvass of Results, Alaska General Election, October 14, 1952," in Office of the Secretary of State, Juneau, Alaska.
6. *The New York Times*, October 18, 1952, p. 18.
7. The *Denver Post*, September 17, 1950, in *Cong. Record*, 83 Cong., 2 Sess., p. 631 (January 22, 1954).
8. Memorandum, E. L. Bartlett to all members of the Alaska Statehood Committee, November 25, 1952, Personal Correspondence, Statehood Committee—X,Y,Z—Gen'l., folder Statehood Committee, Box 39, Anthony J. Dimond Papers, Univeristy of Alaska Archives, College, Alaska.
9. *Cong. Record*, Index, 83 Cong., 1 Sess., p. 799 (H.R. 2684). In addition, statehood bills were introduced by Representative Homer Angell (H.R. 207), Representative Russell V. Mack (H.R. 20), Representative Sam Yorty (H.R. 1746), Representative John P. Saylor (H.R. 2982), and Senator James E. Murray for himself and fourteen colleagues (S. 50), *Ibid.*, pp. 737, 777, 806, 668. Delegate Bartlett introduced a measure for an elective governor and lieutenant-governor (H.R. 1916), *Ibid.*, p. 781.
10. *Ibid.*, 83 Cong., 1 Sess., p. 751 (February 2, 1953).
11. The vote on H.R. 3575 was 274 to 138. In the tabulation, 177 Republicans voted for the bill and 37 voted against; 97 Democrats voted for and 100 against; 1 Independent voted against. *Congress and the Nation, 1945-1964* (Washington: Congressional Quarterly Service, 1965), p. 64a.
12. *The New York Times*, March 10, 1953, p. 19.
13. A. L. Miller to Douglas McKay, April 11, 1953, file 9-1-13, part 12, Alaska-Administrative-General, Records of the Office of the Secretary of the Interior, RG 48, NA.
14. *The Daily Alaska Empire* (Juneau), April 13, 1953, p. 1.
15. See U.S., Congress, House *Statehood for Alaska*, Hearings before the Subcommittee on Interior and Insular Possessions of the Committee on Interior and Insular Affairs on H.R. 20, H.R. 207, H.R. 1746, H.R. 2684, H.R. 2982, H.R. 1916, 83 Cong., 1 Sess. (Washington: Government Printing Office, 1953).
16. *The Daily Alaska Empire* (Juneau), April 14, 1953, p. 1; April 15, 1953, p. 1.
17. U.S., Congress, House, *Providing for the Admission of Alaska Into the Union*, H. Rept. 675 to accompany H.R. 2982, 83 Cong., 1 Sess. (Washington: Government Printing Office, 1953), pp. 1-7, 14-22.
18. *Congressional Quarterly Almanac*, 83 Cong., 1 Sess. (Washington: Congressional Quarterly News Features, 1953), p. 305.
19. *The Daily Alaska Empire* (Juneau), April 3, 1953, p. 1; editorial, August 5, 1953, p. 4.
20. Interview with Victor Fischer, March 17, 1970, College, Alaska; interview with Dr. Niilo Koponen, March 10, 1970, Chena Ridge near College, Alaska.
21. *The Daily Alaska Empire* (Juneau), August 13, 1953, p. 1.
22. Interview with Victor Fischer, March 17, 1970, College, Alaska.
23. U.S., Congress, Senate, *Alaska Statehood and Elective Governorship*, Hearings before the Committee on Interior and Insular Affairs on S. 50 and S. 224, 83 Cong., 1 Sess. (Washington: Government Printing Office, 1953), pp. 176-85, 94, 245, 327-28.

24. Interview with Victor Fischer, March 17, 1970, College, Alaska.

25. *Alaska Statehood and Elective Governorship* (1953), pp. 471-72.

26. Interview with Victor Fischer, March 17, 1970, College, Alaska.

27. *The Daily Alaska Empire* (Juneau), August 27, 1953, p. 1.

28. *Alaska Statehood and Elective Governorship* (1953), pp. 587-94.

29. Interview with Victor Fischer, March 17, 1970, College, Alaska.

30. Christmas card, "Merry Christmas," distributed by Operation Statehood, Anchorage Chapter, copy in the author's files, made available from the private papers of Victor Fischer. Operation Statehood also issued a monthly newsletter and much material in the form of pamphlets, and gave dinners to raise money for lobbying purposes.

31. Interview with Victor Fischer, March 17, 1970, College, Alaska.

32. *The Daily Alaska Empire* (Juneau), September 8, 1953, p. 1.

33. *Ibid.*, September 14, 1953, p. 1.

34. *Cong. Record*, 83 Cong., 2 Sess., p. 82 (January 7, 1954).

35. Editorial, *The Washington Post*, January 10, 1954, Sec. 2, p. 4.

36. U.S., Congress, Senate, *Alaska Statehood*, Hearings before the Committee on Interior and Insular Affairs on S. 50, 83 Cong., 2 Sess. (Washington: Government Printing Office, 1954), pp. 329-39.

37. U.S., Congress, Senate, *Providing for the Admission of Alaska Into the Union*, S. Rept. 1028 to accompany S. 50, 83 Cong., 2 Sess. (Washington: Government Printing Office, 1954), pp. 30-36.

38. *Cong. Record*, 83 Cong., 2 Sess., p. 682 (January 25, 1954); *Congressional Quarterly Almanac*, 83 Cong., 2 Sess., 1954, pp. 395-98.

39. *Cong. Record*, 83 Cong., 2 Sess., p. 2909 (March 9, 1954); p. 3091 (March 11, 1954). The vote followed party lines. Only two Democrats voted against the motion and only two Republicans opposed it. For the debate on Senator Anderson's proposal to join the two bills, see *Ibid.*, pp. 2905-19, 2980-86, 2991-3003, 3065-90 (March 9 to 11, 1954); p. 4343 (April 1, 1954). In the tabulation, 33 Republicans, 23 Democrats, and 1 Independent had voted for, and 9 Republicans and 19 Democrats opposed passage. All of the 19 Democrats came from the Southern and border states.

40. *The Daily Alaska Empire* (Juneau), April 2, 1954, p. 1.

41. *Ibid.*, April 21, 1954, p. 3.

42. For a report on Alaska's resources, see U.S., Congress, House, *Alaska: Reconnaissance Report on the Potential Development of Water Resources in the Territory of Alaska*, H. Doc. 197, 82 Cong., 1 Sess. (Washington: Government Printing Office, 1952).

43. U.S., Congress, House, *Alaska, 1955*, Hearings before the Subcommittee on Territorial and Insular Affairs of the Committee on Interior and Insular Affairs pursuant to H. Res. 30, 84 Cong., 1 Sess. (Washington: Government Printing Office, 1956). Delegate Bartlett stated before the committee that there was "practically a unanimous feeling in Alaska against the partition proposal" which had been advanced by Governor Heintzleman. Bartlett recalled that he could not remember another time "when I have had more mail and telegrams and more unanimously on one side than were sent in opposition to the partition proposal...." *Ibid.*, Part I, p. 252.

44. *The Daily Alaska Empire* (Juneau), April 5, 1954, p. 1; April 6, p. 2; April 7, p. 1.

45. *Cong. Record*, 82 Cong., 2 Sess., p. 1183 (February 20, 1952); *Ibid.*, 83 Cong., 2 Sess., p. 3501 (March 18, 1954).

46. A S. "Mike" Monroney, "Let's Keep It 48," *Collier's*, March 4, 1955, pp. 32-36.

47. One group was the Commonwealth Committee, Inc., Anchorage, Alaska, which produced the pamphlet "Commonwealth for Alaska: Facts and Comments...," Box 668, Records of the Office of the Governor of Alaska, 1884-1958, Federal Records Center, Seattle, Washington. See also *The Daily Alaska Empire* (Juneau) August 9, 1954, p. 3.

48. *Ibid.*, May 3, 1955, p. 2.

49. Richard Strout, "Alaska and Hawaii: Statehood or Commonwealth Status?" *The New Republic*, February 14, 1955, pp. 13-14.

50. Walter Lippmann, "The Hawaii-Alaska Dilemma," *Washington Post and Times Herald*, March 16, 1954, in *Cong. Record.*, 83 Cong., 2 Sess., pp. 3307-08 (March 16, 1954).

51. U.S., Congress, Senate, *Alaska-Hawaii Statehood, Elective Governor, and Commonwealth Status*, Hearings before the Committee on Interior and Insular Affairs on S. 49..., 84 Cong., 1 Sess. (Washington: Government Printing Offfice, 1955), p. 122.

52. Douglas Smith, "The Issue Over Alaska and Hawaii is Basic and Simple," *Washington Daily News*, March 18, 1954, in *Cong. Record*, 83 Cong., 2 Sess., pp. 3491-92 (March 18, 1954).

53. *Alaska, 1955* (1956), p. 279.

54. *Cong. Record*, 83 Cong., 2 Sess., pp. 4325-27 (April 1, 1954); p. 4331 (April 1, 1954).

55. *Ibid.*, 84 Cong., 2 Sess., p. 15477 (July 27, 1956).

56. *Ibid.*, p. 15476 (July 27, 1956).

57. *The Daily Alaska Empire* (Juneau), March 29, 1957, p. 1; Ketchikan Commonwealth Club to Ruth Van Cleve, Legal Assistant to A. M. Edwards, Associate Solicitor for the Territories, April 6, 1957, Acc. No. 66-A-140, Box 169, Interior, Office of The Secretary, Central Files, Section Classified Files, 1954-58, file Territorial Affairs-Alaska-Political Affairs 9, part 1, RG 48, Washington National Records Center, Suitland, Maryland.

58. *The Daily Alaska Empire* (Juneau), April 12, 1954, p. 1.

59. Interview with Victor Fischer, March 17, 1970, College, Alaska.

60. *The Daily Alaska Empire* (Juneau), May 11, 1954, p. 1.

61. The *Anchorage Daily Times*, May 17, 1954, p. 1.

62. *Ibid.*

63. *Ibid.*

64. *Cong. Record*, 84 Cong., 1 Sess., p. 126 (January 6, 1955).

65. *The Daily Alaska Empire* (Juneau), April 1, 1955, p. 1.

CHAPTER X

THE CONSTITUTIONAL CONVENTION

The Republican victory in 1952 had wrought many changes in Alaska's political situation. Ernest Gruening, the Territory's appointed governor for nearly fourteen years, was a casualty of the Republican sweep in 1952. The man who had been a leader and catalyst of the statehood movement left office early in 1953. Alaskans not only wondered who the new governor would be, but equally important, what would be his attitude toward statehood.

President-elect Dwight D. Eisenhower told his Interior Secretary-designate, Douglas McKay, late in December of 1952 that he favored the appointment of a resident of the Territory for the governorship.[1] The last Republican territorial chief executive had been George A. Parks, who had resigned with the inauguration of President Franklin D. Roosevelt in 1933. In the weeks following McKay's announcement of Eisenhower's wishes, a number of candidates were mentioned in territorial Republican circles.[2] The Alaska Republican party, so many years out of power, was unable to agree on one aspirant. In the resulting babel, Secretary McKay recommended that B. Frank Heintzleman, the regional forester for Alaska, be appointed. To the dismay of statehood advocates, Heintzleman declared at the Senate hearings on his confirmation that he was opposed to immediate statehood for Alaska. At his inauguration in Juneau in April, 1953, the new Governor elaborated upon his views. Heintzleman called for objective studies of the issue, particularly of the added costs of state government. He said that Alaskans should ask Congress for a generous land grant, and he urged the drafting of a preliminary state constitution. Attracting and encouraging permanent industries, however, was the most important task ahead, Heintzleman asserted.[3] The new Governor clearly equated economic development with statehood.

While the administrative changeover was still in progress, the Alaska Statehood Committee met in Juneau at the end of January, 1953. The members had to decide what direction the statehood movement should now take. On the same day the meeting began, a bill was introduced in the territorial legislature to abolish the committee and replace it with another one made up of eleven members, eight from the legislature, and selected by that body, and three appointed by the governor. The new organization was to draft an "adequate" statehood bill which would be placed before the voters in a special territory-wide referendum. If accepted, the measure would be handed to Delegate Bartlett for submission to Congress. In addition, the new committee was to write a preliminary constitution which would be given to a constitutional convention as soon as the statehood bill passed Congress.[4]

The bill did not pass the legislature, however, so the Alaska Statehood Committee continued its activities. The committee members decided to oppose the calling of a constitutional convention prior to the passage of an enabling act by Congress. They also declined to support proposals for an elective governor. Such measures, the committee believed, were mere sops which would only serve to delay the attainment of statehood. In a meeting between the Alaska Statehood Committee and members of a special joint committee on statehood of the territorial legislature, Delegate Bartlett warned that Alaska could not ask for too large a land grant. Members of Congress from east of the Mississippi River, Bartlett observed, looked upon the public domain as a national asset, to be managed by the Federal Government for the benefit of all Americans. The Delegate rejected the idea of partitioning the Territory and admitting only the most populous section. Since the Navy reputedly had discovered vast oil reserves on the North Slope, this area promised to become Alaska's most valuable section.[5]

Actually, partition was rejected by Republicans and Democrats alike. But there were still plenty of other differences between the two parties. After long years of dominance, defeat had divided the Democratic party by bringing to the fore matters which formerly had been disregarded in favor of unity. The dispirited Democrats had to find an issue around which they could rally. Alaska's Republicans, in opposition for such a long time and unaccustomed to political responsibility, served Democratic purposes admirably. The Republican majority in the legislature created a controversial McCarthy-like investigative committee. Besides that, little was accomplished in the 1953 session. According to one Democratic observer, ". . . that session was one of the worst in territorial history. . . , members were drunk on the floor..., it was a shambles." The house "never did adjourn, it just disbanded."6

These conditions strengthened the Democrats' determination to reorganize and rejuvenate their leadership. Early in 1954 they held a special territorial convention in Juneau, and one of their decisions was to invite Adlai Stevenson, the recent presidential candidate. His visit, it was hoped, would help unify the party.7 Before Stevenson arrived, however, Secretary of the Interior McKay embarked upon an Alaska inspection trip in July of 1954. While in Anchorage, McKay tongue-lashed an audience who had come to ask him to support statehood. The Secretary gave six reasons why statehood had not been achieved. He told his audience that personally he favored statehood, but that the President made policy and he just worked for him. In addition, the Chief Executive opposed statehood for defense reasons; Alaskans had opposed the partition of the Territory; the Senate had tied the Hawaii and Alaska bills together; there were members of Congress who were opposed to the admission of noncontiguous territory; Alaskans had been too belligerent in their demands; and the Territory was too underdeveloped. The Secretary, not noted for his political tact, told his Anchorage listeners that he was "sick and tired of being kicked around by Alaskans," and that it was time for the people of the Territory to "start acting like ladies and gentlemen." McKay denied as "just a bunch of horsefeathers" reports that his department wanted to maintain control of Alaska and therefore opposed statehood. "I assure you," McKay concluded, "it would take away a lot of headaches if you got statehood tomorrow."8

Stevenson arrived in Alaska a few days after McKay's Anchorage speech. He opened his remarks with an underscored "Ladies and Gentlemen" in an obvious rebuff to the Secretary. Statehood advocates felt elated after the Stevenson visit. The bungling of the territorial legislature, the unfriendly attitude of the national administration toward statehood, and Stevenson's appearance helped the territorial Democrats to victory in the fall elections of 1954.9 After this win, the party faithful gathered in an informal pre-legislative planning session in Fairbanks in the fall of 1954. The group decided to hold a constitutional convention, and in effect, make Alaska a state prior to congressional action. Thomas Stewart, then an Assistant Attorney General of Alaska, was assigned the task of writing a preliminary constitutional convention bill.10

The idea of such a convention was not a new one in the Territory. It had been proposed as early as 1948. At that time, Delegate Anthony J. Dimond had pointed out that such an undertaking should have the active financial support of the territorial legislature in order to make it effective.[11] No such support had been forthcoming. The plan was again promoted in 1951, and, in addition, Alaskans were then urged to elect their congressional delegation without waiting for action from Congress. The Alaska Statehood Committee rejected this idea as inopportune.[12] Early in 1953, Wendell P. Kay, a lawyer and legislator from Anchorage, submitted a bill for a constitutional convention. The lawmakers debated it fruitlessly, and Kay finally withdrew it.[13] He revived the proposal in the fall of the same year, hard on the heels of the statehood hearings which had been held in Alaska.[14] His obvious intention was to keep interest in the issue at a high level. Nothing came of this suggestion either. Early in June of 1954, with the tandem Alaska-Hawaii bill stalled in the House Rules Committee, Representative A. L. Miller, chairman of the House Interior and Insular Affairs Committee, and supposedly opposed to the Territory's admission, suddenly suggested that Alaskans hold a constitutional convention. He indicated that such a positive move might persuade the House Rules Committee to release the measures.[15]

William C. Snedden, publisher of the *Fairbanks Daily News-Miner*, was a strong advocate of a constitutional convention. His experience as one of the first members of the Fairbanks Municipal Utilities District had opened his eyes to the inequities of "second class" citizenship. The board sold two revenue bond issues which totaled $7,000,000. Anywhere in the continental United States, Snedden asserted, these income tax-exempt bonds would have been sold for not more than 3.25 per cent interest. The Eastern banking houses, however, judged the Territory to be politically unstable and charged 4.75 per cent interest on $3,000,000, and 4.25 per cent on the other $4,000,000. This amounted to almost $1,500,000 extra paid by the citizens of Fairbanks over the 25-year life of the bonds for the privilege of living in Alaska. This experience motivated Snedden to question the editorial policies of the paper which he had bought from Austin E. "Cap" Lathrop. The *Fairbanks Daily News-Miner*, under the capable editorship of William C. Strand, had been bitterly and consistently opposed to statehood. When Strand left the paper in early 1952, Snedden hired John C. Ryan as editor. The editorial policy of the paper continued automatically until Snedden, having familiarized himself with Alaska and its problems by late 1953, told Ryan to study the whole statehood question. After a few weeks of solitude, Ryan emerged after Christmas, 1953, as a statehood advocate. Snedden concurred with his editor's decision.[16] In a major editorial on February 27, 1954, Snedden himself changed the paper's stand on statehood, when he stated:

> We are American citizens, . . . and we have the right to enjoy all the privileges for which all our forefathers fought and died . . . . Alaskans should make it clear that we are demanding full Statehood and nothing less. . . . Alaskans should demand STATEHOOD NOW.[17]

On April 9, 1954, Snedden published a collection of his editorials in a special six-page edition which was widely circulated throughout the territory. This switch on statehood cost him the acquisition of *The Daily Alaska Empire* (Juneau), which bitterly opposed statehood. Snedden later recalled that he had made a firm agreement for the purchase of the paper in December of 1953 from Helen Monsen, its owner. After she received a copy of his February 27, 1954, editorial backing statehood, she called him on the phone and asked to be released from the agreement. Snedden agreed to do so.[18] However, the *Fairbanks Daily News-Miner* added a powerful pro-statehood voice to those of other papers in the Territory. And as so often happens, converts to a cause are much more zealous than those who are born to it, and Snedden was no exception.

By 1954, several groups of Alaskans were independently preparing measures for a constitutional convention. One such gathering of interested people, primarily from College, the unincorporated town near the University of Alaska, formed the Constitutional Study League in that year. The members of this organization searched the constitutions of the various States and Canadian provinces for provisions most easily adaptable to Alaskan conditions. A finished bill for a constitutional convention was entrusted to Robert McNealy, a Fairbanks attorney and member of the territorial legislature, who agreed to present the measure in the 1955 session.[19]

Thomas Stewart, an Alaska Assistant Attorney General who had been given the task by the territorial Democrats of preparing a constitutional convention bill, resigned his official position and began to travel widely in the continental United States in his quest to find the best models for his assignment. He visited the political science departments of major universities and sought advice. He talked with those who had been involved in the 1947 New Jersey constitutional convention. Stewart obtained a list of books useful as references for delegates. In addition, he contacted the chief librarian of the Library of Congress and asked him for the names of organizations which could furnish staff services for such a convention. Stewart returned to Juneau at the end of 1954 and began drafting a proposal for a convention to be submitted to the territorial legislature early in 1955.[20]

Throughout 1954 the possibility of such a convention was widely discussed in the Territory. Many of those who were active in the Anchorage-based Operation Statehood questioned the wisdom of such an undertaking. Victor Fischer, vice president of the group, had serious misgivings. He later stated that he and his associates in the organization regarded a constitutional convention strictly as a "gimmick" designed to impress Congress sufficiently to grant statehood. He and his group believed that such a convention would divert energies needed in Washington.[21] Robert B. Atwood, chairman of the Alaska Statehood Committee, while agreeing with Fischer's views that the convention would be a "gimmick," disagreed with him about the efficacy of such an undertaking. Atwood stated that his committee had always looked for new approaches to statehood, and felt that such a convention would greatly aid the cause.[22]

When the legislature met in Juneau early in 1955, territorial Representative Stewart's constitutional convention bill was the first measure submitted in the house. The members of the joint house-senate committee charged with writing a bill acceptable to both houses appointed Stewart their chairman. With the background material he had collected, the copies of the New Jersey and Missouri constitutions, and the document Hawaiians had adopted in 1950, plus the bill prepared by the College group, the joint committee step-by-step completed an acceptable proposal.[23] The provisions of the final measure which emerged from Stewart's joint committee differed greatly from the procedures for a constitutional convention included in the tandem Alaska-Hawaii statehood bill of 1955.[24]

Most importantly, the joint committee agreed to establish twenty-two election districts for choosing delegates. This guaranteed representation for every principal community in the convention, and insured broad support among the various regions of the Territory. The joint committee called for adequate appropriations from the territorial general fund to finance the necessary preliminary staff work and the convention itself and to hire qualified consultants to be utilized by the delegates.[25] The joint committee also fixed a seventy-five day limit for the convention and planned a recess during which the delegates would return home and talk with their constituents. The University of Alaska at College, near Fairbanks, was designated as the meeting place of the convention. This removed it from the political atmosphere which invariably exists in a capital.[26]

In March of 1955, the constitutional convention bill passed the territorial legislature, together with an appropriation of $300,000 for the expenses.[27] With that action, the convention was launched. Alaskans were to go to the polls and elect fifty-five delegates for the November opening of the convention. Robert Atwood was to hire the necessary staff to do the background studies. It had been agreed to secure the services of political scientists from various universities. Instead, early in June, 1955, Atwood selected the Public Administration Service of Chicago, a nonprofit organization associated with the Council of State Governments. Thomas Stewart, for one, was nonplussed at Atwood's decision, since the agreement to hire university political scientists had not been kept. But since time was running short and there still was much to be done, he went along with the choice.[28]

As it turned out, the Public Administration Service hired seven political scientists from various universities for the convention itself, who were to be coordinated by Emil Sady of the organization.[29] Next, the Public Administration Service sent a number of consultants to Alaska who traveled throughout the Territory with Stewart. These consultants spoke at public meetings and to delegate candidates, and they also prepared material about the upcoming convention for local newspapers. These activities helped to stimulate interest and disseminate a great deal of information about the convention.[30]

While preparations for the constitutional convention proceeded apace, four statehood bills were introduced in Congress in 1955, one in the Senate and three in the House.[31] With Republican control ended by the 1954 elections, the new Democratic-controlled House and Senate Interior and Insular Affairs Committees prepared joint

Alaska-Hawaii statehood bills. The House again held hearings, but despite a favorable committee report,[32] the House Rules Committee refused to grant an "open rule," which would have given the House an opportunity to offer amendments and vote for the admission of either Territory. Instead, the Rules Committee gave the tandem bill a "closed rule." A. L. Miller, the mercurial ranking minority member of the House Interior and Insular Affairs Committee, stated, ". . . those who are opposed to both statehood bills in the House Rules Committee reported out a monstrosity of a rule, a Frankenstein type of monster that in their opinion defeats both bills." Miller said that eight of the twelve members of the Rules Committee were against statehood for either Territory. But, he warned, statehood legislation was a privileged matter, and, as such, could be brought to the floor of the House without a rule. The House recommitted the tandem bill on May 10, 1955 by a vote of 218 to 170.[33] Two days later, *The Daily Alaska Empire* (Juneau), one of the few papers opposed to statehood in the Territory, remarked editorially that since the House had killed statehood legislation for the foreseeable future, the $300,000 appropriation for the constitutional convention was a waste of money.[34]

The negative vote in the House did discourage some statehood advocates. The House had passed an Alaska measure in 1950, and statehood proponents had always thought that, if it came to the floor, the House would surely pass a bill again. The Senate was considered to be the real obstacle. In addition, the issue had been before Congress for nearly a decade. But instead of gaining, the last House vote indicated that statehood was losing ground. Congress as well as statehood advocates and opponents had invested much time and energy in the issue. The thousands of pages of testimony were the mute evidence. There seemed to be a mounting danger that the compromise of an elected governor might be agreed upon. This surely would have killed statehood for at least a decade, because Congress undoubtedly would have insisted that Alaskans give this new form of self-government a fair chance. Bills to grant Alaska an elected governor were submitted in every Congress between 1955 and 1957.[35] Delegate Bartlett and the Alaska Statehood Committee refused to endorse such half measures, and none of these bills ever cleared the House or Senate Interior and Insular Affairs Committees. The Alaska constitutional convention thus came at a particularly crucial moment in the statehood movement—when in Congress it had reached its nadir.

In Alaska, the campaign for the election of delegates got under way late in the summer of 1955. There were 55 positions and 171 candidates, indicating the high interest Alaskans showed in this election. Fourteen aspirants were members of the territorial legislature. This posed a dilemma when it was discovered that the Organic Act of 1912 prohibited members of the legislature from serving in positions created by the body of which they had been members. Congress passed a special act to allow these persons to run.[36] The election was nonpartisan. The delegates represented most of Alaska's economic interests.[37] They included lawyers, store owners, fishermen, hotel operators, miners, and housewives. In the Fairbanks district, fifty-five candidates had filed for the seven available positions. According to one observer, the storekeepers, lawyers, politicians, and mining company representatives presented a joint slate designed to maintain their control over Alaska's economy and politics by participating in the writing of the future state's fundamental law. Few of the candidates in the interior area took a public stand on any of the important questions which would come before the constitutional convention. Most declared that they possessed an open mind on the merits of a one- or two-house legislature, the contents of a bill of rights, and other vital questions. Often the election merely centered upon the personal characteristics of the candidates.[38]

A week before the convention opened at the University of Alaska, the Statehood Committee met in Fairbanks and worked out a set of rules and procedures. Approximately ten opening motions were adopted, and when the delegates met, there was a minimum of wasted time. A very smooth beginning was made which was important in setting the tone of the subsequent proceedings. Among the newspapers represented was *The New York Times*, which sent its West Coast representative, Lawrence E. Davies, to cover the event. The *Fairbanks Daily News-Miner* set up a teletype circuit in "Constitution Hall," which it connected with its editorial offices in downtown Fairbanks. The Associated Press wires, which served practically all the newspapers and radio stations in the Territory, thus received a constant flow of convention news.[39]

While these preparations were under way, George H. Lehleitner, a moderately wealthy businessman from New Orleans, arrived in Alaska. He was determined to help the Territory become a state, an undertaking which he had come to consider his civic duty. Lehleitner had originally become interested in Hawaiian statehood while commanding the Navy troopship *Rotanin* in the Second World War. In the ship's library he found a copy of Clarence Streit's book, *Union Now*. The author argued that unless the older democracies combined into a federal union whose strength would deter dictators, greater conflicts would follow. The reasons for a "Union of the Free" impressed Lehleitner profoundly. He visited Hawaii for the first time in 1945 while depositing several hundred Japanese prisoners at Pearl Harbor. He was distressed to see the "wholly un-American system of government" under which Hawaii operated, especially since the military had largely supplanted the civilian governmental functions. Lehleitner was shocked by the irony of the situation. "For here we were," he stated, "supposedly fighting a war to maintain our own freedom and to restore it to others from whom it had been stripped." Yet, he continued, "... we Americans were depriving almost a half million of our fellow citizens of many prime essentials that were the proper entitlements of free men!" He realized that an America which withheld statehood from a segment of its own people because of ancestry and distance from the nearest state was not ready to accept Streit's idea of a union with other people even farther away. The best way to demonstrate the feasibility of such a union, he decided, was to establish a smoothly functioning state of Hawaii. Therefore, statehood for Hawaii was a must, and he determined to promote this idea when he returned to civilian life in 1946. For the next eight years, Lehleitner concentrated his efforts on helping Hawaii through speaking engagements, a campaign of writing letters, and communicating with Congress. In 1951, he read a paper by Dr. Daniel Tuttle, Jr., of the University of Hawaii, on the so-called "Tennessee Plan." Lehleitner thereupon attempted to persuade Hawaiian statehood leaders to adopt this avenue to reach their goal, but it was rejected by them as too aggressive.[40]

This plan was so named because Tennessee had been the first, although not the last, Territory to gain admission by means of it. When it was denied statehood, Tennessee elected its congressional delegation and sent these men to Washington without waiting for an enabling act.

There, the Tennessee delegation made a strong plea for admission, and finally, on June 1, 1796, Tennessee became the sixteenth State of the Union. Six Territories, Michigan, California, Oregon, Tennessee, Kansas, and Iowa, elected senators and representatives to Congress before these Territories were formally admitted to statehood. In Minnesota, a congressional delegation was elected after the passage of an enabling act and the framing of a constitution, but before Congress allowed it to become a State. In each case, statehood was hastened by as much as a few months to several years.[41]

In the fall of 1955, Lehleitner determined to acquaint Alaskans with the Tennessee Plan. While in the Territory, he contacted the delegates and also received the support of the *Fairbanks Daily News-Miner*, although the *Anchorage Daily Times* refused to endorse the scheme. Encouraged by his brief trip, Lehleitner returned to New Orleans, drafted a Tennessee Plan proposal, and sent copies to Alaska's friends in Congress. Receiving uniformly encouraging replies, he photostated some of the letters and put them into packets which he distributed to the convention delegates after he had been invited to address them in January of 1956. By unanimous vote, the convention subsequently adopted the Tennessee Plan in the form of an ordinance attached to the constitution, which would be voted on separately by the people at the ratification of the constitution.[42]

If the ordinance was approved, two senators and one representative were to be chosen at the 1956 general election. Nominations to these positions were to be made at regular party conventions, although independents could file under established procedures. One senator was to serve the full six-year term which would expire on January 3, 1963, and the other a short term which would end on January 3, 1961. If they were seated, however, the United States Senate would actually prescribe the terms. The representative was to be elected for a regular two-year term. Until Alaska's admission, members of the Tennessee Plan delegation would be permitted to hold or be nominated for other offices of the United States or the Territory. The delegates to the constitutional convention apparently included this stipulation to accommodate Delegate Bartlett as well as members of the territorial legislature. In recognition of Lehleitner's efforts, the members of the constitutional convention named him an honorary member, and also designated him ambassador of good will from Alaska to the people of the United States and to Congress.[43]

The fifty-five delegates opened their deliberations in the new Student Union Building on the campus of the University of Alaska on November 8, 1955. The University administration renamed the structure "Constitution Hall" in honor of the occasion. The *Anchorage Daily Times* described the atmosphere as "friendly, folksy, yet serious...." The Student Union was opened on the day the convention began, and the sounds of construction could still be heard. Many delegates thought that these noises were a fitting background for their labors, together with sitting in a new building on a young campus. As the Anchorage paper described the scene:

> The delegates sit in a half circle facing the rostrum on one-armed chairs.... Voluminous literature is stuffed underneath each chair and daily mimeographed reports of the committees are added to these piles. Politics appears to be minimized and President William Egan says that not one delegate has asked him for a committee chairmanship.[44]

Although elected on a nonpartisan basis, Democrats significantly outnumbered Republicans among the delegates, and there were also a few Independents. A close observer of the proceedings has written that the convention members generally respected the expertise of their colleagues as well as that of the hired consultants. As a result, J.C. Boswell, vice president of the U.S. Smelting, Refining, and Mining Company, which had been opposed to statehood, chaired the committee on natural resources; and Leslie Nerland, banker from Fairbanks, the committee on finance and taxation. Veteran members of the territorial legislature headed the committees on apportionment, suffrage and elections, powers of the legislature, and the committee on the executive. Victor Fischer, Anchorage city planner, was secretary of the committee on local government. A political scientist and consultant to the convention, John Bebout, later reported that "few deliberative assemblies have been so fortunate in their choice of chairmen. William A. Egan, veteran territorial legislator and storekeeper from Valdez, "presided with a combination of firmness, fairness and humor" which helped to weld a group of comparative strangers, "inclined to be suspicious of one another, into a body of friends and co-workers united by their mutual respect and common purpose."[45]

Not all went smoothly at the convention, however, and there were differences of opinion. But William A. Egan later asserted that in spite of controversies that often flared into heated debate, "political considerations stayed buried." Lawrence D. Davies, correspondent for *The New York Times*, shared this evaluation of the convention's conduct. He noted the high level of intelligence, understanding, sincerity, dedication, and lack of political partisanship shown by most of the delegates. Their emphasis, Davies reported, was not on party but on "the good of Alaska," and their resistance to pressure groups was noteworthy.[46]

Thoughout the Territory, the convention received phenomenal press coverage. Daily broadcasts told Alaskans about the proceedings, and individual delegates reported to their constituents. During the Christmas-New Year's holiday, the delegates returned home for a recess. At that point, most of the preliminary drafts had been written, and the time was right to consult with the citizenry. Individual members of the convention held hearings and discussions throughout Alaska. These activities helped to maintain the high level of interest.[47] Finally, on February 5, 1956, fifty-four delegates, observed by more than 1,000 spectators, signed the document. The next morning, seventy-five working days after they had begun their labors, the senior ranking delegate, eighty-two-year-old E. B. Collins, who had been a member of Alaska's first territorial legislature in 1913, briefly addressed the delegates. With that the convention adjourned.[48]

Alaska's constitutional convention had produced a brief document of 14,400 words which the National Municipal League termed as "one of the best, if not the best, state constitutions ever written."[49] The document was short and flexible to allow for the changes which the future would bring. It provided for a government that would foster the growth and development of the whole state and the welfare of all its citizens. The constitution was designed to respect and guard the equal rights and dignity of all Alaskans. The basic law called for a legislature consisting of a senate of twenty members elected for four-year terms and a house of representatives of forty members serving for two-year terms, an integrated state administration headed by a governor elected for a four-year term and eligible to succeed himself once, and a unified court system in which judges were selected by the governor on nomination by a judicial council composed of representatives of the bar and the lay public.[50]

A preamble and fifteen articles made up the constitution, and attached to it were three propositions in the form of ordinances. The first of these provided for the ratification of the document at a primary election on April 24, 1956. The second asked the voters to approve the Tennessee Plan. And the third ordinance dealt with the abolition of fish traps in Alaskan waters. The constitution provided for the traditional system of checks and balances, and avoided the inclusion of matters better handled by statutory law and administrative code. A number of consultants stated that it came closer to carrying out the classic pattern of "separation of powers" than had been achieved in any other state.[51] This separation had been accomplished through the establishment of three strong branches of government, the executive, the legislative, and judicial. Only the governor and secretary of state were elective, and they ran on the same ticket. All department heads were appointed by the chief executive. After each federal census, the governor, assisted by a board, was obligated to reapportion the state.

Tradition prevailed in the division of the legislature into an upper and a lower house. The legislative apportionment and apportionment schedule (Articles VI and XIV) were designed to prevent the rural area dominance of most state upper houses. The lower body was based on population in twenty-four election districts, while the upper house was apportioned on the basis of both area and population in sixteen senate districts. These districts were combinations of at least two house election areas. These, in turn, were merged into four larger election districts which roughly corresponded to Alaska's geographical divisions. The legislature was to meet annually as long as necessary, and members were to be paid annual salaries as established by statute. The legislature could override vetoed revenue and appropriation bills or items by a three-fourths vote by immediately calling a joint session upon receipt of the veto. Other bills could be overridden by a two-thirds majority. A legislative council composed of legislators was to function throughout the year.

Article IV, which dealt with the judiciary, was borrowed from the 1947 New Jersey constitution, and established a unified court system. It consisted of a supreme court, a superior court, and such courts as established by the legislature. The judiciary was politically independent, and the administrative head of the court system was to be the chief justice of the supreme court. Judges would be named by a judicial council, composed of three laymen appointed by the governor, three lawyers nominated by the state bar, and a seventh and presiding member who was the chief justice of the supreme court. As a popular check on the judiciary, the framers determined that three years after appointment the name of each supreme court justice and superior court judge would appear on a nonpartisan ballot for approval or rejection by the voters. Thereafter, each superior court judge was to stand for election every six years, and each supreme court justice every tenth year.

Local government (Article X) was placed in boroughs, the Alaska version of unified metropolitan government, and cities. Incorporated boroughs would provide their own local government, while the citizens of unincorporated boroughs assumed limited local responsibility and the state provided whatever assistance was needed.52 Alaska's natural resources (Article VIII) would be developed, wherever possible, according to the sustained yield principle. The State government would retain residual ownership to all State lands and their natural wealth for the benefit of all of its citizens. The initiative and referendum (Article XI) enabled Alaskans to enact laws, and, in the case of the latter, reject acts by the legislature. All elected officials, except judicial officers, were made subject to recall. Article V provided for a voting age of nineteen, provided the citizen could read or speak English. Article IX prevented the creation of funds dedicated for specific purposes, except when this action was required to enable the state to participate in federal programs. In addition, the governor had to submit an annual executive budget for the next fiscal year detailing income and projected expenditures. Amendments to the constitution, as provided for by Article XIII, could be added if approved by a two-thirds vote in each house of the legislature, and subsequently, in a statewide election. Every ten years the question of whether to call a constitutional convention would be automatically placed on the ballot by the secretary of state.53

It was obvious that the framers believed that Alaska should start with the best constitution possible. In addition, many delegates felt that Alaska had the advantage of learning from the experiences and mistakes of other States. In summary, the convention produced a constitution which confined itself to setting basic policy and to establishing a skeletal structure of government. The executive, legislative, and judicial branches of government were entrusted with the task of filling out and adapting the system to changing conditions.

But there was still the matter of ratifying the new constitution. Statehood forces immediately launched a vigorous campaign which lasted until the primary election in April of 1956. They distributed pamphlets throughout the Territory urging Alaskans to vote "yes" on the three ordinances. These pamphlets emphasized the representative role of the delegates through the use of the slogan "You Were There." One pamphlet stated, "Your ideas, your background, your feelings and thoughts were there," and still another said that "What was written was the best YOU could write—the best for YOUR future." Alaskans also received brochures which contained a resume of the constitution to facilitate an understanding of it.[54]

In the spring of 1956, the Democrats and Republicans nominated their candidates for the Tennessee Plan positions. The former selected Ernest Gruening and William A. Egan for the Senate seats, and Ralph J. Rivers of Fairbanks for the House position. Rivers had held a variety of public offices, was a territorial legislator, and had been a delegate to the convention. The Republicans chose John Butrovich, an insurance man and territorial senator from Fairbanks, and Robert B. Atwood of Anchorage for the Senate seats. Charles Burdick, the retired assistant regional forester and a resident of Juneau, received the nomination for the House seat.[55]

When Alaskans went to the polls in April of 1956, they approved the constitution by a vote of 17,447 to 8,180, endorsed the Alaska Tennessee Plan 15,011 to 9,556, and overwhelmingly favored the abolition of fish traps by 21,285 to 4,004 votes.[56] In the October 9, 1956 general election, the voters elected all three Democratic candidates for the Tennessee Plan positions. Ernest Gruening won by 14,169 to 13,301 votes over his rival John Butrovich; William Egan by 15,636 to 11,588 votes for Robert B. Atwood, and Ralph J. Rivers by 15,569 to 11,345 votes for Charles Burdick.[57]

The constitutional convention had been a great success from the standpoint of Alaska's statehood advocates. It dramatized Alaska's plight as a Territory and demonstrated the Territory's political maturity through the "model constitution" the delegates had drafted. In addition, the overwhelming vote to adopt the basic law presented a reaffirmation of the 1946 referendum on the issue, and a vote of confidence in the course Alaska's statehood leaders had been pursuing. Through broad representation in the convention, the Territory's citizens had become involved in the statehood struggle. And finally, with the adoption of the constitution and the approval of the Alaska Tennessee Plan, a full-fledged assault was launched on Congress—the final effort in a long campaign.

FOOTNOTES FOR CHAPTER X

1. *The Daily Alaska Empire* (Juneau), December 23, 1952, p. 1.
2. Mentioned as possibilities were Walter J. Hickel of Anchorage, Lester O. Gore of Ketchikan, B. Frank Heintzleman of Juneau, Elmer Rasmuson of Anchorage, Ralph Lomen of Nome and Seattle, R. E. Robertson of Juneau, Dan Lhamon of Fairbanks, and Charles Burdick of Juneau. Editorial, *Ibid.*, December 23, 1952, p. 4.
3. *The New York Times*, March 14, 1953, p. 10; *The Daily Alaska Empire* (Juneau), April 10, 1953, p. 2.
4. *The Daily Alaska Empire* (Juneau), January 28, 1953, pp. 1, 6.
5. Typewritten carbon copy, Minutes of the Meeting of the Alaska Statehood Committee, Juneau, January 28, 1953, and Meeting of the Joint Special Committee on Statehood of the Alaska Territorial Legislature, Juneau, January 29, 1953, pp. 1-61, 78-119, Alaska Historical Library, Juneau, Alaska.
6. Interview with Thomas Stewart, August 20, 1969, Juneau, Alaska.
7. *Ibid.*
8. *The Daily Alaska Empire* (Juneau), July 21, 1954, p. 1.
9. "Official Canvass of Results, Alaska General Election, Tuesday, October 12, 1954," in Office of the Secretary of State, Juneau, Alaska.
10. Interview with Thomas Stewart, August 20, 1969, Juneau, Alaska.
11. N. R. Walker of Ketchikan to Anthony J. Dimond, May 30, 1948, Personal Correspondence, Statehood Committee—X,Y,Z—Gen'l.—Folder Statehood for Alaska, General Correspondence, Box 39, Anthony J. Dimond Papers, University of Alaska Archives, College, Alaska.
12. Minutes of the Meeting of the Alaska Statehood Committee, Anchorage, Alaska, January 6-7, 1951, Box 668, Records of the Office of the Governor of Alaska, 1884-1958, Federal Records Center, Seattle, Washington.
13. H.B. No. 7 *Journal of the House of Representatives*, 21st session, 1953, pp. 50-51.
14. *The Daily Alaska Empire* (Juneau), November 27, 1953, p. 1.
15. *Ibid.*, June 3, 1954, p. 1. Delegate Bartlett stated that such a move would bring statehood no earlier, and might even delay it. He agreed, however, that a constitutional convention should be held "whether or not Congress approved statehood at this session." *Ibid.*, June 4, 1954, p. 6.
16. Interview with William C. Snedden, March 25, 1970, Fairbanks, Alaska; editorial, *Fairbanks Daily News-Miner*, February 27, 1954, p. 1; U.S., Congress, House, *Statehood for Alaska*, Hearings before the Subcommittee on Territorial and Insular Affairs on H.R. 50. . . , 85 Cong., 1 Sess. (Washington: Government Printing Office, 1957), p. 154. For the part Alaska's press played in the struggle for statehood, see Carroll V. Glines, Jr., "Alaska's Press and the Battle for Statehood" (unpublished M.S. thesis, American University, 1969).
17. *Fairbanks Daily News-Miner*, February 27, 1954, p. 1.

18. *Fairbanks Daily News-Miner*, April 9, 1954, pp. 1-6.

19. Niilo E. Koponen, "The History of Education in Alaska: With Special Reference to the Relationship between the Bureau of Indian Affairs Schools and the State School System" (unpublished "special paper" presented in partial fullfillment of the requirements for a Doctoral degree in Education, Harvard University, Graduate School of Education, June, 1964), pp. 68-69; and interview with Dr. Niilo Koponen, March 10, 1970, Chena Ridge near College, Alaska.

20. Interview with Thomas Stewart, August 20, 1969, Juneau, Alaska.

21. Interview with Victor Fischer, March 17, 1970, College, Alaska.

22. Interview with Robert B. Atwood, August 26, 1969, Anchorage, Alaska.

23. Interview with Thomas Stewart, August 20, 1969, Juneau, Alaska.

24. U.S., Congress, House, *Hawaii-Alaska Statehood*, Hearings before the Committee on Interior and Insular Affairs on H.R. 2535 and H.R. 2536..., 84 Cong., 1 Sess. (Washington: Government Printing Office, 1955), pp. 8-9. The Alaska bill provided for twenty-seven delegates to a constitutional convention, apportioned among the four judicial divisions of Alaska as follows: six delegates from the first, three from the second, ten from the third, and five from the fourth; and three delegates to be elected at large. The convention was to meet in the capital of Alaska at Juneau, and not to exceed seventy-five days in length.

25. See Chapter 46, *Session Laws of Alaska*, 1955.

26. Interview with Thomas Stewart, August 20, 1969, Juneau, Alaska.

27. *The Daily Alaska Empire* (Juneau), March 11, 1955, p. 1.

28. Interview with Thomas Stewart, August 20, 1969, Juneau, Alaska.

29. The seven were Drs. Ernest R. Bartley, University of Florida; Dayton D. McKean, University of Colorado; Vincent Ostrom, University of Oregon; Weldon Cooper, University of Virginia; Kimbrough Owen, Louisiana State University; Sheldon Elliot, Institute of Judicial Administration, New York University; and John E. Bebout, National Municipal League. Emil Sady, the representative of the Public Administration Service, remained at College throughout the convention. John E. Bebout, "Charter for Last Frontier," *National Municipal Review*, April, 1956, p. 160. For the background studies prepared for the convention delegates, see Public Administration Service, *Constitutional Studies*, vols. I-III, prepared on behalf of the Alaska Statehood Committee for the Alaska Constitutional Convention, November, 1955. (Mimeographed.)

30. Interview with Thomas Stewart, August 20, 1969, Juneau, Alaska.

31. *Cong. Record*, Index, 84 Cong., 1 Sess., p. 641. The bill, S. 452, was introduced by Senators William Langer, Estes Kefauver, and Warren Magnuson; *Ibid.*, H.R. 185, p. 715 (introduced by Representative John P. Saylor); *Ibid.*, F.R. 248, p. 717 (submitted by Delegate Bartlett); *Ibid.*, H.R. 825, p. 732 (introduced by Representative Russell V. Mack).

32. *Hawaii-Alaska Statehood* (1955); U.S., Congress, House *Enabling...Hawaii and Alaska... to be Admitted Into the Union*, H. Rept. 88 to accompany H.R. 2535, 84 Cong., 1 Sess. (Washington: Government Printing Office, 1955). This report includes the minority views.

33. *Cong. Record*, 84 Cong., 1 Sess., p. 5880 (May 9, 1955); pp. 5975-76 (May 10, 1955).

34. *The Daily Alaska Empire* (Juneau), May 12, 1955.

35. *Cong. Record*, Index, 84 Cong., 1 Sess., S. 399, p. 640 (introduced by Senator George W. Malone); *Ibid.*, 84 Cong., 2 Sess., H.R. 8113, p. 750 (submitted by Representative William Dawson); *Ibid.*, H.R. 8287, p. 754 (introduced by Representative James B. Utt); *Ibid.*, 85 Cong., 1 Sess., S. 35, p. 856 (introduced by Senator George W. Malone). That support for such a compromise bill existed is indicated in the request from the Director of the Office of Territories to the Department of the Interior to submit a favorable report on S. 399. Memorandum from Legislative Counsel, Office of the Solicitor, July 14, 1955 on S. 399, Acc. No. 62-A-401, Box 95, Department of the Interior, Office of Territories, file Alaska-Political Affairs—Election—Legislation, 2, part 1, RG 126, Washington Federal Records Center, Suitland, Maryland. Walter J. Hickel, Alaska Republican National Committeeman, endorsed the elective governor bill. He reminded the Department of the Interior that both parties had come out in favor of it. Hickel to Kirkley Coulter, Assistant Director of the Office of Territories, July 8, 1955, *Ibid.*

36. *Anchorage Daily Times*, September 10, 1955, p. 1; U.S. *Stats. at Large* 299 (1955).

37. *Fairbanks Daily News-Miner*, February 6, 1956, Alaska Constitution Section, p. 1.

38. Koponen, "The History of Education in Alaska," pp. 71-73.

39. Interview with Thomas Stewart, August 20, 1969, Juneau, Alaska; *Fairbanks Daily News-Miner*, February 6, 1956, Alaska Constitution Section, p. 5.

40. George H. Lehleitner to Representative James C. Wright, Jr., of Texas, September 12, 1963, Statehood File, University of Alaska Archives, College, Alaska.

41. George H. Lehleitner, "Alaska Seeks Statehood the Tennessee Way," *Freedom and Union, Journal of the World Republic*, II (April, 1956), 16; Mary Lee Council, "Alaska Statehood" (unpublished manuscript, n.d.), p. 19, copy in author's files; William R. Tansill, "Election of Congressional Delegations Prior to the According of Statehood," October, 1955, copy in author's files.

42. George H. Lehleitner to Representative James C. Wright, Jr., of Texas, September 12, 1963, Statehood File, University of Alaska Archives, College, Alaska. The vote after a five-hour debate was 53 to 0. *Anchorage Daily Times*, January 30, 1956, pp. 1, 7. The Alaska Tennessee Plan also received recognition in an editorial in *Life*, May 14, 1956, p. 48.

43. *Anchorage Daily Times*, January 30, 1956, p. 7.

44. *Ibid.*, November 16, 1955, p. 16.

45. Koponen, "The History of Education in Alaska," p. 74; John E. Bebout, "Charter for Last Frontier," *National Municipal Review*, April, 1956, p. 161.

46. William A. Egan, "The Constitution of the New State of Alaska," *State Government*, Fall, 1958, p. 210; *The New York Times*, February 5, 1956, p. 76. For further details on the constitutional convention, see Alaska Legislative Council, *Alaska Constitutional Convention, Proceedings*, November 8, 1955 to February 5, 1956.

47. Interview with Victor Fischer, March 17, 1970, College, Alaska. Dr. Niilo Koponen had an entirely different view of the constitutional convention. He believed that many of those who had been opposed to statehood for Alaska jumped on the bandwagon and co-opted the movement in order to keep it conservative and safe. The convention, he thought, never considered any real issues and never discussed a one house legislature, proportional representation, or a modern bill of rights. Interview with Dr. Niilo Koponen, March 10, 1970, Chena Ridge near College, Alaska.

48. Delegate R. E. Robertson resigned from the convention two days before the signing ceremonies because he objected to the ordinance which called for the abolition of fish traps, the failure of the convention to include a right-to-work clause, and the inclusion of a new apportionment system which abolished the traditional four judicial divisions, giving more representation to the less populated areas. *The New York Times*, February 6, 1956, p. 14; *Fairbanks Daily News-Miner*, February 6, 1956, pp. 1-2.

49. Editorial, *National Municipal Review*, April, 1956, p. 156.

50. Pamphlet, *Proposed Constitution for the State of Alaska: A Report to the People of Alaska from the Alaska Constitutional Convention* (Fairbanks, Alaska: Commercial Printing Co., Inc., 1956); hereafter cited as *Proposed Constitution for the State of Alaska, 1956*. Victor Fischer made a copy of this publication available to the author.

51. *Fairbanks Daily News-Miner*, February 6, 1956, Alaska Constitution Section, p. 1.

52. For a perceptive critique of the local government article of the Alaska constitution, see Morehouse and Fischer, *The State and the Local Governmental System*, chaps. I, IV-IX. The implementation of the local government article is treated in Ronald C. Cease, "Area-wide Local Government in the State of Alaska: The Genesis, Establishment, and Organization of Borough Government" (unpublished Ph. D. dissertation, Claremont Graduate School, 1964); and Ronald C. Cease and Jerome R. Saroff, eds., *The Metropolitan Experiment in Alaska: A Study of Borough Government* (New York: Frederick A. Praeger, 1968).

53. *The Constitution of the State of Alaska.*

54. Pamphlet, *You Are Looking at Alaska's Future: What Do You See In It?"* (Fairbanks, Alaska: Commercial Printing Co., Inc., 1956). Victor Fischer made a copy of this publication available to the author. See also, *Proposed Constitution for the State of Alaska, 1956.*

55. Gruening, *The State of Alaska*, p. 500.

56. Election Results, Acc. No. 66A-140, Box 169, Interior, Office of the Secretary, Central Files Section, Classified Files, 1954-58, file Territorial Affairs—Alaska—Political Affairs, 9, part 1, RG 48, Washington National Records Center, Suitland, Maryland.

57. "Official Canvass of Results, Alaska General Election, Tuesday, October 9, 1956," in Office of the Secretary of State, Juneau, Alaska.

CHAPTER XI

STATEHOOD ACHIEVED

Between 1947 and 1956, hearings on Alaska statehood were conducted on seven different occasions in Washington and three times in Alaska. The printed record of these investigations amounted to approximately 4,000 pages. Statehood bills were before Congress almost continuously after 1943. Both Democratic and Republican party platforms included promises of statehood for Alaska and Hawaii. The Democrats had mentioned eventual statehood for the two Territories since 1940, and since 1948 had urged the immediate admission of both. In 1948, the Republican platform favored eventual statehood for both, and in 1952, it promised immediate statehood for Hawaii, and eventual statehood for Alaska under an equitable enabling act. In 1956, the statehood plank in the Republican platform reiterated the pledge to Hawaii, and held out admission to Alaska if adequate provisions for defense requirements could be made. In late 1955, a Gallup poll showed that 82 per cent of Americans supported the admission of Alaska, while 78 per cent favored Hawaii's cause. In addition, some 32 national organizations, such as the American Legion, the American Federation of Labor, and the General Federation of Women Clubs, as well as approximately 95 per cent of the nation's newspapers, endorsed statehood for both Territories.[1]

Despite President Truman's strong support, an Alaska statehood bill did not come to the House floor for a vote until 1950, at which time it passed. It only reached the floor then because of the previously mentioned twenty-one day rule which had been adopted in 1949. Two years later, this reform of the Rules Committee was repealed.[2] Not until 1955 did a combined Alaska-Hawaii statehood bill come to a vote again in the House. That time it reached the floor because the Rules Committee was fairly certain that under the "closed" rule it had granted, statehood would be defeated. And, as expected, the tandem measure was recommitted.

Between 1953 and 1955, the Eisenhower administration, eager to admit Republican-leaning Hawaii but cool to Democratic Alaska, and a hostile conservative Republican-Southern Democratic coalition blocked statehood for both Territories. The arguments against Alaska's admission focused on several basic themes. The Territory's sparse population did not justify representation in Congress and could not support a state government. Alaska's noncontiguity not only isolated the Territory from the main currents of American life, but its admission would set an undesirable precedent, opening the door to statehood for such lands as the Philippines, Guam, and Okinawa. The current defense construction boom in Alaska would end some day, it was said, depriving the Territory of its major source of revenue. The Territory's resources were still too underdeveloped to attract enough private industry to take the place of federal expenditures. And, finally, statehood would cause sharp increases in various governmental costs which would lead to higher taxes and discourage economic development.

Racism and civil rights also played a vital role in the opposition of some members of Congress. Ernest Gruening reported in 1953 that a common inquiry in private conversations about Hawaiian statehood, was a whispered "How would you like to have a United States Senator called Moto?" Representative John C. Davis of Georgia perhaps best summed up the Southern attitude toward statehood in a speech before the House. He cited the 1950 census figures for Alaska and Hawaii. The former had a population of 128,643, of whom 33,000 were Indians and Eskimos. The latter had a population of 499,799, which was composed of 183,000 Japanese, 33,000 Chinese, 114,000 whites, 87,000 Hawaiians, and 88,000 of other racial or ethnic backgrounds. Davis concluded that his figures did not reflect on the nonwhite population of either Territory, but he did contend that "... the crosscurrents of racial feeling create political and administrative whirlpools too dangerous to yet be allowed the authoritative voice in the American Government that goes with full statehood."[3]

These anti-statehood arguments were used successfully year after year, but, in 1956, several events occurred which set the stage for the final statehood drive, for Alaska in 1958 and for Hawaii in 1959. In his 1956 State of the Union message, President Eisenhower, as on previous occasions, urgently requested Congress to grant statehood to Hawaii, "a community that is a successful laboratory of brotherhood." As for Alaska, the Chief Executive was less enthusiastic as he stated, "... in harmony with the provisions I last year communicated to the Senate and House Committees on Interior and Insular Affairs, I trust that progress toward statehood for Alaska can be made in this session."[4] Eisenhower apparently referred to letters he had written in 1955 to Senator Henry M. Jackson, chairman of the Senate Interior and Insular Affairs Committee, and Representative A. L. Miller, the ranking Republican on the House Interior and Insular Affairs Committee. In these letters, the President had said that Alaska's strategic importance required full freedom for federal action. Statehood would impair it. Therefore, unless a formula could be devised and approved by Congress which adequately met these defense needs, it would be imprudent to confer statehood on Alaska. The President had also observed:

> I am in doubt that any form of legislation can wholly remove my apprehensions about granting statehood immediately. However, a proposal seeking to accommodate the many complex considerations entering into the statehood question has been made by Secretary of the Interior McKay, and should legislation of this type be approved by the Congress, I assure you that I shall give it earnest consideration.[5]

The so-called McKay line, referred to by Eisenhower, modified the partition proposal made by Governor Heintzleman in 1953. McKay's plan intended to set aside, within the boundaries of the new State, some 276,000 square miles which would be subject to defense withdrawals by the President. These areas were located in the sparsely settled northern and northwestern parts of Alaska. No acceptable compromise solution had been found in 1955, and the House, as previously stated, had recommitted the combined Alaska-Hawaii measure by a vote of 218 to 170.[6]

As a result, Eisenhower's comment on Alaska statehood in his 1956 message brought an immediate Democratic response. Senator Jackson remarked, "... if the President comes out flatfooted for Alaska we'll report both it and Hawaii out." Representative Clair Engle, chairman of the House Interior and Insular Affairs Committee, expressed willingness "to give the statehood bills another try if I get definite word what the White House wants in an Alaska statehood bill and assurance that the President will sign it." On the other hand, Delegate Bartlett was encouraged because he felt that Eisenhower's prestige could now be used to rally Republican support for Alaska's cause.[7]

An event of considerable importance in the statehood movement was the resignation of Secretary of the Interior McKay on June 8, 1956 to run for the Senate seat in Oregon held by Wayne Morse. The Secretary, although not personally unfriendly to Alaska's aspirations, had reflected the administration's unfavorable attitude toward statehood for the Territory. The President appointed Fred A. Seaton of Nebraska, a statehood advocate, to replace McKay.[8] Alaskans, who knew only too well how important the Department of the Interior was in territorial affairs, realized that the attitude of the Secretary could either impede or enhance statehood chances. Secretary Seaton strengthened Alaskan optimism when he told the Senate Interior and Insular Affairs Committee that he would try to persuade the President to favor the immediate admission of Alaska.[9] On the territorial level, Alaskans had already overwhelmingly approved the proposed State constitution. Since this fact was a matter of record, it simplified the drafting of subsequent statehood bills because, rather than enabling acts, they merely became potential admission measures. In effect, the gap between territorial status and statehood was closing.

William C. Snedden, publisher of the *Fairbanks Daily News-Miner*, was especially elated about the appointment of Secretary Seaton. The two had known each other for some time, and with a friend of statehood as Interior Secretary, Snedden decided that the time had come to pursue admission in an orderly and systematic fashion. Snedden later recalled that until the constitutional convention, Alaska's statehood forces had never really concentrated their efforts to achieve the goal. Instead, they had too often used a shot-gun approach by making occasional trips to Washington to testify at congressional hearings and by rallying support for local hearings in Alaska. Snedden asserted that the Alaska Statehood Committee had rendered yeoman work in obtaining the support of the various national organizations, such as the Elks, the Kiwanis, the American Legion, and the Chamber of Commerce of America, in addition to the active help of many newspapers. But nobody, with the exception of Delegate Bartlett and ex-Governor Gruening, had pursued the matter steadily and singlemindedly. Now Snedden was determined to launch an intensive effort to attain the goal.[10]

As a first step in this direction, he phoned the new Interior Secretary a day after his appointment and suggested that the time had come to make methodical and calculated moves toward statehood.

Seaton agreed, and asked Snedden to recommend an informed Alaskan who could work in Washington for the Department of the Interior. Upon Snedden's recommendation, Theodore Stevens, then United States Attorney in Fairbanks, was hired and went to Washington to work as legislative counsel for Interior. On his next trip to the national capital, Snedden found a hand-lettered, cardboard sign on Stevens' office door reading "Alaskan Headquarters." Stevens quickly became known as "Mr. Alaska" in the department.[11] And, as a Republican of some standing, Stevens maintained communications between Alaska party members and the Eisenhower administration.

In the meantime, a group of statehood enthusiasts in Washington were making preparations to assist Alaska's Tennessee Plan delegation, which was to arrive for the opening of the Eighty-fifth Congress in January, 1957. An unofficial committee, consisting of Delegate Bartlett, Dr. Ernest Bartley, a professor of political science at the University of Florida, who had been a consultant to the Alaska constitutional convention, and George Lehleitner compiled dossiers on every member of Congress. These files included, among much other information, the attitudes of senators and representatives toward Alaska statehood.[12] George Lehleitner also had written a pamphlet which described the historical antecedents of the Tennessee Plan. Together with a cover letter, this booklet was sent to every member of Congress, and was also widely distributed to the editors of daily newspapers, to radio and television network news programs, and to all principal news magazines and periodicals.[13] John Adams, who had been a White House correspondent for the Columbia Broadcasting System during the Truman administration, was hired by Lehleitner as the public relations man for the Alaska Tennessee Plan delegation.[14]

In order to create as broad a base as possible for the congressional lobbying effort, Snedden and Stevens began to compile a card file on every member of Congress for their own use. This file, like the one being prepared for the Alaska Tennessee Plan delegates, contained not only information about the attitudes of senators and representatives but also extensive personal information on individual members of Congress. Snedden took up residence in Washington on a more or less permanent basis in 1956. To deal with those senators and representatives who still remained doubtful or opposed to the Territory's cause, he engaged a detective agency, which was assigned to unearth information on uncooperative legislators which might be used as leverage in obtaining affirmative votes for statehood. "In a few cases," Snedden recalled, "we stumbled across situations where we knew beyond a shadow of a doubt that...[if revealed, it] would end...[a man's career] in public service." As remembered by Snedden, the problem was how to put this intelligence to its best use:

> And then the delicate part came in, what to do with it, how to handle it? We got excellent cooperation from all the top people in the press in Washington. Some of the nation's top columnists gave us a hand there.

In short, the information was passed to some sympathetic columnists who would call the person involved and "make a trade." The caller would usually say, "Here's something I ran across. I just wondered whether [I should reveal]... it. It concerns so and so back in such and such time."[15] As a result, several pledges for a vote in support of statehood were obtained.

Snedden also capitalized on his friendship with editors of small newspapers throughout the United States. A poll, which he conducted among these papers and some magazines, was published in *The New York Times* and circulated widely on Capitol Hill. It showed unanimous support for Alaska's admission.[16] The Hearst and Scripps-Howard newspaper chains and *Time* and *Life* joined the struggle. Snedden has said that once he was able to get the attention of a particular newspaperman, statehood "was just like motherhood and being against sin when you explained to them what the situation was." The statehood cause was, as Snedden explained it, "200,000 Alaskans, Americans all, who were held in colonial bondage by the United States government." Secretary Seaton used the power and influence of his office to gather pledges for statehood votes from wavering and undecided members of Congress. The Secretary used additions to National Park facilities and personnel increases for the Geological Survey or the Bureau of Land Management, among other incentives, in the districts or states of the senators and representatives in question. According to Snedden, "Fred Seaton did a marvelous job of rounding up a very impressive assortment of pawns."[17]

While the friends of statehood were rounding up votes, Senators-elect Gruening and Egan and Representative-elect Rivers left the Territory late in 1956 in cars which had been painted white for dramatic effect. The three cars had the Alaska flag, eight stars of gold in a field of blue, painted on each door, in addition to the name and office of each man and a sign proclaiming, "Alaska, the 49th State." The Alaska Tennessee Plan delegation drove down the ALCAN Highway and through the capitals of the States which had used the Tennessee Plan, arriving in Nashville, Tennessee, where the governor entertained them at a reception and dinner.[18] Gruening, Egan, and Rivers finally reached Washington in January, 1957, in time for the opening of the first session of the Eighty-fifth Congress. On the fourteenth day of that month, during the noon hour, Florida's Senator Spessard L. Holland asked for the floor. He was recognized by the Senate's presiding officer and secured unanimous consent to read an unusual memorial from the Alaska constitutional convention. This document, dated December 9, 1956, asked Congress to "seat our duly-elected representatives and... [to] enact legislation enabling the admission of Alaska to the Union of States."[19] Senator Holland then introduced Alaska's congressional delegation, which was seated in the diplomatic gallery with their families. Gruening, Egan, and Rivers rose and were greeted with a burst of applause which was followed by speeches from the Senate floor, all forcefully endorsing Alaska statehood.[20]

Despite this magnificent introduction, the Alaska Tennessee Plan delegates were not officially recognized or seated. This refusal did not deter them from pursuing their task as lobbyists. Ralph Rivers later recalled that the delegation at first used Delegate Bartlett's office, and finally rented their own quarters a few blocks from Capitol Hill. Gruening took on the job of contacting the editors of major newspapers in the United States, and both he and Egan visited all of the senators. Meanwhile, Rivers observed, "I walked those marble halls and talked with the representatives. It took two years to do it."[21]

Two days after the Alaska delegation had been introduced in the upper house by Senator Holland, President Eisenhower delivered his budget message to Congress. He again recommended the admission of Hawaii, and, "subject to area limitations and other safeguards for the conduct of defense activities so vitally necessary to our national security, statehood...[for] Alaska."[22] With the introduction of half a dozen statehood bills in January of 1957, the struggle for Alaskan statehood resumed.[23] Four of these measures differed from previous ones in that they were admission bills rather than enabling acts, thereby recognizing that Alaskans had written and ratified a constitution.

In a speech at the University of Alaska at the end of January, 1957, Secretary Seaton underscored the fact that the Eisenhower administration was serious about admitting Alaska. However, if the defense measures deemed necessary by Washington were rejected, he warned his audience, statehood might be delayed for scores of years. In an address to a joint session of the territorial legislature in Juneau on the following day, Seaton told the lawmakers that the battle for statehood faced a "long and uphill fight" in Congress. The legislators rose and gave him a standing ovation when he asserted that the statehood fight was one "the administration does not intend to lose."[24]

In March, the House Subcommittee on Territorial and Insular Affairs held ten days of hearings, while the Senate Interior and Insular Affairs Committee devoted two days to the subject.[25] On March 11, the first day, Undersecretary of the Interior Hatfield Chilson appeared before the House subcommittee and explained the area limitations President Eisenhower had in mind for defense purposes. Chilson made it clear that the Administration did not intend to partition Alaska, a statement which laid to rest fears about such a scheme. Instead, the Undersecretary submitted an amendment which asked Congress to grant the President, as Commander-in-Chief, the authority to create special defense withdrawals in case of national necessity in an area of approximately 276,000 square miles. This land was located in the northern and northwestern portion of the territory. In these military reservations the Federal Government was to assume exclusive jurisdiction.[26] Senator Gruening later remarked that this was a wholly unnecessary request since the President, as head of the armed forces, already had the power to make such withdrawals. "What in time amounted to a face-saving formula for the Administration," Gruening asserted, "was provided as an amendment. . . . It remained in the Statehood Act. . . and has been meaningless. . . ever since."[27]

Among the favorable testimony given before the House subcommittee was that of General Nathan Twining, acting chairman of the Joint Chiefs of Staff. Twining reminded the subcommittee that once before, in 1950, he had testified in favor of Alaska statehood. "I am happy, therefore," the General stated, "to be able to say in my official capacity, in this month of March, 1957 that. . . the time is ripe for Alaska to become a State."29 Among the territory's citizens who spoke out in favor of admission were the Tennessee Plan delegates and Mildred R. Hermann, secretary of the Alaska Statehood Committee. Alaskans who expressed opposition were Glen D. Franklin, chairman of the legislative committee of the Alaska Miners Association of Fairbanks; A. W. Boddy, president of the Alaska Sportsmen's Council; and Alice Stuart, editor and publisher of the *Alaska Calendar of Engagements.* 29

Generally, the two hearings were perfunctory because many members of the House and Senate committees felt that nothing much that had not already been said could be added to the record. The House Interior and Insular Affairs Committee reported its bill on June 25, 1957, and recommended that the Territory be admitted. The committee observed that the traditionally accepted requirements for admission of incorporated Territories to statehood appeared to be:

> That the inhabitants of the proposed new State are imbued with and sympathetic toward the principles of democracy as exemplified in the American form of government. That a majority of the electorate wish statehood. That the proposed new State has sufficient population and resources to support State government and at the same time carry its share of the cost of the Federal Government.

Under this historic pattern, Territories had become states. By each of these historic standards, the committee asserted, "Alaska is ready and qualified for statehood now." The House bill also provided that Congress accept the Alaskan constitution, and granted to the proposed state some 182,800,000 acres of vacant, unappropriated, and unreserved land to be selected within a period of twenty-five years after admittance. The aboriginal land claims were left in status quo, to be dealt with by future legislative or judicial action.30 In August, the Senate committee reported its Alaska statehood measure favorably. In one of its major provisions, Alaska was given the right to select some 103,350,000 million acres from the public domain within a twenty-five year period after statehood had been achieved.31

In the meantime, in July of 1957, House Speaker Sam Rayburn of Texas, hitherto a foe of Alaska statehood, changed his mind and promised to give the Territory "its day in court." This decision sent the hopes of statehood advocates soaring. Representative Leo W. O'Brien of New York, chairman of the House Subcommittee on Territorial and Insular Affairs, predicted that the Speaker's support would add "at least 20 votes" to the bill when it reached the House floor. Rayburn recommended, however, that the Alaska measure not be brought to the floor of the House in the last days of the session when members of Congress were in no mood to consider major legislation but merely wanted to hurry home.[32] Rayburn's advice was accepted by the statehood forces in the House, and the Alaska bill was put off for consideration until 1958.

There are several versions of why Rayburn changed his mind about the Territory's admission. Mary Lee Council stated that when the Speaker was asked about it he replied, "I can tell you in two words, 'Bob Bartlett.' " Another version relates that Lyndon B. Johnson was interested in the Democratic presidential nomination as early as 1957, but being a Southerner, his close friend and mentor Rayburn felt he would encounter opposition from Northern liberal Democrats. To help overcome this resistance, the Speaker decided to promote a few pieces of legislation favored by these liberals, such as Alaska statehood. Still another explanation was given after Bartlett's death by a journalist of the *Anchorage Daily News*. He disclosed that Bartlett "apparently pledged complete support for Johnson in return for an all-out drive to put the statehood bill over the top...." According to this writer, Bartlett kept notes on the agreement which would be found in his papers.[33] In any event, Rayburn's support proved to be crucial in the House in overcoming the opposition of the House Rules Committee.

Finally, in his 1958 budget message, President Eisenhower for the first time fully supported Alaska statehood. The President urged "that the Congress complete action on appropriate legislation admitting Hawaii and Alaska into the Union as States."[34] But shortly after his message, Eisenhower again dimmed the hopes of Alaska statehood proponents when he advocated that the Hawaii bill should be brought up simultaneously with the Alaska measure. The implications of such a move were obvious to many. *The New York Times* declared that if the two statehood measures were tied together again, neither would get through.[35] At this critical juncture, Delegate John A. Burns of Hawaii came to Alaska's help. Burns asserted that "nothing should interfere with success in the consideration of [the] Alaska... [statehood bill]." The Delegate promised to remove the Hawaii bill from the Senate debate if it was necessary to insure the success of Alaska. Senator Frank Church, Democrat of Idaho, an ardent supporter of statehood for both Territories, supported Burns' stand when he warned his colleagues that any attempt to link the two bills would merely have "the effect of combining the opponents of statehood for either Territory, and thus of uniting them against either bill."[36] The two statehood bills were not combined.

Although the danger of linking the two measures seemed to have been avoided, the Alaska bill still faced many uncertainties. In early February of 1958, therefore, Delegate Bartlett met with Senate Majority Leader Lyndon B. Johnson, Democrat of Texas, in an attempt to eliminate some of these hazards. The Senator was noncommittal. He related to Bartlett that his office had been swamped by anti-statehood mail. Additionally, bitter opponents such as Senator Richard B. Russell, Democrat of Georgia, and William Prescott Allen, a Texan and the publisher of the anti-statehood *The Daily Alaska Empire* (Juneau), had been besieging Johnson. Under these circumstances the Senator did not know what he would do and even might find it necessary to vote against the measure when it came to the Senate floor. Yet ambiguously the Majority Leader stated that he intended to act as "a midwife" for Alaska statehood, although he definitely did not plan to be the "doctor" who would "deliver" it. Pressed by Bartlett whether or not Alaska would achieve its goal in 1958, the Senator replied with a firm "no." As if this was not disheartening enough, the Alaska measure still faced the opposition of the House Rules Committee, and particularly its chairman, Howard W. Smith, Democrat of Virginia. *Life* magazine remarked editorially that passage of the Alaska statehood bill was being "held up by the willfulness of one Howard Smith, a Virginia gentleman whose impeccable manners include little real respect for either free enterprise or democracy." Smith had vehemently expressed his feelings toward statehood for either Alaska or Hawaii in 1955 when he had stated:

> I am opposed to statehood for Alaska. I am opposed to statehood for Hawaii, I am opposed to both of them together, I am opposed to them separately. I am opposed to bringing in Puerto Rico, which has been promised statehood by both of the great political parties like these two outlying Territories have. I am opposed to Puerto Rico, I am opposed to the Virgin Islands, I am opposed to all of them. I want to keep the United States of America on the American continent. I hope I have made my position clear.[37]

Smith had not changed his mind by 1958. On May 6 of that year, he appealed to his colleagues in the House to oppose the Alaska statehood bill. He had been informed, he related, that the measure would be called up in the House on May 14 as a "privileged bill." Smith asserted that there were many valid and compelling reasons why statehood should not be granted to Alaska, but the strongest was that the contemplated measure constituted the greatest giveaway of natural resources in American history. Smith objected to the land grant of 182,800,000 acres, including all mineral resources, to the new State. But the real "gimmick" of the bill, Smith observed, was the clause which gave the new State the right for a period of twenty-five years to make its own selections of land in blocks of not less than 5,760 acres. During that period of time, the chairman of the Rules Committee complained, Alaska would only have to watch where the most valuable discoveries of mineral resources were made and then choose accordingly. "These natural resources," Smith righteously concluded, "belong to all of the people of the United States!"[38]

Smith failed to mention that as early as June 26, 1957, Representative Clair Engle, Democrat of California, chairman of the House Interior and Insular Affairs Committee, had requested him to grant the Alaska bill consideration on the floor. As late as February, 1958, not even a time for a hearing had been set. Engle, therefore, had been authorized by the members of his committee "to use all parliamentary methods to secure passage of H.R. 7999," the Alaska statehood bill. In a letter to Smith, Engle asserted that the statehood bill before the House enjoyed privileged status. "I would much prefer to follow the regular procedure and take the bill on the floor under a rule," Engle stated. But unless there was some indication that the Alaska measure would get the "green light" by the middle of March, he would have to bypass the Rules Committee. The procedure Engle had in mind was a little-used device. Under it, statehood and a few other types of legislation were deemed as privileged.[39] This maneuver required that the Speaker of the House recognize the chairman of the legislative committee concerned with this legislation and permit each member of the House, if he wished, to speak for one hour on any amendment.

The Alaska statehood bill was brought up on May 21, 1958 as privileged matter by Representative Wayne Aspinall, who spoke for Engle's committee. He moved that the House resolve itself into the

Committee of the Whole House on the State of the Union. Clarence Cannon of Missouri immediately objected on a point of order. Certain matters, such as the appropriation of federal funds to the new State, deprived the measure of its privileged status, he said. Cannon hoped that he might "have the attention of the Speaker who had looked all along as if he had made up his mind and was not going to change it. I trust he will give attention with an open mind."[40] Speaker Rayburn listened patiently to various other complaints voiced by Representatives Howard V. Smith, Noah M. Mason, and John Taber. Finally, Rayburn ruled that the major features of the Alaska statehood bill dealt with the Territory's admission as a State. Lesser provisions did not destroy the privileged status, and the point of order and other objections were overruled. The House, by a roll-call vote of 217 to 172, thereupon agreed to consider the Alaska statehood bill.[41]

With this action the debate on Alaska statehood opened. It was frequently interrupted by delaying tactics from statehood opponents, such as twenty-five minute quorum calls and attempts to attach crippling amendments or to kill the bill outright. John R. Pillion of New York, a bitter statehood foe, found the tactics which had been used by Alaskans to further the cause highly objectionable. Inflammatory slogans such as patriotism, the right to vote, colonialism, second-class citizenship, and taxation without representation, if true, would be a reflection upon "the integrity and wisdom of Congress," and particularly the Committee on Interior and Insular Affairs. Pillion doubted that it was proper for a territorial government to use vast public funds to publicize and promote a purely political objective. "The election by Alaska of three Tennessee plan Congressmen," Pillion declared, "was not only presumptuous but ... also a brazen attempt to coerce Congress."[42]

The House accepted an amendment by Representative William A. Dawson 91 to 8 which reduced the land grant to the new state from 182,800,000 to 102,500,000 acres. An attempt by Walter Rogers of Texas to limit further the acreage to 21,000,000 was defeated. A. L. Miller's proposal to require Alaskans to vote on whether or not the Territory should immediately be admitted to statehood was accepted, as was an amendment by Representative Jack Westland of Washington to temporarily retain federal authority over Alaska's fish and wildlife resources. A proposal by Craig Hosmer of California to delay statehood until the Territory had attained a population of 250,000 was defeated, as was an attempt by Herbert C. Bonner to reduce from 70 per cent to 25 per cent Alaska's share in the proceeds from the sales of sealskins. On May 28, Representatives Rogers and Pillion tried to recommit the measure, but were defeated on roll-call votes of 199 to 174 and 202 to 172, respectively.[43]

Victor Fischer, who was working in Washington in 1958, has described the House vote:

> I remember walking down the long corridor from the House Office Building through the underground corridor to the Capitol Building, and I had Marge Smith [Bartlett's personal secretary] on my arm, and Bartlett and Mary Lee [Council] were walking ahead. And Marge was just broken up, she was shaking, she said: "I just can't take this anymore. I just can't take it. If we don't make it now, I just can't go through this again." We sat there, our group, in the House gallery ... Mary Lee, and Marge, and I don't know who else was there. And Bartlett sat with [New York Representative Leo W.] O'Brien at that point, and it was really a tremendously tense affair. Representatives kept filing in and out ... [and it] looked like a turmoil on the floor, and Bartlett and O'Brien sitting there tallying all this time. And then, finally, Bartlett looks up at us, and gives the thumbs-up sign. The gals just sort of broke down at that point. It was such a phenomenally emotional experience.[44]

The roll-call vote was 210 to 166, and with that the House sent the amended Alaska statehood bill to the Senate for action.

In 1950, the only other time an Alaska measure had passed the House, it had subsequently died in the Senate. This time, *The New York Times* observed, the bill was "considered to have a good fighting chance" in the upper house. That body now had before it the House bill as well as its own version. If the Senate went ahead and passed a measure which varied in any particular from the House bill, Delegate Bartlett worried, the statehood forces would "be catapulted into a morass." Any change in the House bill, he observed, meant that the measure would have to go to conference. Such a step necessitated unanimous consent, a remote possibility which only provoked "laughter" in this case. Another alternative was to ask the House Rules Committee to take charge and provide a rule which would allow the measure to go to conference. In view of chairman Howard Smith's hostility, Bartlett stated, there was "about as much likelihood of that as of unanimous consent." Still another chance lay in sending the bill back to the House Interior and Insular Affairs Committee and persuade it to accept the Senate amendments, then take the measure again to the floor under privileged status and try for passage. In the Delegate's view the foregoing alternatives did not look promising. He therefore arranged a meeting with Senator Henry "Scoop" Jackson, Democrat of Washington and floor manager of the Alaska bill. Bartlett, Representative Leo O'Brien, and Ernest Gruening, among others, tried at the meeting "to persuade Scoop to ditch the Senate bill and take the House measure." The Delegate anticipated grave difficulties because Senator Jackson and his subcommittee had made many improvements in the Senate version. To everybody's relief, however, Senator Jackson accepted the House bill.[45]

The Senate debated the statehood bill in the latter half of May and throughout June. In that month, the Southern senators caucused to consider action on the pending measure, and a proposal was made to defeat Alaska statehood with a filibuster. Senator Russell Long opposed this course of action, indicating that he would not only argue against his colleagues but also invoke cloture. Such talk was heresy for a Southerner. The result was that a number of the most intensely opposed senators made long speeches against the bill "for the record," that is, for home consumption, but a Southern filibuster did not develop.[46]

On June 27, 1958 Senator Monroney submitted an amendment to substitute commonwealth status for the statehood measure. It was rejected by a vote of 50 to 29. Senator Eastland's point of order to delete, as unconstitutional, the bill's provision that would permit the President to make defense withdrawals was also defeated by a count of 53 to 28. On June 30, Senator Eastland introduced his second point of order on the basis that Alaska's constitution, endorsed in the statehood bill, violated the United States Constitution because it specified that one senator was to be elected for a regular term and one for a short term. It also missed approval by a vote of 62 to 22. Next, Senator John Stennis' motion to refer the Alaska statehood bill to the Senate Armed Services Committee with instructions to report it back within thirty days also failed by 55 to 31. Senator Strom Thurmond thereupon introduced an amendment to exclude the proposed defense area from the boundaries of the new State. It likewise suffered defeat on a vote of 67 to 16. At that point Senator Eastland gave up. He had intended, Eastland stated, to offer a motion to refer the statehood bill to the Senate Committee on the Judiciary. But in view of the voting trend so far, "such a motion would be useless...." Instead, he merely asked that his speech be printed in the *Congressional Record*.47

With Eastland's move the Southern opposition collapsed, and Senator Henry M. Jackson summarized the Senate effort up to that point:

> Our work to date has not been the product of a single party. It has been the product of a bipartisan majority. This demonstrates again that America can close ranks in the truly great issues. This is not a Republican victory; it is not a Democratic victory; it is not simply a victory for Alaskans. Mr. President, it is a victory for all Americans and for the Democratic process.48

Several Senators called "vote, vote," and with Senator Richard Neuberger presiding, the roll-call began. Aiken—yes; Allott—yes; Anderson—yes. There were four more ayes, and then the first nayes—Bridges, Bush, Butler, Byrd—then back to the ayes and on until there were 64 ayes and 20 nayes. William C. Snedden, one of the many Alaskans in the Senate gallery that day, recalled that when the vote was about half over, "people began to talk. They began to see that we had it, and well, we did. There was spontaneous applause from the galleries and also from the floor." The time at which the roll-call vote ended was 8:02 p.m. Eastern Standard Time.49 Soon after the vote, Delegate Bartlett and many of the Alaskans who had been sitting in the galleries all day long, headed for the Senate chapel to give thanks for the fulfillment of their hopes and aspirations. For Mary Lee Council, June 30, 1958 was a memorable day:

> In all ways it turned out to be a perfect Monday, blue of sky but not blue of mood. So many years had gone into the fight, so many heartbreaks and setbacks had occurred. Success was almost unbelievable—a numbing experience for all who had participated. Something like 8,018,160 minutes passed between April 2, 1943, and June 30, 1958. The first date represents the introduction of the Langer bill and the second the day...[when] the bill passed.50

Word reached editor George Sundborg in Fairbanks at the moment the last vote was taken. It was a little past two o'clock in the afternoon in Alaska's interior city, but the staff of publisher Snedden's *Fairbanks Daily News-Miner* worked tirelessly throughout the rest of that day and part of the night in order to make a token air shipment of the special statehood issue to Washington. It was "for delivery to every member of Congress...as a demonstration of the nearness, under modern transportation conditions, of the nation's capital to the heart of Alaska, the 49th state."[51] The special issue was on the desks of members of Congress on July 1, 1958.

Reaction was jubilant in Alaska. In Fairbanks, "for five full minutes the combined blast of every civil defense siren from College to North Pole [a small community south of Fairbanks] cried out the news that the U.S. Senate had passed the Alaska statehood bill," reported the *Fairbanks Daily News-Miner*. "Anchorage blows its lid," announced the *Anchorage Daily Times*, as "Alaska's largest city rocked and rolled as the air was split by the sound of sirens, horns, bells, firecrackers, guns—and everything else that could be used to make a noise."[52]

Statehood had been achieved—almost. President Eisenhower still had to sign the measure. He did so on July 7, 1958. But instead of signing the admission bill in public, as was customary, the Chief Executive decided to do so privately. This action was severely criticized by Senator James E. Murray, Democrat of Montana, who complained to Ernest Gruening:

> Rather than to have had pictures taken in the presence of yourself and all those other fine Democrats who played such instrumental roles in bringing about the admission of the 49th State into the Union, he chose to handle this momentous matter as though he were merely signing a private bill for the relief of Mr. "X." Lord knows where he's going to find two Republicans who were sufficiently important in bringing about statehood for Alaska to whom to present the two pens he used in the signing.[53]

Murray exaggerated, of course, because statehood had been very much a bipartisan effort.

On August 26, 1958, Alaskans went to the polls in a referendum and overwhelmingly accepted three propositions which had been inserted in the statehood bill: (1) Shall Alaska immediately be admitted in to the Union as a State? (2) Shall the boundaries of the new State be approved? (3) Shall all the boundaries of the statehood act, such as those reserving rights and powers to the United States, as well as those prescribing the terms and conditions of the land grants and other property, be consented to? The three propositions were approved, receiving 40,452 to 8,010; 40,421 to 7,766; and 40,739 to 7,500 votes, respectively.[54]

On January 3, 1959, President Eisenhower formally admitted Alaska as the forty-ninth State when he signed the official proclamation. The statehood proclamation recited the action of Congress in 1958 to admit Alaska and the vote of the people in the new State to carry out the provisions of the statehood act. It declared that Alaskans had complied with the requirements set forth by Congress in all respects, and that "admission of the State of Alaska into the Union on an equal footing with the other States of the Union is now accomplished."[55] The President then unfurled the new American flag containing a field of seven staggered rows of seven stars each. The Chief Executive, briefly addressing himself to the historic occasion, remarked that he felt highly privileged and honored to welcome the forty-ninth State into the Union. To the State itself and to its people, he extended, "on behalf of all their [sic] sister states, best wishes and hope of prosperity and success."[56]

It is one of the ironic twists of history that finds Alaska, once jestingly referred to as a nearly worthless piece of real estate, now in a position of national, indeed international prominence. In an age when oil determines political and economic relations between countries, "black gold" has been discovered on the North Slope. In 1970, hardly anyone questions the wisdom of Alaska statehood.

In retrospect, the arguments used against Alaska statehood are of less significance today than during the struggle. Although the size of the population was always an issue in the admission of Territories to statehood, the question actually was settled during the Constitutional Convention in the Connecticut Compromise of 1787, which created two houses, one with equal and the other with proportional representation. Many members of Congress used this argument to conceal their real concern. Not the size, but the racial composition and the supposedly liberal political philosophy of this frontier area worried the Southern bloc.

Over the years, especially after the Second World War, with its attendant revolution in transportation and communications, the objection that Alaska was noncontiguous and too remote became irrelevant. The advances in air transportation and the realization that some of the shortest routes to Europe and Asia were over Alaskan soil lent special significance to the territory. Americans were more anxious to have Alaska as their full-fledged front porch than to worry about it as Asia's and Europe's backdoor to the North American Continent. Another argument, that Alaska did not have a sufficiently large population to support State government, was true in some respects. It was especially true because the delegates to the convention drafted a "model constitution" in order to demonstrate the Territory's maturity to Congress. But this document would have been more suitable for a heavily populated, urban, industrialized state like New York or Pennsylvania. The overwhelming majority of Alaskans did indeed live in relatively small, yet surprisingly sophisticated and modern, urban communities, the myth of the rugged "last frontier" notwithstanding. A government such as the one embodied in the Alaska constitution, however, with its complete range of governmental services, was expensive for a State with limited sources of taxation. Alaska could only boast of a couple of pulp mills. There were a few producing oil and gas wells, possibilities of hydroelectric power development, the likelihood of diversification in the fishing industry, some mining, and prospects for a vastly increased tourist trade. The State's business enterprises were small and catered mostly to local needs. In addition, Alaska's population was modest and hardly amounted to more than that of a medium-sized city in the continental United States.

Accordingly, revenues were small. Yet, the demands were great. The State government had to provide all the governmental services and social overhead required by modern American society. For instance, it would have been relatively simple to build a few roads, furnish normal police protection, and establish the customary school facilities. But nothing was normal in Alaska; it was and remains a land of superlatives. Subarctic engineering is relatively new, but the State would have to face the problem of permafrost conditions that frequently cause the roadtop to buckle and heave. Police protection would have to be provided for an area one-fifth the size of the forty-eight United States but with very few roads available. Flying would become a way of life for law enforcement officials as well as other Alaskans—an expensive way of life. "Bush schools" scattered along the Aleutian chain, through the Yukon Valley, and on the Seward Peninsula and the islands of southeastern Alaska were expensive to maintain. It was not until the discovery of oil on a large scale that the picture changed. By 1970, Alaska's small population had become a virtue rather than a handicap. The potential oil revenues and a modest population will make it possible for the State, if it so desires, to pioneer in building a unique model community with the comforts and conveniences of twentieth-century life in proximity to and in harmony with the natural environment.

Basically, the same arguments against Alaskan statehood appeared in every discussion and at every hearing between 1915 and 1958. How close were these objections to the real issues? Prior to the Second World War, the lack of action was mostly due to Alaska's small population and physical remoteness, as well as to the opposition and lobbying activity of the special interests. The Second World War rushed Alaska headlong into the modern age and drastically changed the composition of its citizenry. With this population influx came a new awareness, and many of the new arrivals were not so willing to acquiesce to the status quo, but wanted to pull Alaska into the mainstream of American life.

Despite the new involvement of Alaskans, the attitude of Congress had not changed enough. The old guard in Congress viewed Alaska and Hawaii as potential dangers. For instance, senators and representatives from these two new States, many feared, would threaten the tradition of the filibuster and endanger cloture. Indeed, in combination with Western, Northern and Eastern liberal support, these new votes could conceivably be sufficient to abolish Senate Rule XXII. There also was the fear that the admission of Alaska and Hawaii would integrate the hallowed Congressional chambers.

In 1957, Congress, after prolonged debate, passed a new civil rights law, the first since 1870. This new act was meant to protect the Negroes' right to vote by removing some of the obstacles created by state and local officials. Although at first far too weak to overcome the numerous devices used to circumvent it, the new act was indicative of the revolution in race relations and in American society generally. These changes led many members of Congress to reassess the limitations of their power and influence. Led by such modern political leaders as Senator Lyndon B. Johnson, these politicians grudgingly acceded to the admission of Alaska, and finally, Hawaii as well.

With Alaska statehood in 1958 and Hawaii statehood in 1959, the land domain of the United States had been rounded out. There are no more new frontiers in a geographical sense. Hopefully, the State of Alaska, especially in view of its newly-found wealth, will be able to pioneer new realms in the fields of economics and social relationships, and possibly demonstrate that technology and nature are not incompatible.

FOOTNOTES FOR CHAPTER XI

1. Porter and Johnson, *National Party Platforms*, 1840-1956 pp. 388, 403, 435, 386, 537, 453, 504, 553; *Cong. Record*, 84 Cong., 1 Sess., p. 5883 (May 9, 1955).
2. Galloway, *The Legislative Process in Congress*, p. 344.
3. Ernest Gruening, "Statehood for Alaska," *Harper's Magazine*, May, 1953, p. 73; *Cong. Record*, 84 Cong., 1 Sess., p. 5938 (May 10, 1955).
4. *Ibid.*, 84 Cong., 2 Sess., p. 143 (January 5, 1956).
5. Dwight D. Eisenhower to Representative A. L. Miller, March 31, 1955, in *Cong. Record*, 84 Cong., 1 Sess., p. 5880 (May 9, 1955). The same letter was sent to Senator Jackson.
6. For the details of the various debates on the defense safeguard amendments, see *Hawaii-Alaska Statehood* (1955), pp. 336-55, 396-432.
7. *The Daily Alaska Empire* (Juneau), January 6, 1956, p. 1; January 5, 1956, p. 1.
8. *Congress and the Nation*, p. 99a.
9. *The Daily Alaska Empire* (Juneau), June 5, 1956, p. 1.
10. Interview with William C. Snedden, March 25, 1970, Fairbanks, Alaska.
11. *Ibid.*
12. George H. Lehleitner to Representative James C. Wright, Jr., September 12, 1963, Statehood file, University of Alaska Archives, College, Alaska.
13. Pamphlet, George H. Lehleitner, *The Tennessee Plan: How the Bold Became States* (New Orleans, La., 1956). Copy in author's files.
14. George H. Lehleitner to Representative James C. Wright, Jr., September 12, 1963, Statehood File, University of Alaska Archives, College, Alaska.
15. Interview with William C. Snedden, March 25, 1970, Fairbanks, Alaska.
16. *The New York Times*, October 7, 1956, p. 60.
17. Interview with William C. Snedden, March 25, 1970, Fairbanks, Alaska.
18. George H. Lehleitner to Representative James C. Wright, Jr., September 12, 1963, Statehood File, University of Alaska Archives, College, Alaska.
19. *Cong. Record*, 85 Cong., 1 Sess., pp. 466-67 (January 14, 1957).
20. *Ibid.*, pp. 467-69. For editorials from Tennessee newspapers favoring Alaska statehood, see *ibid.*, p. 475.
21. Interview with Ralph J. Rivers, December 31, 1969, Fairbanks, Alaska.
22. *Cong. Record*, 85 Cong., 1 Sess., p. 608 (January 16, 1957).

23. These bills were S. 49, *Cong. Record*, Index 85 Cong., 1 Sess., p. 856 (introduced by Senator James E. Murray for himself and 23 colleagues); H.R. 50 *ibid.*, p. 943 (introduced by Delegate Bartlett); H.R. 340, *ibid.*, p. 951 (introduced by Representative Russell V. Mack); H.R. 628, *ibid.*, p. 958 (introduced by Representative Clair Engle); H.R. 849, *ibid.*, p. 964 (submitted by Representative Leo O'Brien); H.R. 1242, *ibid.*, p. 974 (introduced by Representative John P. Saylor); H.R. 7999, *ibid.*, p. 1130 (submitted by Representative Leo W. O'Brien); H.R. 1243, *ibid.*, p. 974 (a tandem Alaska-Hawaii measure submitted by Representative John P. Saylor).

24. *The Daily Alaska Empire* (Juneau), January 29, 1957, p. 1; February 1, 1957, p. 1.

25. *Statehood for Alaska* (1957); U.S., Congress, Senate, *Alaska Statehood*, Hearings before the Committee on Interior and Insular Affairs on S. 49 and S. 35, 85 Cong., 1 Sess. (Washington: Government Printing Office, 1957).

26. *Statehood for Alaska* (1957), pp. 94-98, 104-06.

27. Gruening, *The Battle for Alaska Statehood*, p. 95.

28. *Statehood for Alaska* (1957), p. 103.

29. *Ibid.*, pp. 188-213, 180-84, 303-47, 355-75, 168-76, 217-47, 248-65, 276-302.

30. U.S., Congress, House, *Providing for the Admission of the State of Alaska Into the Union*, H. Rept. 624 to accompany H.R. 7999 with Minority Report on H.R. 7999 and Minority Views on H.R. 7999 expressed by Hon. Craig Hosmer of California, 85 Cong., 1 Sess. (Washington: Government Printing Office, 1957), pp. 10, 18-19.

31. U.S., Congress, Senate, *Providing for the Admission of the State of Alaska Into the Union*, S. Rept. 1163 to accompany S. 49, 85 Cong., 1 Sess. (Washington: Government Printing Office, 1957), p. 2.

32. *The Daily Alaska Empire* (Juneau), July 26, 1957, p. 1.

33. Interview with Mary Lee Council, July 20, 1969, Washington, D.C.; Alfred Steinberg, *Sam Johnson's Boy: A Close-Up of the President from Texas* (New York and London: The Macmillan Company and Collier-Macmillan Ltd., 1968), p. 485; *Anchorage Daily Times*, December 12, 1968, in *Memorial Services Held in the Senate and House of Representatives for Lewis Edward Bartlett, Late a Delegate from the Territory of Alaska and a Senator from Alaska*, 91 Cong., 1 Sess. (Washington: Government Printing Office, 1969), p. 81. Bartlett's papers were deposited in the University of Alaska Archives, College. Although still in the process of being indexed and not open for research, the author received permission to check the late Senator's statehood file. No evidence was found which might have corroborated the assertion of the *Anchorage Daily Times* writer.

34. *Cong. Record*, 85 Cong., 2 Sess., p. 404 (January 13, 1958).

35. Editorial, *New York Times*, February 10, 1958, in *Cong. Record*, 85 Cong., 2 Sess., p. 1905 (February 10, 1958).

36. John A. Burns to Senator Frank Church, February 5, 1958, in *Cong. Record*, 85 Cong., 2 Sess., p. 7988 (May 5, 1958). Senator Church added his remarks at this time, *Ibid.*, pp. 7983-94.

37. Confidential Memorandum for Bartlett's own file, February 7, 1958, Statehood File, Legislative History, January-April 1958, Box 19, E. L. Bartlett Papers, University of Alaska Archives, College, Alaska; Editorial, *Life*, May 5, 1958, clipping in H85A-D8, papers accompanying H.R. 7999, 85 Cong., 1 Sess., NA; *Cong. Record*, 84 Cong., 1 Sess., p. 5881 (May 9, 1955).

38. Howard W. Smith to colleagues in the House of Representatives, May 6, 1958, H85A-D8, papers accompanying H.R. 7999, 85 Cong., 1 Sess., NA.

39. Clair Engle, chairman, Committee on Interior and Insular Affairs, to Howard W. Smith, chairman, House Rules Committee, February 25, 1958, in Excerpt from Full Committee Minutes

(Executive Session) of January 18, 1957, H85A-D8, papers accompanying H.R. 7999, 85 Cong., 1 Sess., NA; *Ibid.* The procedure Engle had in mind was a rarely used device allowed under Rule XI, clause 20, of the rules of the House of Representatives.

40. *Cong. Record*, 85 Cong., 2 Sess., p. 9213 (May 21, 1958).

41. *Ibid.*, p. 9212-17 (May 21, 1958).

42. *Ibid.*, p. 9225 (May 21, 1958).

43. *Congressional Quarterly Almanac*, 85 Cong., 2 Sess., p. 284; *Cong. Record*, 85 Cong., 2 Sess., pp. 9597-9612, 9743-57 (May 27 to 28, 1958).

44. Interview with Victor Fischer, March 17, 1970, College, Alaska. For the scene on the House floor, see *Cong. Record*, 85 Cong., 2 Sess., pp. 9756-57 (May 29, 1958).

45. *The New York Times*, May 29, 1958, p. 1; E. L. Bartlett to Robert B. Atwood, Confidential, June 5, 1958, Statehood File, Legislative History, June, 1958, Box 20, E. L. Bartlett Papers, University of Alaska Archives, College, Alaska.

46. George H. Lehleitner to Representative James C. Wright, Jr., of Texas, September 12, 1963, Statehood File, University of Alaska Archives, College, Alaska. For the opposition speeches, see *Cong. Record*, 85 Cong., 2 Sess., pp. 12015-21 (Senator A. Willis Robertson, Democrat of Virginia), 12047-54 (Senator Strom Thurmond, Democrat of South Carolina), 12175-79 (Senator James O. Eastland, Democrat of Mississippi), 12292-98 (Senator Herman E. Talmadge, Democrat of Georgia), 12299-304 (Senator John Stennis, Democrat of Mississippi), 12292-98 (Senator A. A. "Mike" Monroney, Democrat of Oklahoma), 12338-46 (Senator Thurmond), 12441-47 (Senator Olin D. Johnston, Democrat of South Carolina)—(June 24 to 27, 1958).

47. *Ibid.*, pp. 12449-53, 12454-71, 12602-11, 12617-32, 12634, 12637-41 (June 27 to 30, 1958).

48. *Ibid.*, 85 Cong., 2 Sess., p. 12650 (June 30, 1958).

49. Interview with William C. Snedden, March 25, 1970, Fairbanks, Alaska.

50. Council, "Alaska Statehood," pp. 1-3.

51. *Fairbanks Daily News-Miner*, June 30, 1958, p. 1.

52. *Ibid.*, *Anchorage Daily Times*, June 30, 1958, p. 1.

53. Senator James E. Murray to Ernest Gruening, Alaska Statehood Committee, July 9, 1958, Alaska Statehood File, Alaska Historical Library, Juneau, Alaska.

54. Memorandum on Statehood Election in 1958, Acc. No. 62-A-401, Box 95, file Alaska-Political-Affairs-Election, file 2, part 1, Department of the Interior, Office of Territories, RG 126, Washington Federal Records Center, Suitland, Maryland.

55. "Admission of the State of Alaska into the Union: A Proclamation by the President of the United States of America," White House Press Release, January 3, 1959. In author's files.

56. *Anchorage Daily News*, January 3, 1959, p. 1.

BIBLIOGRAPHY

I. Manuscripts

Alaska Historical Library, Juneau, Alaska. Senator James E. Murray to Ernest Gruening, Alaska Statehood Committee, July 9, 1958.

———. Typewritten carbon copy. Minutes of the Meeting of the Alaska Statehood Committee, Juneau, January 28, 1953, and Meeting of the Joint Special Committee on Statehood of the Alaska Territorial Legislature, Juneau, January 29, 1953.

Federal Records Center, Seattle, Washington. Records of the Office of the Governor of Alaska, 1884-1958.

National Archives, Washington, D. C. Record Group 46, Papers accompanying Senate bills.

———. Record Group 48, Records of the Department of the Interior.

———. Record Group 126, Records of the Office of Territories.

———. Record Group 233, Papers accompanying House bills.

University of Alaska. Archives, Personal papers of E. L. Bartlett.

———. Archives, Personal papers of Anthony J. Dimond.

———. Archives, Personal papers of Margaret Harrais.

———. Archives, Diary (on microfilm) of James Wickersham.

Washington National Records Center, Suitland, Maryland. Record Group 48, Records of the Department of the Interior.

———. Record Group 126, Records of the Office of Territories.

II. Government Publications

Alaska Law Compilation Commission. *Compiled Laws of Alaska, 1949, Containing the General Laws of the Territory of Alaska, Annotated with Decisions of the District Courts of Alaska, the Circuit Court of Appeals, and the Supreme Court of the United States.* San Francisco: Bancroft-Whitney Co., 1948.

Alaska Legislative Council. *Alaska Constitutional Convention, Proceedings.* November 8, 1955 to February 5, 1956.

Alaska Statehood Committee. *Alaska Statehood: Analysis and Refutation of Minority Views on S. 50.* Juneau, Alaska, January, 1952.

———. *Handbook for Delegates to the Alaska Constitutional Convention.* 1955.

———. *Statehood for Alaska: A Report on Four Years of Achievement.* Juneau, Alaska, 1953.

Annual Report of the Governor of Alaska. Washington: Government Printing Office, 1885-1940.

Congressional Record. 1896, 1914, 1916, 1923-1931, 1933-1958.

The Constitution of the State of Alaska. 1956.

Memorial Services Held in the Senate and House of Representatives for Lewis Edward Bartlett, Late a Delegate from the Territory of Alaska and a Senator from Alaska. 91 Cong., 1 Sess. Washington: Government Printing Office, 1969.

Message from the President of the United States to the Congress of the United States Relative to Enactment of Necessary Legislation to Admit Alaska to Statehood at the Earliest Possible Date. 80 Cong., 2 Sess. Washington: Government Printing Office, 1948.

Murphy, James W., ed. *Speeches and Addresses of Warren G. Harding, President of the United States.* Washington: Government Printing Office, 1923.

National Resources Committee. *Regional Planning—Part VII, Alaska—Its Resources and Development.* Washington: Government Printing Office, 1938.

National Resources Planning Board. *"Postwar Economic Development of Alaska,"* in Regional Development Plan—Report for 1942. Washington: Government Printing Office, December, 1941.

Office of the Secretary of State. "Official Returns, Territorial Canvassing Board, General Election, 1944-56." Juneau, Alaska.

Proposed Constitution for the State of Alaska: A Report to the People of Alaska from the Alaska Constitutional Convention. Fairbanks, Alaska: Commercial Printing Co., Inc., 1956. (Pamphlet.)

Public Administration Service. *Constitutional Studies,* vols. I-III. Prepared on behalf of the Alaska Statehood Committee for the Alaska Constitutional Convention, November, 1955. (Mimeographed.)

United States Army. Alaska. *The Army's Role in the Building of Alaska.* Headquarters, United States Army, Alaska: Public Information Officer, Pamphlet 360-5, April, 1969.

U.S. Congress. House. *Alaska.* Hearings before the Subcommittee on Territories and Insular Possessions of the Committee on Public Lands pursuant to H. Res. 93, Committee Hearing No. 31, 80 Cong., 1 Sess. Washington: Government Printing Office, 1948.

———. *Alaska, 1955.* Hearings before the Subcommittee on Territorial and Insular Affairs of the Committee on Interior and Insular Affairs pursuant to H. Res. 30, Part I, 84 Cong., 1 Sess. Washington: Government Printing Office, 1956.

———. *Alaska Reconnaissance Report on the Potential Development of Water Resources in the Territory of Alaska.* H. Doc. 197, 82 Cong., 1 Sess. Washington: Government Printing Office, 1952.

———. *Biographical Directory of the American Congress, 1774-1961.* H. Doc. 442, 85 Cong., 2 Sess. Washington: Government Printing Office, 1961.

———. *Enabling the People of Hawaii and Alaska Each to Form a Constitution and State Government and to Be Admitted Into the Union.* H. Rept. 88 to accompany H.R. 2535, 84 Cong., 1 Sess. Washington: Government Printing Office, 1955.

———. *Hawaii-Alaska Statehood.* Hearings before the Committee on Interior and Insular Affairs on H.R. 2535 and H.R. 2536..., 84 Cong., 1 Sess. Washington: Government Printing Office, 1955.

U.S. Congress. House. *Official Trip to Conduct a Study and Investigation of the Various Questions and Problems Relating to the Territory of Alaska.* Committee on the Territories, H. Rept. 1583 pursuant to H. Res. 236, 79 Cong., 2 Sess. Washington: Government Printing Office, 1946.

———. *Official Trip of Examination of Federal Activities in Alaska and the Pacific Coast States.* Subcommittee of the Committee on Appropriations, 79 Cong., 1 Sess. Washington: Government Printing Office, 1945.

———. *Providing for the Admission of Alaska Into the Union.* H. Rept. 1731 to accompany H.R. 5666, 80 Cong., 2 Sess. Washington: Government Printing Office, 1948.

———. *Providing for the Admission of Alaska Into the Union.* H. Rept. 225 to accompany H.R. 331, 81 Cong., 1 Sess. Washington: Government Printing Office, 1949.

———. *Providing for the Admission of Alaska Into the Union.* H. Rept. 675 to accompany H.R. 2982, 82 Cong., 1 Sess. Washington: Government Printing Office, 1953.

———. *Providing for the Admission of the State of Alaska Into the Union.* H Rept. 624 to accompany H.R. 7999 with Minority Report on H.R. 7999 and Minority Views on H.R. 7999 expressed by Hon. Craig Hosmer of California, 85 Cong., 1 Sess. Washington: Government Printing Office, 1957.

____. *Reapportionment of the Alaska Legislature.* Hearings. 68 Cong., 1 Sess. Washington: Government Printing Office, 1924.

____. "Speech of Hon. Charles Sumner of Massachusetts, on the Cession of Russian America to the United States." House Executive Document No. 177, 40 Cong., 2 Sess. Washington: Government Printing Office, 1868.

____. *Statehood for Alaska.* Hearings before the Subcommittee on Territories and Insular Possessions of the Committee on Public Lands. Committee Hearing No. 9, 80 Cong., 1 Sess. Washington: Government Printing Office, 1947.

____. *Statehood for Alaska.* Hearings before the Subcommittee on Territories and Insular Possessions of the Committee on Public Lands on H.R. 331 and related bills, Committee Hearing Serial No. 3, 81 Cong., 1 Sess. Washington: Government Printing Office, 1949.

____. *Statehood for Alaska.* Hearings before the Subcommittee on Territorial and Insular Possessions of the Committee on Interior and Insular Affairs on H.R. 20..., 83 Cong., 1 Sess. Washington: Government Printing Office, 1953.

U.S. Congress. House. *Statehood for Alaska.* Hearings before the Subcommittee on Interior and Insular Affairs on H.R. 50..., 85 Cong., 1 Sess. Washington: Government Printing Office, 1957.

U.S. Congress. Senate. *Alaska Statehood and Elective Governorship.* Hearings before the Committee on Interior and Insular Affairs on S. 50 and S. 224, 83 Cong., 1 Sess. Washington: Government Printing Office, 1953.

____. *Alaska Statehood.* Hearings before the Committee on Interior and Insular Affairs on H.R. 331 and S. 2036, 81 Cong., 2 Sess. Washington: Government Printing Office, 1950.

____. *Alaska Statehood.* Hearings before the Committee on Interior and Insular Affairs on S. 50, 83 Cong., 2 Sess. Washington: Government Printing Office, 1954.

____. *Alaska Statehood.* Hearings before the Committee on Interior and Insular Affairs on S. 49 and S. 35, 85 Cong., 1 Sess. Washington: Government Printing Office, 1957.

____. *Alaska-Hawaii Statehood, Elective Governor, and Commonwealth Status.* Hearings before the Committee on Interior and Insular Affairs on S. 49..., 84 Cong., 1 Sess. Washington: Government Printing Office, 1955.

____. *Conditions in Alaska.* Committee on Territories, S. Rept. 282 to accompany S. Res. 16, 58 Cong., 2 Sess. Washington: Government Printing Office, 1904.

____. *Investigation of the Department of the Interior and of the Bureau of Forestry.* S. Doc. 719 pursuant to H.J. Res. 103, 61 Cong., 3 Sess. Washington: Government Printing Office, 1910.

____. *Needs of Alaska in Matters of Legislation and Government* S. Doc. No. 14, 59 Cong., 2 Sess. Washington: Government Printing Office, 1906.

____. *Providing for the Admission of Alaska Into the Union.* S. Rept. 1929 to accompany H.R. 331, 81 Cong., 2 Sess. Washington: Government Printing Office, 1950.

____. *Providing for the Admission of Alaska Into the Union.* S. Rept 315 to accompany S. 50, 82 Cong., 1 Sess. Washington: Government Printing Office, 1951.

____. *Providing for the Admission of Alaska Into the Union.* S. Rept. 1028 to accompany S. 50, 83 Cong., 2 Sess. Washington: Government Printing Office, 1954.

U.S. Congress. Senate. *Providing for the Admission of the State of Alaska Into the Union.* S. Rept. 1163 to accompany S. 49, 85 Cong., 1 Sess. Washington: Government Printing Office, 1957.

U.S. *Statutes at Large.*
You Are Looking at Alaska's Future: What Do You See in It?
   Fairbanks, Alaska: Commercial Printing Co., Inc., 1956.
   (Pamphlet.)

III. Court Cases

Balzac v. People of Porto Rico, 258 U.S. 298 (1922).
De Lima v. Bidwell, 182 U.S. 1 (1901).
Downes v. Bidwell, 182 U.S. 244 (1901).
McAllister v. United States, 141 U.S. 174, 188 (1891).
Nagle v. United States, 191 Fed. 141 (1911).
O.Donoghue v. United States, 289 U.S. 516, 537 (1933).
Rasmussen v. United States, 197 U.S. 516 (1905).
United States v. Farwell, 76 F. Supp. 35 (1948).

IV. Personal Interviews

Arnold, Winton C., Anchorage, Alaska, August 25, 1969.
Atwood, Robert B., Anchorage, Alaska, August 26, 1969.
Council, Mary Lee, Washington, D.C., July 20, 1969.
Faulkner, Herbert L., Anchorage, Alaska, August 11, 1969.
Fischer, Victor., College, Alaska, March 17, 1970.
Gruening, Ernest, Washington, D.C., July 16, 1969.
Koponen, Dr. Niilo, Chena Ridge, Alaska, March 10, 1970.
Rivers, Ralph J., Fairbanks, Alaska, December 31, 1969.
Rogers, Dr. George W., College, Alaska, January 19, 1970.
Snedden, William C., Fairbanks, Alaska, March 25, 1970.
Stewart, Thomas, Juneau, Alaska, August 20, 1969.

V. Newspapers

The Alaska Daily Empire (Juneau). 1915-1916.
Alaska Daily Times (Fairbanks). 1911, 1954.
Alaska Record (Juneau). 1908.
The Commercial and Financial Chronicle. 1923.
The Daily Alaska Dispatch (Juneau). 1916.
The Daily Alaska Empire (Juneau). 1950-1958.
Fairbanks Daily News-Miner. 1950-1958.
Fairbanks Times. 1909.
The Forty-Ninth Star (Valdez). 1915-1916.
Ketchikan Alaska Chronicle. 1946-1947.
The New York Times. 1920-1958.
The Seattle Times. 1957-1958.
Washington Post. 1954.

VI. Periodical Articles

"About Statehood" (Letters to the Editor), *Alaska Life*, March, 1944, pp. 2, 57-59.
"Alaska: Our Next State; Bolstering Arctic Frontier," *U.S. News and World Report*, September 13, 1946, pp. 19-20.
"Alaska Statehood Delay Asked," *Alaska Life*, May, 1944, p. 52.
"Alaska to Be Fortified Against Japanese Invasion: New Northern Airplane Route Envisaged," *The China Weekly Review*, May 10, 1941, pp. 318-319.
"Alaskan Defenses Alter Strategic Map of the Pacific," *The China Weekly Review*, October 11, 1941, p. 160.
"The Alaskan Story," *Congressional Digest*, November, 1947, pp. 272-275.

"Alaska's Future Is the Responsibility of the U.S.," *Fortune*, March, 1942, p. 114.
"Alaska's Pitt Talking Home Rule," *Alaska-Yukon Magazine*, March, 1911, p. 50.
"Alaska's Plea for Home Rule," *The Literary Digest*, August 21, 1920, pp. 20-21.
"Alaska's Problem as President Harding Saw It," *The Literary Digest*, August 18, 1923, pp. 17-18.
Andrews, C. L. "Alaska Beginning to Loom Large in Great Problem of the Pacific," *The China Weekly Review*, December 17, 1938, pp. 72-74.
———. "Why Alaska Has Troubles," *Alaska-Yukon Magazine*, August, 1911, pp. 9-15.
Atherton, Brownell. "Wanted: A Government for Alaska," *Outlook*, February 26, 1910, pp. 431-440.
Atwood, Robert B. "Alaska's Struggle for Statehood," *State Government*, Autumn, 1958, pp. 202-208.
Bailey, Thomas A. "Why the United States Purchased Alaska," *Pacific Historical Review*, III (March, 1934), 39-49.
Baldwin, George E. "Conservation Faddists Arrest Progress and Seek to Surplant Self-Government with Bureaucracy," *Alaska-Yukon Magazine*, February, 1912, pp. 44-46.
———. "What Are the Needs of Alaska," *Alaska-Yukon Magazine*, December, 1911, pp. 341-348.
Ballinger, R. A. "A Portrayal of Bureaucratic Government in Alaska," *Alaska-Yukon Magazine*, November, 1911, pp. 253-262.
Bebout, John E. "Charter for Last Frontier," *National Municipal Review*, April, 1956, pp. 158-163.
Beers, W. F., Jr. "The Government of Alaska," *Alaska-Yukon Magazine*, January, 1908, pp. 370-375.
Bone, Scott C. "Alaska from the Inside," *Saturday Evening Post*, August 8, 1926, p. 130.
———. "The Land That Uncle Sam Bought and Then Forgot," *Review of Reviews*, April, 1922, pp. 402-410.
"Conservation Gone Crazy," *Alaska-Yukon Magazine*, February, 1910, pp. 171-173.
"Conservation That Locks Up," *Alaska-Yukon Magazine*, April, 1910, pp. 290-293.
Crain, Mel. "When the Navy Ruled Alaska," *U.S. Naval Institute Proceedings*, LXXXI (February, 1955), 199.
Dall, William H. "Is Alaska a Paying Investment?" *Harper's*, January, 1872, pp. 252-257.
Doherty, Bella and Arthur Hepner. "Alaska: Last American Frontier," *Foreign Policy Reports*, December 1, 1942, pp. 328-347.
Dunning, William A. "Paying for Alaska; Some Unfamiliar Incidents in the Process," *Political Science Quarterly*, XXVII (September, 1912), 385-398.
Dyer, F. J. "Saving at the Spigot," *Alaska-Yukon Magazine*, May, 1910, pp. 357-363.
Eby, S. C. "Home Rule in Conservation," *Alaska-Yukon Magazine*, May, 1910, pp. 354-356.
"Editorial," *Life*, May 14, 1956, p. 48.
"Editorial," *National Municipal Review*, April, 1956, p. 156.
Egan, William A. "The Constitution of the New State of Alaska," *State Government*, Fall, 1958, pp. 209-214.
Elliott, Henry W. "Ten Year's Acquaintance with Alaska," *Harper's*, November, 1877, pp. 801-816.
"Falcon Joslin Before the House Committee on Territories," *Alaska-Yukon Magazine*, May, 1910, pp. 364-367.

Farrand, Max. "Territory and District," *The American Historical Review*, V (July, 1900), 676-681.

Farrar, Victor J. "Joseph Lane McDonald and the Purchase of Alaska," *Washington Historical Quarterly*, XII (April, 1921), 83-90.

———. "The Background of the Purchase of Alaska," *Washington Historical Quarterly*, XIII (April, 1922), 93-104.

Foster, W. S. "Statehood Would Benefit Alaskan Cities," *The American City*, August, 1954, pp. 104-106.

Frykman, George A. "The Alaska-Yukon-Pacific Exposition, 1909," *Pacific Northwest Quarterly*, LIII (July, 1962), 89-99.

Gates, Charles M. "Human Interest Notes on Seattle and the Alaskan Gold Rush," *Pacific Northwest Quarterly*, XXXIV (April, 1943), 205-211.

Golder, Frank A. "The Purchase of Alaska," *The American Historical Review*, XXV (April, 1920), 411-425.

Gruening, Ernest. "Alaska Fights for Statehood," *Atlantic*, January, 1957, pp. 66-69.

———. "Should Congress Now Grant Statehood to the Territory of Alaska," *Congressional Digest*, November, 1947, pp. 282-288.

———. "Statehood for Alaska," *Harper's*, May, 1953, pp. 72-77.

Harrais, Margaret Keenan. "Statehood Letter," *Alaska Life*, December, 1944, pp. 57-59.

Holman, Alfred. "Alaska As a Territory of the United States," *Century Magazine*, February, 1913, pp. 582-601.

Huber, Louis R. "Alaska: Our Deep Freeze," *Atlantic Monthly*, September, 1945, pp. 79-83.

Huddle, Frank P. "Admission of New States," *Editorial Research Reports*, March 20, 1946, pp. 185-198.

Hulbert, William D. "In the Haunts of the Syndicate," *Outlook*, April 20, 1912, pp. 866-872.

———. "What Is Really Going On in Alaska," *Outlook*, December 23, 1912, pp. 949-962.

Jordan, David S. "Colonial Lessons of Alaska," *Atlantic Monthly*, November, 1898, pp. 582, 591.

Joslin, Falcon. "The Conservation Policy in Alaska," *Alaska-Yukon Magazine*, May, 1910, pp. 341-349.

Kenny, E. "Is an International State the Answer," *Alaska Life*, August, 1943, pp. 15-18.

Kluckholm, Frank L. "Alaska Fights for Statehood," *American Mercury*, May, 1949, pp. 555-562.

Lane, Franklin K. "Freeing Alaska from Red-Tape," *North American Review*, June, 1915, pp. 172-174.

———. "Red Tape in Alaska," *Outlook*, January 20, 1915, pp. 135-140.

Langer, William. "The Forty-ninth Star," *Alaska Life*, June, 1943, pp. 7-11.

Leehey, Maurice D. "A Story of Government Wrongdoing," *Alaska-Yukon Magazine*, November, 1911, pp. 269-279.

Lehleitner, George H. "Alaska Seeks Statehood the Tennessee Way," *Freedom and Union, Journal of the World Republic*, II (April, 1956), 16.

Lindley, Ernest K. "Alaska: Strategic Stepchild of the Continent," *Newsweek*, March 16, 1942, p. 28.

Lowney, Paul B. "Report from Washington," *Alaska Life*, January, 1946, pp. 39-41.

———. "What Congress Thinks of Statehood for Alaska," *Alaska Life*, May, 1946, pp. 16-17, 28.

Luthin, R. H. "Sale of Alaska," *Slavonic Review*, XVI (July, 1937), 168-182.
Manders, John L. "Statehood for Alaska," *Alaska Life*, September, 1946, pp. 8-9.
Marchon, Piere. "Should Alaska Have Full Territorial Government?" *Alaska-Yukon Magazine*, February, 1910, pp. 162-166.
Mazour, Anatole G. "The Prelude to Russia's Departure from America," *Pacific Historical Review*, X (September, 1941), 311-319.
McCoy, Donald R. "The Special Indian Agency in Alaska, 1973-1874: Its Origins and Operation," *Pacific Historical Review*, XXV (November, 1956), 355-367.
Meller, Norman, "Hawaii: The Fiftieth State," *Parliamentary Affairs*, XIII (1959/1960), 489-508.
Monroney, A. S. "Mike." "Let's Keep It 48," *Collier's*, March 4, 1955, pp. 32-36.
Moran, Casey. "A Land to Loot," *Collier's*, August 6, 1910, pp. 19-24.
Neuberger, Richard L. "Alaska—Northern Front," *Survey Graphic*, February, 1942, pp. 57-62.
———. "Gruening of Alaska," *Survey Graphic*, October, 1947, p. 513.
———. "The State of Alaska," *Survey Graphic*, February, 1947, pp. 75-88.
Noyes, Charles E. "Present and Future Development of Alaska," *Editorial Research Reports*, August, 1939, pp. 171-184.
"President Taft Does Not Favor Home Rule," *Alaska-Yukon Magazine*, August, 1909, pp. 470-471.
"Progress of the Northland," *Alaska-Yukon Magazine*, August, 1911, pp. 61-72.
"The Question of Granting Statehood to Hawaii: Pro and Con," *Congressional Digest*, January, 1959, pp. 3-32.
"Question of Statehood for Hawaii, Alaska," *Congressional Digest*, April-May, 1954, p. 170.
"Red-Tape Riddance for Alaska," *The Literary Digest*, June 27, 1914, p. 1530.
Richardson, Wilds P. "Alaska," *Atlantic Monthly*, January, 1928, pp. 111-121.
Rivers, Ralph J. "Alaska... The 49th State?" *Alaska Life*, December, 1945, pp. 8-11.
———. "Transition to Statehood," *Alaska Life*, May, 1946, pp. 17, 29.
Rogers, Sherman. "The Problem of Alaska's Government," *Outlook*, January 23, 1923, pp. 172-174.
St. Clair, D. P. "The Struggle for Alaska," *Van Norden Magazine*, January, 1909, pp. 446-451.
"Seward's Folly—a Cold Look," *Monthly Review, Federal Reserve Bank of San Francisco*, September, 1958, pp. 130-140.
Sherman, Dean. "Statehood for the Asking," *Alaska Life*, November, 1943, pp. 3-7.
———. "The Statehood Question," *Alaska Life*, June, 1944, pp. 14-19.
Sikes, Bob. "A Congressman's View of Alaska," *Alaska Life*, May, 1947, p. 5.
Smith, Richard Austin. "Alaska: The Last Frontier," *Fortune*, September, 1955, pp. 104-113.
"Statehood-for-Alaska Clubs," *Alaska Life*, February, 1944, p. 2.
"The Statehood Referendum," *Alaska Frontier*, May-June, 1941, p. 3.

Stefansson, Vilhjalmur. "Alaska, American Outpost No. 4," *Harper's*, June, 1941, pp. 83-92.
Stewart, Thomas B. "The Meaning of Statehood to Alaska," *State Government*, Autumn, 1958, pp. 215-219.
Strong, J. F. A. "The Development of Alaska," *Alaska-Yukon Magazine*, May, 1910, pp. 350-353.
Strout, Richard. "Alaska and Hawaii: Statehood or Commonwealth Status?" *The New Republic*, February 14, 1955, pp. 13-14.
Tarr, Ralph S. "The Alaskan Problem," *North American Review*, January, 1912, pp. 40-55.
Thompson, W. F. "Strong Words from Alaska," *Sunset Magazine*, September, 1923, pp. 15, 91-92.
"U.S. Strengthens Defenses in Alaska and Bering Straits to Meet Twin Threat of Russian and Japanese Action," *The China Weekly Review*, January 11, 1941, pp. 186-187.
"What Alaskans Say About Statehood," *Alaska Life*, September, 1946, p. 9.
"Where Opportunity Runs Wild," *Alaska-Yukon Magazine*, December, 1909, pp. 120-121.
Wickersham, James. "The Forty-Ninth Star," *Collier's*, August 6, 1910, p. 17.
Wilbur, Ray Lyman. "A New Alaska in the Making," *Current History*, XXXV (October, 1931), 81-84.
Woehlke, Walter V. "Warren Harding's Bequest," *Sunset Magazine*, October, 1923, pp. 9-11, 104-105.

VIII. Books

Atwood, Evangeline B. *Alaska's Struggle for Self-government... 83 Years of Neglect*. Anchorage, Alaska: Anchorage Daily Times, 1950.
Berton, Pierre. *The Klondike Fever: The Life and Death of the Last Great Gold Rush*. New York: Alfred A. Knopf, 1958.
Billington, Ray Allen. *Westward Expansion: A History of the American Frontier*. 3rd ed. New York: The Macmillan Company, 1967.
Brooks, Alfred Hulse. *Blazing Alaska's Trails*. Edited by Burton L. Fryxell. Published jointly by the University of Alaska and the Arctic Institute of North America. Caldwell, Idaho: The Caxton Printers, Ltd., 1953.
Brown, Everett S. *The Territorial Delegate to Congress and Other Essays*. Ann Arbor, Michigan: The George Wahr Publishing Co., 1950.
Cease, Ronald C. and Jerome R. Saroff, eds. *The Metropolitan Experiment in Alaska: A Study of Borough Government*. New York: Frederick A. Praeger, 1968.
Clark, Henry W. *History of Alaska*. New York: The Macmillan Company, 1930.
Congress and the Nation. 1945-1964. Washington: Congressional Quarterly Service, 1965.
Congressional Quarterly Almanac. Washington: Washington Congressional Quarterly News Features, 1948-1958.
Dall, William H. *Alaska and Its Resources*. Cambridge, Massachusetts: Cambridge University Press, John Wilson and Son, 1870.
Driscoll, Joseph. *War Discovers Alaska*, Philadelphia: J. B. Lippincott Company, 1943.
Eblen, Jack E. *The First and Second United States Empires: Governors and Territorial Government, 1784-1912*. Pittsburgh: University of Pittsburgh Press, 1968.

Frontier Alaska. Anchorage, Alaska: Alaska Methodist University Press, 1968.

Galloway, George B. *The Legislative Process in Congress.* New York: Thomas Y. Crowell Company, 1955.

Gruening, Ernest. *The Battle for Alaska Statehood.* College, Alaska: The University of Alaska Press in cooperation with the Alaska Purchase Centennial Commission, 1967.

———. *The State of Alaska.* 2nd ed. New York: Random House, 1968.

Hellenthal, J. A. *The Alaskan Melodrama*, New York: Liveright Publishing Corporation, 1936.

Hilscher, Herbert H. *Alaska Now.* Rev. ed. Boston: Little, Brown and Company, 1950.

Joy, Edmund Steele. *The Right of the Territories to Become States of the Union.* Newark, New Jersey: Advertiser Printing House, 1892.

Morehouse, Thomas A. and Victor Fischer. *The State and the Local Governmental System.* College, Alaska: Institute of Social, Economic and Government Research, March, 1970.

Murray, Robert K. *The Harding Era: Warren G. Harding and His Administration.* Minneapolis: University of Minnesota Press, 1969.

Nichols, Jeannette Paddock. *Alaska: A History of Its Administration, Exploitation, and Industrial Development During the First Half Century under the Rule of the United States.* Cleveland: The Arthur H. Clark Company, 1924.

Noggle, Burl. *Teapot Dome: Oil and Politics in the 1920's.* Baton Rouge: Louisiana State University Press, 1962.

O'Connor, Harvey. *The Guggenheims: The Making of an American Dynasty.* New York: Covici Friede, 1937.

Penick, James, Jr. *Progressive Politics and Conservation: The Ballinger-Pinchot Affair.* Chicago and London: The University of Chicago Press, 1968.

Pinchot, Gifford. *Breaking New Ground.* New York: Harcourt, Brace and Company, 1947.

Pomeroy, Earl S. *The Territories and the United States 1861-1890: Studies in Colonial Administration.* Philadelphia: University of Pennsylvania Press, 1947.

Porter, Kirk H. and Donald Bruce Johnson, compilers. *National Party Platforms, 1840-1956.* Urbana: The University of Illinois Press, 1956.

Potter, Jean. *Alaska Under Arms.* New York: The Macmillan Company, 1943.

Richardson, James D., ed. *A Compilation of the Messages and Papers of the Presidents.* New York: Bureau of National Literature, 1912.

Riley, Burke. *Federal Land Policy and Its Effect on Development and Settlement in Alaska.* Juneau: Alaska Development Board, January, 1948.

Rogers, George W. *Alaska in Transition: The Southeast Region.* Baltimore: The Johns Hopkins Press, 1960.

———. *The Future of Alaska: Economic Consequences of Statehood.* Baltimore: The Johns Hopkins Press, 1962.

Rogers, George W. and Richard A. Cooley. *Alaska's Population and Economy.* Vol. I, *Analyses*, Vol II, *Statistical Handbook.* College, Alaska: Institute of Business, Economics and Government Research, 1963.

Ross, Sherwood. *Gruening of Alaska.* New York: Best Books, Inc., 1968.

Russell, Francis. *The Shadow of Blooming Grove: Warren G. Harding in His Times.* New York and Toronto: McGraw-Hill Book Company, 1968.
Sherwood, Morgan B., ed. *Alaska and Its History.* Seattle and London: University of Washington Press, 1967.
Speech of Hon. James Wickersham, Delegate to Congress. Juneau, Alaska, March 10, 1931.
Speech of William H. Seward at Sitka, August 12, 1868. Washington: Philips and Solomons, 1869.
Spicer, George Washington. *The Constitutional Status and Government of Alaska.* Baltimore: The Johns Hopkins University Press, 1927.
Steinberg, Alfred. *Sam Johnson's Boy: A Close-Up of the President from Texas.* New York: The Macmillan Company, 1968.
Sundborg, George. *Statehood for Alaska: The Issues Involved and the Facts About the Issues.* Anchorage, Alaska: Alaska Statehood Association, August, 1946.
Swineford, A. P. *Alaska: Its History, Climate and Natural Resources.* Chicago and New York: Rand, McNally and Co., 1898.
Tompkins, Stuart Ramsey. *Alaska, Promyshlennik and Sourdough.* Norman: University of Oklahoma Press, 1945.
Tugwell, Rexford Guy. *The Stricken Land: The Story of Puerto Rico.* New York: Greenwood Press, Publishers, 1968.
Wickersham, James A. *Bibliography of Alaskan Literature, 1724-1924.* Cordova, Alaska: Cordova Daily Times, 1927.
Wiebe, Robert H. *The Search for Order 1877-1920.* New York: Hill and Wang, 1967.

VIII. Theses

Bailey, Ronald B. "The Admission of Alaska Into the United States: Adjustments in the Federal System." Unpublished Ph. D. thesis, University of Illinois, 1965.
Cease, Ronald C. "Areawide Local Government in the State of Alaska: The Genesis, Establishment, and Organization of Borough Government," Unpublished Ph.D. thesis, Claremont Graduate School, 1964.
Crain, Melvin. "Governance for Alaska: Some Aspects of Representation." Unpublished Ph.D. thesis, University of Southern California, 1957.
Fisher, Joseph L. "Alaska: The Development of Our Arctic Frontier," Unpublished Ph. D. thesis, Harvard University, 1947.
Glines, Carroll V., Jr. "Alaska's Press and the Battle for Statehood," Unpublished Master's thesis, American University, 1969.
Koponen, Niilo E. "The History of Education in Alaska: With Special Reference to the Relationship Between the Bureau of Indian Affairs and the State School System," An unpublished "special paper" presented in partial fullfillment of the requirements for a Doctoral degree in Education, Harvard University, Graduate School of Education, June, 1964.
MacDonald, Donald Alexander. "Seattle's Economic Development 1880-1910." Unpublished Ph.D. thesis, University of Washington, 1959.
Miller, Orlando Wesley. "The Frontier in Alaska and the Matanuska Valley Colony." Unpublished Ph.D. thesis, Columbia University, 1965.

IX. Miscellaneous

Christmas card. "Merry Christmas," sponsored by Operation Statehood, Anchorage Chapter, Anchorage, Alaska.

Council, Mary Lee. "Alaska Statehood." Unpublished manuscript, n.d.

Lehleitner, George H. *The Tennessee Plan: How the Bold Became States*. New Orleans, Louisiana, 1956. (Pamphlet.)

Memorial of the People of the First Judicial Division of Alaska. Juneau, Alaska, n.d. [1923].

INDEX

Abood, Mitchell, 117
A 'Court, Capt. H. Holmes, 2
Adak Island, 58
Adams, John, 155
ALCAN (see Alaska-Canada Military Highway)
Alaska:
 designated U. S. Customs District, 1;
 troops withdrawn, 1;
 designated civil and judicial district, 2;
 Oregon laws adopted for, 2;
 gold rush, 4;
 federal laws affecting homestead laws, 4;
 railroad construction provisions made, 4;
 Criminal Procedure Code established, 4;
 Oregon laws codified/modified for 4;
 taxation system levied, 5;
 Civil Code enacted for, 5, 19;
 Code of Civil procedure enacted, 5, 19;
 incorporation of municipalities made possible, 5;
 highways, 58;
 economy booms 1940-1950, 59;
 employment 1940-1950, 59;
 Legislature, in (designed in Constitution) 143
Alaska Daily Empire (Juneau), 38, 42, 135, 138, 161
Alaska-Canada Military Highway, 57, 58, 157
Alaska Calendar of Engagements, 159
Alaska Cession Day, 29
Alaska Daily Dispatch, 39
Alaska Daily Times, 30
Alaska Development Board, 74
Alaska Fish Trust, 40
Alaska geographic areas:
 Interior—practically inaccessible, 1880, 15.
 Southeastern—majority of State's white population, 1880, 15,
 separate Statehood considered, 42, 43;
 referendum results, 73.
 Western—practically inaccessible 1880, 15.

Alaska-Hawaii statehood bill, 96, 126, 133, 136, 138, 151, 153
Alaska Home Rule Association, 60
Alaska Miners' Association, 77, 95, 159
Alaska Railroad, 41, 59, 73, 77
Alaska Salmon Industry, Inc., 10, 77, 95, 97
Alaska Sportsmen's Council, 159
Alaska State Constitution, adopted in 1956, 10, 146
Alaska Statehood Act, passed in 1958, 10, 167, 168
Alaska Statehood Association, 70
Alaska Statehood Committee, 9, 90, 91, 97, 105, 114, 115, 123, 125, 131, 132, 134, 136, 138, 139, 154, 159
Alaska Steamship Company, 86
Alaska Syndicate, 23, 26, 27
Alaska-Tennessee Plan (see Tennessee Plan)
Alaska Weekly, 78
Alaska Women's Club, 78
Alaska-Yukon-Pacific Exposition, 28
Aleutian Chain, 57
Aleutian Islands, 57, 75
Aleuts, 8, 14, 38, 76, 92
Alexander Archipelago, 15
Allen, Edward W., 99
Allen, William Prescott, 161
Allott, Senator Gordon, 166
Amchitka Island, 58
American Federation of Labor, 151
American Federation of Labor Unions and Councils of Alaska, 75
American Legion, 151, 154
American Mercury, 87
Anchorage, 41, 56, 57, 73, 74, 77, 87, 89, 115-117, 125
Anchorage Daily News, 60
Anchorage Daily Times, 42, 60, 70, 78, 91, 115, 141, 142, 167
Anderson, Al, 77, 78, 95
Anderson, Senator Clinton P. 114, 119, 120, 123, 166
Arizona, 8
Arnold, Gen. Henry H., 56
Arnold, Winton C., 77, 78, 85, 95, 97-102
Aspinall, Rep. Wayne N., 162
Associated Press, 139

187

Atlantic Monthly, 19
Attu, 57, 58, 75
Atwood, Evangeline, 70
Atwood, Robert B., 60, 61, 91, 92, 123, 136, 137, 146

Baker, William L., 90, 91
Ballinger, Richard A., 29
Ballinger-Pinchot controversy, 23, 29
Bartlett, Senator Edward L. ("Bob"), 7, 68-79, 90, 92, 95, 97, 102, 105, 106, 111, 112, 115, 121, 123, 124, 132, 138, 141, 153-155, 157, 160, 161, 164-166
Bartley, Dr. Ernest, 155
Beach, Rex, 93
Beardslee, Comdr. Lester Anthony, 2
Bebout, John, 142
Bennett, James Gordon, 3, 4
Bering River, 29
Bering Sea, 3, 89
Bering Strait, 13
Bettinger, Lee C., 91
Beveridge, Senator Albert J., 30
Big Delta, 58
Boddy, A. W., 159
Bonanza Creek, 17
Bone, Governor Scott C., 41, 51
Bonner, Rep. Herbert C., 164
Bonneville Power Administration, 70
Boroughs, Alaska, created, 145
Boston American, 67
Boswell, J. C., 142
Brady, Governor John G., 18
Bridges, Harry, 103
Bridges, Senator Styles, 166
Brookings Institute, 70
Brooks, Alfred H., 15
Bryan, William J., 30
Buck, Pearl S., 93
Burdick, Charles, 146
Burns, John A., 160
Bush, Senator Prescott, 166
Butler, Senator Hugh, 79, 101-105, 112, 115-117, 119, 120, 166
Butler, Maj. Gen. Smedley D., 57
Butrovich, John, 125, 146
Byrd, Senator Harry F., 166
Byrd, Rear Admiral Richard E., 93

Cagney, James, 93
Cale, Thomas, 23-26
California, 40
Cannon, Rep. Clarence, 163
Cape Nome, 18
Cariboo District, B.C., 14
Carmack, George Washington, 17
Carmack, Mrs. George Washington, 17

Chamber of Commerce of America, 154
Chapman, Secy. of Interior Oscar L., 97, 98
Chilberg, Joseph, 26
Chilkoot Barracks, 56
Chilkoot Pass, 14
Chilson, Halfield, 158
Church, Senator Frank, 160
Circle City, 15
Civil Aeronautics Administration, 59
Civilian Conservation Corps, 54
Civil War, 3, 9
Clark, Henry W., 47
Clark, Governor W. E., 31
Clements, Senator Earle C., 119
Clum, J. P., 26
Cold War, 9, 75
College, Alaska, 135, 137, 167
Collier's, 36
Collins, E. B., 143
Columbia Broadcasting System, 155
Commonwealth for Alaska, Inc., 122
Congressional Record, 166
Connecticut Compromise of 1787, 168
"Constitution Hall," 139, **142**
Constitutional Convention, Alaska, 10, 131-147
Constitutional Study League, 135
Copper River and Northwestern Railroad, 26
Cordon, Senator Guy, 103, 104, 119, 124
Corson, "Seattle John," 26, 27
Council, Mary Lee, 100, 160, 164, 166
Council of State Governments (See also Public Administration Service) 137
Cunningham, Clarence, 29

Davies, Lawrence E., 139, 143
Davis, General Jefferson C., 1
Davis, Rep. John C., 152
Dawson Creek, B.C., 58
Dawson, Rep. William A., 163
Dawson, Y.T., 25
Dearborn Independent, 42
Delegate Act (1906), 23
Democratic National Convention of 1888, 17
Denmark, 56
Depression (1929), 51, 52
Dimond, Anthony J., 52-54, 56, 57, 59, 61, 68, 69, 75, 77, 90, 134
Dirksen, Senator Everett McKinley, 103
Division of Territories and Island Possessions, 67, 71

Douglas, 54
Douglas Island, 54
Douglas, James H., 114
Downes v. Bidwell, "Insular Case," 8
Dutch Harbor, 57

Egan, Senator William A., 78, 142, 146, 156, 157
Eagle, Alaska, 5, 24
Eagle City—see Eagle, Alaska
Eastland, Senator James, 102, 165
Eblen, Jack E., 3
Edmonton, Alta., 58
Eisenhower, President Dwight D., 111-113, 119, 121, 125, 126, 131, 151-153, 155, 157, 158, 160, 167, 168
Elks (club), 154
Engle, Rep. Clair, 153, 162
Eskimos, 8, 14, 38, 74, 76, 90-92, 152
Evening Public Ledger, (Philadelphia) 42

Fahy, Jack B., 71
Fairbanks, 18, 24, 41, 57, 70, 74, 77, 78, 87, 115, 116, 133, 167
Fairbanks Daily News-Miner, 68, 134, 135, 139, 141, 154, 166, 167
Fairbanks Municipal Utilities District, 134
Fairbanks Times, 28
Fall, Secy. of Interior Albert B., 41, 42, 50
Farrington, Delegate Joseph R., 106
Faulkner, Herbert L., 76
Federal Aid Highway Act of 1916, 53, 60
Federal Emergency Relief Administration, 54
Federal Housing Administration, 68
Federation of Women's Clubs (territorial), 91
Fischer, Victor, 74, 115-119, 136, 142, 164
Flood, Rep. Henry D., 30
Fortas, Abe, 71
Forty-Ninth Star, 36, 37
Franklin, Glen D., 159
Fraser River, B.C., 14
Fur seals, 13

Gallup, George, 72
Gallup poll, 72, 104, 151
Gardner, Warner W., 76
Garfield, Secy. of Interior James R., 29
Gastineau Channel, 54
General Federation of Women's Clubs (national) 92, 151
Glavis, Louis, 29

Gold Rush, 4, 5, 18
Groh, Cliff, 115
Gruening, Dorothy, 67
Gruening, Governor Ernest, 47, 55, 61, 67-79, 85, 87, 88, 90, 91, 96, 97, 100, 103, 106, 111, 115, 131, 146, 152, 154, 156-158
Guggenheim interests, 26, 27, 29, 31
"Guggies" (see Guggenheim interests)
Gunther, John, 93

Haines, 56, 116
Halleck, Rep. Charles, 92
Hamilton, Rep. E. L., 30
Harding, President Warren G. 9, 40-41, 42, 43
Harris, Richard T., 14
Harrisburg, 17
Harrison, Senator Benjamin, 14
Hawaii, 8, 56, 79, 96-126, 133, 136, 138, 140, 151-153, 160, 161, 170
Hearst newspaper, 105, 156
Heinmiller, Carl W., 116
Heintzleman, Governor B. Frank, 120, 121, 131, 153
Hellenthal, J. A., 47, 49
Henderson, U.S.S., 41
Hermann, Mildred R., 78, 90, 92, 98, 159
Hinckley, Ted C., 14, 16
Hoggatt, Governor Wilford B., 23-25
Holland, Senator Spessard L., 157
Homestead laws, Federal extended to Alaska (1898), 4
Honolulu, Hi., 56
Hoover, Herbert: as Secy. of Commerce, 51;
as President, 52
Hosmer, Craig, 163
Hubbard, Rev. Bernard R., 98
Hubbard, Senator O. P., 36
Hudson's Bay Company, 14
Hyder, 77

Ickes, Secy. of Interior Harold L., 57, 67, 71
Iliamna Bay, 55
Indians, 8, 14, 38, 74, 76, 78, 90-92, 152
"Insular Cases," 8
International Fisheries Commission, 99
International Longshoremen's and Warehousemen's Union, 103
Ipalook, Percy, 91

Jackson, Senator Henry M. ("Scoop"), 153, 165

JAMESTOWN, U.S.S., 2
Jarvis, David H., 26
Johnson, President Andrew, 1
Johnson, President Lyndon B., 160, 161, 170
Jones Act (see Maritime Act of 1920)
Jones, Senator Wesley, 68
Jordan, David S., 19
Judicial Districts, 5, 73, 74
Judicial System, 72, 143
Juneau, 14, 17, 39, 41, 54, 70, 78, 116, 158
Juneau Bar Association, 61
Juneau Chamber of Commerce, 61
Juneau, Joseph, 14

Kay, Wendell P., 134
Kenai Peninsula, 55
Kennecott-Bonanza copper mine, 26
Ketchikan, 70, 78, 91, 116
Ketchikan Bar Association, 61
Ketchikan Central Labor Council, 75
Ketchikan Chronicle, 42, 75, 78, 90
Ketchikan Commonwealth Club, 124
Kiska, 57, 58, 75
Kiwanis (club), 154
Klawock, 13, 90
Klondike, 4
Klondike River, 18
Kluckhohn, Frank L., 87
Knowland, Senator William F., 79
Kodiak, 56, 70, 89, 91
Kodiak Island, 57
Koponen, Niilo, 115, 116
Korean War, 104, 111
Krug, Secy. of Interior Julius A., 72

Lane, Secy. of Interior Franklin L., 49
Langer, Senator William L., 60
Langer-McCarran Bill, 60, 61, 166, 171
Lathrop, Austin E. ("Cap") 87, 134
Lehleitner, George H., 140, 141, 155
Library of Congress, 70, 136
Life, 156, 161
Linck, Mrs. Alaska, 77
Lindley, Ernest K., 57
Lippmann, Walter, 123
"Little Men for Statehood," 115, 116, 118, 125
Lomen, Carl, 87
Lomen, Ralph, 87
Long, Senator Russell, 165
Lucas, Senator Scott, 102, 103
Lyng, Howard, 91

MacArthur, General Douglas, 93
Mackenzie River, 14

Magnuson, Senator Warren G., 102, 106
Malone, Senator George W., 97, 114
Manders, John E., 69, 122
Maritime Act of 1920, 68, 75
Marshall, General George C., 56
Martin, Rep. Joseph W., 96, 120, 125
Mason, Noah M., 163
Matanuska Valley Colonization, 54
McCarran Act 1952, 117
McCarran, Senator Pat, 60
McClellan, Senator John L., 103
McCormack, Rep. John, 92
McCutcheon, Stanley J., 91
McFarland, Senator Ernest W., 99
McKay, Secy. of Interior Douglas, 113, 114, 124, 131, 133, 153, 154
McKinley, President William, 4, 24
McNealy, Robert J., 135
McWilkins, Weber and Cole, 97
Metlakatla, 41
Michigan, 54
Miller, Rep. A. L. "Doc," 113, 125, 134, 138, 153, 163
Mills, Rep. Wilbur D., 124
Miners' Code, 14, 15
Minnesota, 54
Missouri Constitution, 136
Mitchell, General "Billy," 57
Monroney, Senator A. S. "Mike," 107, 121, 123, 165
Monsen, Helen, 135
Morgan, J. P., 26
Morse, Senator Wayne, 154
Mount McKinley National Park, 41
Mundt-Ferguson bill, 102
Murray, Senator James E., 167

Nation, 67
National Municipal League, 143
National Reforestation Act of 1933, 54
National Resources Committee, 55
National Resources Planning Board, 6
Nenana, 41
Nerland, Andrew, 91
Nerland, Leslie, 142
Neuberger, Senator Richard L., 57, 86, 166
Nevada, 9, 97
New Deal, 55, 67, 85, 112
"New Dealers," 77
New Eldorado, 18
New Jersey Constitution, 136, 144
New Mexico, 8
New Republic, 122
Newsweek, 57
New York Herald, 3

New York Journal-American, 97
New York, 122
New York Stock Exchange, 51
New York Sun, 42
New York Times, 52, 111, 112, 139, 143, 156, 160, 164
Nez Percé uprising, 1
Nichols, Jeannette Paddock, 93
Niebuhr, Reinhold, 93
Nome, 24, 26, 74, 87, 88, 91
North Pole, 167
North Slope, 132, 168
Northern Commercial Company, 39
Northland Transportation Co., 86
Northwest Ordinance of 1787, 7
Norway, 57

O'Brien, Rep. Leo W., 159, 164, 165
O'Mahoney, Senator Joseph C., 104, 106,
"Operation Statehood," 118, 125, 136
Order of Railway Conductors of America, 98
Oregon, 2, 4
Oregonian, (Portland), 42
Organic Act, First (1884), 2, 5, 14-17, 19, 31
Organic Act, Second (1912), 6, 7, 31, 35, 36, 39, 40, 60, 69, 74, 139
Osprey, H.M.S., 2
Outlook, 51

Palmer, 54, 70
Parks, Governor George A., 52, 131
Pearl Harbor, Hi., 57, 75, 140
Peden, Rep. Preston E., 87
Pelly, Rep. Thomas M., 124
Peratrovich, Senator Frank, 90, 91
Peterson, Almer J., 73
Peterson, Rep. J. Hardin, 96
Philadelphia Record, 42
Pillion, Rep. John R., 163, 164
Pinchot, Gifford, 29
Pitman, Senator Key, 38
Pittman, Governor Vail, 97
Plummer, Raymond E., 126
Pomeroy, Earl S., 3
Portland Telegram, 40
Pribilof Islands, 13, 75
Prince of Wales Island, 13
Prince Rupert, B.C., 69
Public Administration Service, 137
Public Works Administration, 54
Puerto Rico, 8, 103, 122, 124

Rabbit Creek (See Bonanza Creek)
Rayburn, Rep. Sam, 92, 96, 125, 159, 163

Reeve, Robert, 111
Rivers, Rep. Ralph J., 72, 78, 100, 146, 156, 157
Rivers, Victor C., 90, 91
Roden, Henry, 69
Rogers, Dr. George W., 16, 100
Rogers, Sherman, 51
Rogers, Rep. Walter, 163, 164
Ronan, John, 26, 27
Rooney, Rep. John, 71
Roosevelt, Eleanor, 93
Roosevelt, Franklin D.:
 as Governor of New York, 52;
 as President, 54, 55, 67, 131
Roosevelt, President Theodore, 20, 24, 29, 30
Root, Secretary of War Elihu, 8
Rousseau, General Lovell H., 1
Russell, Senator Richard B., 102, 161
Rutledge, Margaret, 117
Ryan, John C., 135

Sady, Emil, 137
San Francisco Chronicle, 40
Saturday Evening Post, 51
Schlesinger, Arthur M., Jr., 93
Scripps-Howard newspapers, 105, 156
Seaton, Fred R.:
 as Senator, 106;
 as Secy. of Interior, 154, 155, 158
Seattle, Wa., 17, 28, 68, 69, 77, 106
Seattle-Tacoma Airport, Wa., 117
Senate Armed Services Committee, 165
Senate Democratic Policy Committee, 102
Seventh Inter-American Conference, 67
Seward, 41, 70, 77
Seward, William Henry, 1, 4
Seward Peninsula, 18, 23
Shattuck, Allen, 116
Shemya, 58
Shenandoah, C.S.S., 3
Sitka, 1, 2, 5, 14, 15, 56, 57, 70
Skagway, 26, 58
Skagway Alaskan, 20
Skinner family, 86
Skookum Jim, 17
Smathers, Senator George A., 107
Smith, Douglas, 123
Smith, Rep. Howard W., 161-164
Smith, Marge, 164
Snedden, William C., 134, 135, 154-156, 166
Spanish-American War (1898), 8
Stefansson, Vilhjalmur, 93
Stennis, Senator John C., 103, 165

191

Stevenson, Governor Adlai, 111, 133
Stevens, Theodore, 155
Stewart, Thomas, 133, 135-137
Stikine River, 14
Stimson, Secy. of War Henry L., 57
Stines, Norman, 77
Stock, R. H., 88
Stoeckl, Baron Edouard, 1
Strand, William C., 134
Streit, Clarence, 140
Strout, Richard, 122
Stuart, Alice, 159
Sumner, Senator Charles, 3
Sundborg, George, 70, 74, 166
Sunset Magazine, 43
Sutherland, Dan A., 48
Swineford, Governor Alfred P., 16

Taber, Rep. John, 163
Taft, President William H., 23, 27-31
Tagish Charlie, 17
Tanana Valley, 18, 23, 25, 95
Taylor, Warren A., 91
"Tennessee Plan," 140, 141, 144, 146, 147, 155-157, 159, 163
Thomas, Dr. Joe, 55
Thompson, Secretary of Navy R.W., 2
Thompson River, B.C., 14
Thurmond, Senator Strom, 165
Time, 156
Tongass National Forest, 119
Treaty of Cession of Russian-America, 1, 37
Troy, John W.; 38; as Governor, 85
Truman, President Harry S., 72, 79, 101, 102, 151, 155
Tugwell, Rexford G., 67
Tuttle, Dr. Daniel, Jr., 140
Twining, Lt. Gen. Nathan F., 98, 99, 158

Umnak Island, 58
Unalaska, 56
Underwood, Oscar, 30
"Union Now" (book by Clarence Streit), 140
United Congo Improvement Association, 55
U. S. Bureau of the Budget, 120
U. S. Bureau of Land Management, 156
U. S. Department of Agriculture, 79, 95
U. S. Department of Commerce, 120
U. S. Department of Defense, 114
U. S. Department of Interior, 75, 78, 79, 86, 99, 120, 124, 154

U. S. Department of State, 120
U. S. Fish and Wildlife Service, 71
U. S. Forest Service, 41
U. S. Geological Survey, 15, 71, 156
U. S. News and World Report, 72
U. S. Public Road Administration, 58
U. S. Smelting, Refining and Mining Co., 88, 142
U. S. Supreme Court, 36
U. S. Treasury Department, 1
University of Alaska, 88, 120, 135, 137, 139, 142, 158
University of Florida, 155
University of Hawaii, 140

Valdez, 20, 24, 26, 36, 70, 78
Valdez News, 20
Vancouver, B.C., 69
Veterans of Foreign Wars, 98
Virgin Islands, 103, 122, 124

Wade, Jerry, 116
Wallace, Secy. of Agriculture Henry C., 41
Warren, Governor Earl, 98
Washington Daily News, 123
Washington Post, 119
Waskey, Frank, 23-25
Waskey-Cale platform, 23
Westland, Rep. Jack, 163
Wherry, Senator Kenneth, 106
White Act (1924), 69
White, Barrie M., 115
White Pass & Yukon Railway, 58
Whitehorse, Y.T., 58
Wickersham, James, 7, 9, 23-29, 31, 35-40, 49, 52
Wills, Rep. Wilbur D., 124
Wilson, President Woodrow, 30, 35, 49
Wisconsin, 54
Wood, Rear-Admiral Ralph, 99
Work, Secy. of Interior Hubert, 50
Work Projects Administration, 54
World War I, 47, 50
World War II, 9, 70, 73, 75, 99, 115, 140, 168, 170
Wrangell, 70
Wrangell Chamber of Commerce, 61
Wright, Leslie B., 92

Yukon River, 5, 14, 17, 18, 24

Ziegler, H., 69